"*Remote, Inc.* is a timely and practical guide to remote work, explaining how we can recharge, reset, and bring our full attention to the work that really matters."

—Arianna Huffington, founder and CEO of Thrive Global

"The world has gone remote and is not going back. This book is an extraordinarily helpful guide to this new world."

—David Rubenstein, cofounder and co–chief executive, the Carlyle Group

"Working remotely is a learned skill, and *Remote, Inc.* is the perfect guide to accelerate your learning. A quick read that will have you and your team working smarter tomorrow morning!"

—Barb Bidan, senior vice president, global talent, Peloton

"*Remote, Inc.* provides a needed road map, enabling salaried employees, managers, and freelancers alike to be successful. It's a must-read for today's professionals."

—Jenny Rooney, communities director and
chair of the CMO Network, *Forbes*

"If you need to understand how leaders and employees can thrive no matter where or how the work gets done, *Remote Inc.* is the book for you."

—Ragy Thomas, CEO of Sprinklr

REMOTE, INC.

REMOTE, INC.

HOW TO THRIVE AT WORK . . . WHEREVER YOU ARE

ROBERT C. POZEN AND ALEXANDRA SAMUEL

HARPER
BUSINESS

An Imprint of HarperCollinsPublishers

REMOTE, INC. Copyright © 2021 by Robert C. Pozen and Alexandra Samuel. All rights reserved. Printed in the United States of America. No part of this book may be used or reproduced in any manner whatsoever without written permission except in the case of brief quotations embodied in critical articles and reviews. For information, address HarperCollins Publishers, 195 Broadway, New York, NY 10007.

HarperCollins books may be purchased for educational, business, or sales promotional use. For information, please email the Special Markets Department at SPsales@harper collins.com.

FIRST EDITION

Designed by Kyle O'Brien

Library of Congress Cataloging-in-Publication Data
Names: Pozen, Robert C., author. | Samuel, Alexandra, 1962– author.
Title: Remote, Inc.: how to thrive at work . . . wherever you are / Robert C. Pozen and Alexandra Samuel.
Description: First edition. | New York, NY: Harper Business, [2021] | Includes bibliographical references. | Summary: "Two experienced productivity authors team up to reveal how proven strategies and a little tech savvy can help you level up your efficiency and transform you into a remote-work expert"—provided by publisher.
Identifiers: LCCN 2021001341 (print) | LCCN 2021001342 (ebook) | ISBN 9780063079373 (hardcover) | ISBN 9780063079380 (ebook)
Subjects: LCSH: Telecommuting. | Virtual work teams. | Information technology—Management.
Classification: LCC HD2336.3.P69 2021 (print) | LCC HD2336.3 (ebook) | DDC 658.3/123—dc23
LC record available at https://lccn.loc.gov/2021001341
LC ebook record available at https://lccn.loc.gov/2021001342

21 22 23 24 25 LSC 10 9 8 7 6 5 4 3 2 1

For Liz and Rob,
who make it a joy to work from home

CONTENTS

Highlighting the practical how-tos you'll find in each chapter

CHAPTER 9: ORGANIZING YOUR SPACE...129
How to . . .

- Share workspace with family or roommates
- Find new spaces to get your work done
- Get the most out of coworking spaces
- Dress for home office success

PART IV: ESSENTIAL SKILLS FOR REMOTE WORKERS

CHAPTER 10: MAKING THE MOST OF MEETINGS...143
How to . . .

- Have fewer and shorter meetings
- Make online meetings more effective
- Avoid low-value meetings diplomatically
- Leave a meeting with clear next steps

CHAPTER 11: READING ONLINE AND OFFLINE...163
How to . . .

- Keep up with industry news while you're at home
- Beat the disadvantages of reading online
- Use audio tools to fit more reading into your day
- Build a read-it-later file and a clipping file

CHAPTER 12: WRITING SOLO AND WITH OTHERS...177
How to . . .

- Use outlines to overcome writer's block
- Work with colleagues to draft documents online
- Give and get feedback through online collaboration
- Choose the right software for any writing project

PART V: EFFECTIVE ONLINE COMMUNICATION

CHAPTER 13: EMAIL AND MESSAGING: BEATING OVERLOAD...197
How to . . .

- Know when to email, call, or message
- Conquer email overload by automating your attention
- Write emails that drive people to action
- Use team messaging to get answers quickly

INTRODUCTION

Should you check your email before you eat breakfast, or carve out some personal time before you sit down at your home computer? Do you need to talk with each of your remote reports every day, or can you trust that they're making progress toward their deliverables? Should you block off a day to get your memo written, or try to fit the work into the gaps between your various online meetings? Do you need to turn on your camera for this Zoom call, or can you listen in while quietly doing the dishes?

These are the typical dilemmas that characterize our day-to-day experiences as home-based workers. Many of us are working from home for the first time, due to Covid, and still hoping it's temporary; others of us have worked remotely, either full- or part-time, for many years.

In either case, we now have to grapple with a world in which remote work has become, if not the rule, then certainly no longer the exception. And we are also learning to do remote work without being able to count on the haven of coworking spaces or the sanctuary of the local coffee shop. Even folks who have long worked remotely may struggle to adapt to the expectations and norms that emerge as remote work goes mainstream.

It's a very challenging context in which to figure out the work habits and collaboration strategies that can make you most productive as a remote worker. But you're not a remote worker: you're *Remote, Inc.*

Remote, Inc. means thinking like what we call a "Business of One." Whether you're early in your career with a large organization, managing a small team, or a self-employed freelancer, you should try to adopt the mindset and habits of a small business owner.

That's because every single home office is, essentially, its own freestanding enterprise. Your boss is effectively your client, and you are effectively in the position of a vendor or supplier. Your boss gives you the orders for products and services, and it is up to you to complete those orders on time and on budget.

That means you should approach your work as a series of deliverables: you're accountable for each deliverable, whether it is a marketing plan for a product launch, a new feature for a software program, or an ethics manual for new hires.

Thinking of yourself as *Remote, Inc.* means you have the responsibility and accountability of a business owner, but also the flexibility and independence. It means thinking in terms of outcomes and final products, instead of schedules and billable hours. It means organizing the pace and timing of your work around your own priorities and goals, instead of being forced to bend your priorities to fit into the straitjacket of the modern nine-to-five workplace.

Far from consigning you to a lifetime of working from home, the productivity skills and mental habits that you develop as *Remote, Inc.* will serve you very well if and when you return to working in an office, even if it's only part-time. Learning to think like a business owner will make you more efficient and more focused, and it will strengthen your time management skills in ways that help you get the most out of every day.

Just as important, thinking like a Business of One will make you more valuable to your employer and clients. Managing a distributed team that requires constant hand-holding is an enormous drain on any organization, but that is what's required if remote employees depend on daily or even hourly direction in order to make effective use of their time. By embracing the Business of One mindset, remote workers address this management challenge by delivering consistent, high-quality results while requiring far less overhead in the form of supervision and infrastructure. Your goal is to make *Remote, Inc.* into your boss's favorite subsidiary: the supplier who can be relied upon to think proactively, collaborate effectively, and deliver great results.

SOLVING THE PROBLEM OF REMOTE WORK

To provide you with practical strategies and tools that will make you more productive as a remote worker, and more valuable to your employer or clients, we need to start by looking at what makes remote work different from a traditional workplace, and at the particular challenges you need to address in order to do your best outside the office.

The modern workplace, which has its roots in the Industrial Revolution and the shift to factory production, exists to solve one main problem: How do you coordinate a disparate group of people so they can get more done together than they could separately?

For a long time, the centralized workplace (and the hierarchically integrated organization) was our best answer to that question. Get everybody into the same building, or line them up side by side in rows of cubicles, and it's easier for them to exchange information (on paper), generate ideas (face-to-face) or collaborate (on a whiteboard).

The advent of computers and the Internet changed that answer: within just a few decades it's become possible to exchange information instantly (via email, links, or messaging), generate ideas remotely (over Zoom calls or on Slack), or collaborate globally (via Miro or Google Docs).

At first it was big corporations that tapped this potential for a globally integrated workforce, using intranets to connect centrally organized workplaces that were spread across the globe, like spokes around a hub. But eventually, people and organizations figured out that if a Manhattan HQ could connect to satellite offices in Berlin or Bangalore, it could also connect to branch offices in Boston or Birmingham. And so the era of remote work was born.

While Covid has accelerated the transition, the shift to remote work is an inevitable result of information technologies that give us a superior alternative to the centralized, hierarchical firm. Technology makes it possible to coordinate with one another—but we still need to figure out the how, both technically and socially.

When you're at the office, the problem of coordination is solved by everybody being in the same place at the same time. When you're at home, the problem of coordination has to be solved by you.

That's where this book comes in. Remote work is a learned skill: it takes time and effort to unlock the productivity gains that come from working from home. Once people turn that corner, however, they develop a strong preference for working remotely. To turn that corner, you should start think-ing like *Remote, Inc.*—adopting the mindset and skills to excel as a Business of One.

Remote, Inc. will help you build the key competencies you need to thrive while you're working remotely. The specific strategies and tactics we recom-mend rest on a fundamental shift in how you think about your work, so that you can operate as if you were running your own business.

ADAPTING THIS BOOK TO YOUR NEEDS

The shift to thinking like a Business of One will be easiest for people who are white-collar workers or professionals with some degree of market power, as well as those who are already self-employed. Our Business of One model will be less readily applicable to people in support or junior roles, whose tasks are set for them on a daily or hourly basis by their managers: administrative staff, customer service agents, and telemarketers are unlikely to achieve significant autonomy in their daily work, even when they're remote. And of course not everyone can work remotely, period—though moving to a hybrid model may allow many more jobs to be done partially remotely by people who spend at least some time in the office.

Your ability to implement the Business of One model will also depend on the overall approach of your organization or manager. Some organizations have rapidly embraced remote work as a way to boost productivity, lower costs, and increase employee engagement. By providing their teams with the autonomy and support they need to work effectively from home, these orga-nizations create a win-win scenario: employees enjoy greater flexibility and work-life balance, while the organization gets better results and a more stable workforce. If you work with an organization that has taken this approach to its remote team, you will find it easier to take the Business of One approach, because your employer will support your efforts to take ownership of your own productivity and results.

Even if you are relatively junior or work with an organization that has yet to adopt a more decentralized model, however, our approach, strategies, and tactics can still be useful to you. Learning to prioritize your goals, focus on the final product, and stop sweating the small stuff will help you make effective use of your time and deliver better results; mastering foundational skills and modern communication tools will boost your efficiency. As you demonstrate your ability to deliver excellent results, and as your organization becomes more effective at remote work, you will be able to move toward working like a Business of One.

MEET THE BOARD OF ADVISERS
FOR YOUR BUSINESS OF ONE

If this still sounds like a big shift in how you think about your work, be assured that *Remote, Inc.* has a strong team of advisers: Us! We each bring particular experience and knowledge to the job of retooling for remote work, and we want to help you make your Business of One successful.

Bob is a careful planner who has worked in large companies and managed sizable teams. His passion for productivity dates to the earliest part of his career, when he taught law and economics at NYU Law School, and then served as associate general counsel of the SEC. From there, Bob was recruited to Fidelity Investments when it was a relatively small firm with only $65 billion in assets under management. Through careful management of his time and attention, he rose to become president of the investment company and, by the time he retired, had helped grow the company's assets under management to almost $1 trillion.

In the process of leaving Fidelity, Bob was asked to join the President's Commission to Strengthen Social Security, and later served as Massachusetts's secretary of economic affairs—roles that allowed him to apply the productivity strategies he'd honed in the financial sector to the very different context of government and policy work. He moved on to a role as executive chair of MFS Investment Management, where he helped double its assets under management to almost $300 billion—while also serving on several corporate boards and teaching a full course load at Harvard Business School.

Bob's reputation for productivity led to an invitation to write a *Harvard*

Business Review article in which he shared some of the secrets that drove his own professional achievements. The response to his *HBR* article was so overwhelming that he wrote an entire book explaining his recipe for success. *Extreme Productivity* hit number three on *Fast Company*'s list of best business books for 2012 and was translated into ten languages. He now teaches at MIT's Sloan School of Management, including courses on personal productivity for executives from around the world.

Alex is a passionate technologist who has worked with some of the world's biggest tech and media companies. She has worked remotely for most of her career: As a PhD student at Harvard in the 1990s, she wrote one of the first dissertations on the Internet while leading a digital governance research program for a consortium of countries from around the world. She then founded Social Signal, one of the world's first social media agencies, and built online communities for national and international organizations—many of them launched from her living room.

As the mother of two young children, Alex returned to the conventional workplace as the research director for the Social + Interactive Media Centre at Emily Carr University and, later, as the vice president of social media for the customer intelligence company Vision Critical. Throughout these years Alex relied on a growing range of tech tools to juggle her professional and personal responsibilities, writing about her tactics for Oprah.com, the *Atlantic*, and the *Harvard Business Review*.

Alex returned to working remotely in 2012 so that she could homeschool her autistic son while working full-time as a technology and data journalist. She is now a regular contributor to the *Wall Street Journal*, where she writes frequently about tech-enabled productivity and remote work. She has authored the *Work Smarter with Social Media* series for Harvard Business Review Press, and served as the data journalist for the past four editions of the *Forbes* annual *World's Most Influential CMOs* report. More than five thousand students have taken her Skillshare class, "Email Productivity: Work Smarter with Your Inbox."

This book distills the strategies and tactics we have developed through these two very different careers. We also draw on the experiences of our colleagues and, to the extent that they exist, on studies and surveys about this new world of remote work. Where we make a research-driven recommendation, we note the relevant sources in a citation.

A ROAD MAP TO THIS BOOK

We have provided you with a broad handbook on how to maximize your productivity when working remotely. But we know that being productive at home involves some of the same fundamental skills that are required to succeed in the modern workplace—like managing your time, optimizing your technology, conducting effective meetings, writing persuasive emails, and using social media. So we offer you key concepts and tools in all these areas, while focusing on the special challenges that confront you when you work remotely. We have highlighted some of these practical how-tos in the table of contents, so you can quickly find the solutions you need.

Let us offer some guidance on how to make the most of all this content. If you want to get just the highlights of the book, you can simply read the "Takeaways" list at the end of each chapter. That is the very quick, though superficial, approach, which may help you decide where to read more thoroughly.

To understand the core concepts underlying our approach to productivity, read part 1 on the Business of One model and how to apply it. We strongly recommend reading chapters 1 and 2 thoroughly, because they provide the foundation for the whole book. To strengthen your fundamental approach to productivity, read part 2, "Three Key Strategies for Remote Workers," on goal-setting, focusing on the final product, and sweeping away the small stuff. These first two parts of the book provide you with a new way of thinking about remote work and your personal productivity, so you can make use of the practical advice that follows.

After that, the book becomes much more tactical: it is aimed at readers who want to learn specific practices and techniques in key areas. You can concentrate on the chapters that address your most serious challenges or help you unlock major productivity wins.

Part 3, "Getting Organized as a Remote Worker," will show you how to organize your time, your tech, and your home workspace. (If you are looking for tech fixes or improvements, keep an eye out for the "Tech Deep Dive" features that appear throughout these chapters, as well as in parts 4 and 5.) Part 4 covers the essential skills of meeting, reading, and writing: these are important to any knowledge worker, but we offer additional suggestions that are specific to the challenges and opportunities of working remotely. Part 5 covers the modern communication methods that most bedevil or empower remote workers: email, messaging, social media, and presentations.

Part 6, "Thriving in a World of Remote Work," helps you apply everything you've learned from this book to the next year or decade of your career. We look at the future of work in a hybrid environment where people work partly at home and partly at the office, and help you understand what that means for your own career choices.

In the conclusion, we show you the benefits you and your organization can expect to see when you start working like *Remote, Inc.*

At the end of each chapter, you will find "From a Remote Worker" profiles of people who have navigated the complexities of working from home. They've shared their experiences and insights so that they can make remote work easier and more fulfilling for other people. Although each profile is loosely related to the themes of its chapter, these profiles are part of a broader story. So even if you're going to skim a chapter, consider reading these profiles for inspiration.

As you set out on this journey, we encourage you to find a group of colleagues who also are thinking about how to improve their productivity and experience with working from home. A virtual reading or discussion group will help you get more out of the book, and it can be a great way for your team to connect and bond over the challenges of remote work. Even more important, working through these strategies together will help you develop some shared vocabulary and approaches that will be even more effective if you have them in common. As you adopt the mindset, strategies, and skills you find in this book, you will all tap in to the power of working as *Remote, Inc.*

PART I

THE BUSINESS OF ONE

This is a practical book with guidance on how to solve the kinds of problems you are likely to face when working remotely. But the truth is that you can't really address those problems if you keep working the way you did when you went into the office every day. That's why we need to start by changing that mental model, and introducing you to a new way of thinking that will help you be happier and more productive when you're working from home.

This model hinges on thinking of yourself as a Business of One, adopting the mental habits and skills of a small business owner. This model allows you to deliver results that wow your boss or clients, while enjoying the flexibility that is the best part of home-based work. The first chapter in this section walks you through what it means to think like a Business of One, and shows you the data that underlies the promise of this new model.

Understanding this model is key to making effective use of the strategies, skills, and tips you find in the rest of the book. But we know that the Business of One model will work differently depending on your role and circumstances, so the next two chapters dig in more deeply and help you think about how to make the model suit your needs.

In chapter 2, "Making the New Model Work," we look at how your approach to remote work will be shaped by your employment structure (that is, whether you're an employee or a freelancer) as well as by your market power (how difficult it is for your clients or employer to replace you). We introduce the idea of punctuated collaboration, which will help you create a little more freedom from your team, and to a few tactics that can help you get a little more freedom from your boss.

In chapter 3, "Managing a Remote Team," we flip that around, because we know you might be a remote worker *and* a team leader. If you're a manager, you need to figure out how to make this model work for your whole team. If you're not a manager, you may want to be one someday—and, meanwhile, reading this chapter should give you a better understanding of the challenges faced by your boss.

CHAPTER 1

YOUR BUSINESS OF ONE

How do you know if you're productive?

This question is at the heart of how we think about remote work.

After all, when people talk about "productivity," what they're usually talking about is how much you get done in a day. If you say you've had a really productive day, what you mean is that you got more done than you usually do. If people describe you as a productive person, what they mean is that you get more accomplished than most other people in your job or field: you're productive if you deliver bigger and better results on any given workday.

But what is your workday, exactly? When you're in the office, it's an easy question to answer: it's measured from the time you walk through the door until the time you leave. (Plus whatever additional work you squeeze in before or after hours, if you put in some extra time at home.)

Once you switch to working remotely, however, the idea of a workday gets a lot messier. Is your workday defined by the time you spend sitting at your desk? What about the business call you took while you were doing the dishes? How about the bolt of inspiration that hit you in the shower, and which you then scribbled down the moment you got to your phone? Do they count as part of your productive workday?

In this chapter, we'll help you rethink your notion of productivity so that it's no longer defined by the dated concept of a workday. We'll start by looking at where the eight-hour workday came from, and the limitations of that metric in today's economy, especially for remote work. Next, we'll show you a different model, which we call thinking like a "Business of One": it helps you achieve more for yourself and your organization by focusing on your accomplishments, rather than the ticking clock. Finally, we'll show you survey data that helps illuminate the productivity gains from providing remote workers with more autonomy, so they can operate like *Remote, Inc.*

BEYOND THE WORKDAY

Most organizations still define productivity by the eight-hour workday, even as millions of people have transitioned to remote work that makes those eight hours awfully hard to track. Nonetheless, salaried employees are often held accountable for each day's work in the form of a timesheet, recording how they spent every hour. If you're a service professional like a lawyer or accountant, you may even be accountable for each and every billable quarter hour. Even if you're running your own business, you may find yourself focusing on where your hours go, either because you're billing on an hourly basis or because the visible hours you spend on video calls are the way you demonstrate effort to your clients or staff.

This obsession with the eight-hour workday is an obsolete leftover from a previous era in which the nine-to-five day was a crucial tool for maximizing productivity, ensuring employee accountability, and measuring output. When the Industrial Revolution brought us factories and assembly lines, factory owners looked at hours worked as the key to maximizing the profits from their investments. Once union organizers won a forty-hour work week, managers focused on getting the greatest possible output from every eight-hour shift.[1]

As the industrial economy yielded to the digital and information-based economy, however, hours ceased to be a sensible way to measure productivity or hold employees accountable.[2] Employees could generate a great result in a few hours, or a poor result in a few days. Indeed, a growing number of studies suggested that piling on additional work hours produces smaller and smaller gains as hours increase.[3]

You can see the problem with equating hours and productivity in just about any form of knowledge work. If you hire an advertising agency to come up with an ad concept for your new video game, do you feel like the ad is worth more if it took longer to produce—or do you mainly care about whether the ad itself is original and compelling? If you ask your director of sales to find you ten new recurring clients, do you judge those contracts based on how many hours it took to land them—or based on the dollar value of each individual client agreement? If you ask someone on your team to produce the slide deck for your upcoming board presentation, do you want a big deck that represents many hours of work—or do you just want the most effective, well-designed presentation?

Despite the obvious flaws of using hours to measure productivity, some employers have tried to find new ways of counting the hours put in by remote employees: tracking mouse movements and keyboard strokes, taking video snapshots of employees at their desks, or just keeping people so tied up with phone and video calls that they don't have any free time to waste.[4] But that kind of scrutiny is more likely to lead to employee burnout than increased productivity: just one month into the remote work shift triggered by the Covid pandemic, one survey found that 45 percent of employees were already feeling burned out.[5]

If the eight-hour workday is so ill-suited to measuring the productivity of knowledge-based workers, why do so many employers obsess over counting hours? Blame history: Two hundred years of bean counting won't evaporate overnight. Hours offer an easy way to measure and bill your services. And for managers, hours provide a plausible if crude way to track what the team is doing: if you're spending eight hours on back-to-back video calls, at least your boss knows you're not going to the beach!

As outdated as the hour-tracking system may be, it's not going anywhere until organizations find another way to ensure the accountability of their employees—especially those who are working remotely. The right approach to accountability also needs to be better for employees: enabling them to work productively, deliver stronger results, and achieve more control over how they spend their time. That's exactly what will happen if remote workers think like a Business of One.

THINKING LIKE A BUSINESS OF ONE

Thinking like a Business of One means thinking of yourself as if you are your own small business, even if you're actually an employee working for a larger organization. Your "products" are made up of the work you are delivering for your clients—and if you're an employee, your number one client is your boss. You are the CEO, the chief marketing officer, the director of HR *and* the entire workforce of this business: it's your job not only to get the work done, but also to think strategically, manage your "brand," and keep your workforce— that's you!—happy and productive.

Thinking as a Business of One lets you focus on outcomes instead of hours worked, and outcomes are what should matter to both you and your employer. By helping you rethink and reorganize the way you work remotely, this model solves the problems of accountability, productivity, and output measurement—but in a totally different way from the outdated obsession with the eight-hour day.

- ACCOUNTABILITY . . . FOR OBJECTIVES. As the CEO of your Business of One, you are accountable for achieving or supporting the objectives your clients have set out. If you are an employee, that means that you are accountable for the objectives that have been set by your boss or employer: that's your client. (If you are a freelancer or business owner, your customers are your clients.) You and your boss/client will negotiate agreements that ensure these objectives are crystal clear, so that you actually can be accountable for delivering on them.
- PRODUCTIVITY . . . FOR YOU. As the head of HR for your Business of One, it is your job to fully understand what maximizes the productivity of your workforce. You should organize your time and space to bring out your best, even if what is best for you might be a little different from how you've worked in the past, or how you've related to the rest of your team. If you're an employee, you and your boss will need to agree on a mode of working that lets you deliver the best results in a way that's in everybody's interests.
- MEASUREMENT . . . OF OUTCOMES. As the chief marketing officer, you need to protect and further the reputation of your business by delivering measurable results. When you're clarifying the objectives of your boss or client, you will also discuss how to measure your progress toward these objectives. To create a true meeting of the minds, the

remote worker and the boss should agree on what we call success metrics: a written list of deliverables with time targets. Then you will organize your work in a way that yields those measurable results, and regularly communicate with your boss to share your progress.

Managing Accountability, Productivity, and Measurement

Let's look at how thinking like a Business of One might change the day-to-day work of a customer account manager at a medical supply company. In the old model, the head of the department ensures accountability by witnessing the account manager hard at work all day at the office, either in meetings or on calls at her desk. The boss manages productivity by walking around the floor just often enough to discourage chitchat and personal calls, so that everybody stays focused on customer-centered work. And the boss may simply reach a subjective judgment about whether certain employees *seem* productive— perhaps based on how much time they spend in the break room.

When that customer account manager shifts to remote work, however, those accountability mechanisms and subjective judgments fall apart, because she's no longer under the boss's nose. Instead it's up to the account manager to think like a Business of One—figuring out the best way to organize her work at home to deliver measurable results for the company.

Her client—that is, her boss—sets the objectives for which she will be accountable. Perhaps this quarter, the chief objective is to improve customer service. While everyone would agree that improving customer service is a worthwhile goal, what does it mean in this context? And who is the customer? It could be the hospital administrator, the doctors, the medical technicians, or the patients, or a combination of these people.

To ensure she really can be accountable for delivering on these objectives, our customer account manager negotiates with her client—the boss—to bring clarity to their objectives. Through a series of conversations, they agree the manager will be accountable for improving service to hospital administrators who buy the equipment as well as the doctors who actually use it. That means providing more training and support, as well as faster responses to any inquiries. This process of negotiating metrics looks much like the work any business owner would do when negotiating a contract: you can't sign a contract unless you know what you'll be expected to deliver.

Next, our account manager needs to think about her own productivity. She realizes that she'll need some uninterrupted time to work on the training strategy and materials her business will be delivering. She will also need to be more responsive to incoming calls from hospital administrators. Since she mainly manages East Coast accounts but works from California, she needs to be available to return customer calls for at least the first half of the day. She proposes blocking off her time in the company calendar so that her afternoons are reserved for focused work, while her meetings are booked in the morning—with enough slack time between meetings that she can return incoming calls from East Coast customers.

Finally, it's time to talk about measurement: How will the boss know if the account manager is being productive? Rather than relying on subjective judgments, they agree on a set of success metrics that will allow them both to measure progress toward the objective of improving customer service. After reviewing a range of options, they land on a few measurable indicators: a decrease in the number of equipment returns, a reduction in the time it takes to resolve a customer issue, and higher revenues as measured by the additional orders for their equipment placed by hospital customers. Once she knows how the success of her Business of One will be measured, the account manager can focus her work on the tasks and projects that will move the needle.

The Benefits of Thinking Like a Business of One

As you can see from the story of our account manager, thinking like a Business of One can transform the way you as a remote worker control your schedule and relate to your boss. Reaching negotiated agreements on your accountability, productivity, and measurement practices can help you . . .

- FOCUS ON WHAT MATTERS. Once you and your boss or clients agree on exactly what is to be achieved, as well as on how progress will be measured, it's much easier for you to stay focused on what really matters—because you'll know what that is!

- BUILD TRUST WITH YOUR BOSS OR CLIENTS. The process of negotiating your objectives and metrics, as well as reporting on them regularly, builds transparency and trust. When you have clear metrics that let your boss or client assess your progress on your key objectives, they will be much less inclined to micromanage you.

- TAKE CONTROL OF YOUR TIME. When you think like a Business of One, you redefine the notion of a workday so that it's about what you accomplish, not the number of hours you spend sitting at your desk. You are "profitable" if you can deliver those accomplishments in the time you're being paid to work—or possibly even less than that amount of time. The time you free up is time you can then reinvest in your career—taking on additional projects that improve your promotion prospects. Or you can use that time to pursue personal priorities instead, so that you're regenerated and fulfilled.

- TAKE CONTROL OF THE WAY YOU WORK. When you're responsible for results instead of hours, you can work where, when, and how you work best. So much of the productivity struggle around remote work comes from the fact that people are twisting themselves into pretzels with the effort of working within a management system that was designed for office work. When you start thinking like a Business of One, you can organize your work in a way that actually makes sense for your remote life.

- DELIVER STRONGER RESULTS. The ultimate value of working like a Business of One lies in what you can accomplish. When you are working in the way that makes you most effective, aligning your use of time with your goals and priorities, and taking advantage of your home-based solitude to undertake focused, in-depth work, you will be able to produce better outcomes in less time. Your employer and clients will see the impact of your *Remote, Inc.* mindset in the quality and consistency of your output.

You can now see why we advocate thinking like a Business of One. Whether you're a remote employee or a freelancer, this is the mindset that will help you work effectively. You can define your workday in terms of completing key tasks and projects for your boss or clients, not spending a certain number of hours at your desk.

THE CASE FOR THINKING LIKE A BUSINESS OF ONE

We all know people who seem to thrive when they work from home—as well as people who seem to struggle. That's because remote productivity is a learned skill, and it takes some time to learn it.

Research shows that the productivity of people working remotely changes over time, as does their preference for long-term remote work. Polling firm Maru/Blue surveyed 2,183 Americans in four waves from April through September of 2020, asking about their productivity and long-term appetite for remote work at four different moments in the pandemic.[6] Both productivity and satisfaction with remote work rose steadily in the first four months, before leveling out as remote work became the new normal.

Employees, employers, and self-employed people all have a strong interest in ensuring that new remote workers adapt their productivity practices as quickly as possible, and that experienced remote workers continue to hone their remote productivity skills. Providing remote workers with some degree of autonomy—what we call the Business of One mode—appears to facilitate this process of learning and adaptation to remote work.[7]

To understand the adaptation process, we asked Maru/Blue to survey more than a thousand remote workers on their autonomy, productivity, and feelings about remote work (see this book's appendix, "About the Data"). Two results from this survey stand out.

Remote Work Is a Learned Skill

First, the longer people work remotely, the more likely they are to feel at least as productive at home as they were in the workplace. In other words, remote productivity is a learned skill.

You can see this most clearly when you look at figure 1.1. Even after the initial learning curve of 2020, newer remote workers (those who started working remotely only after the Covid pandemic began) did not feel as productive at home as those who'd been working remotely for a long time. This comparison suggests that newcomers to remote work still had a lot to learn about home-based productivity.

What changes over time is not only the number of workers who feel like they can be as productive at home as they were at the office, but also the number of workers who say they are *more* productive at home than they were at the office. Among new remote workers, only a quarter say they're more productive at home than they were in the workplace. By contrast, among long-term remote workers, more than half say that remote work lets them do their best (see figure 1.1). This mirrors what Maru/Blue found in its time series surveys: the proportion of workers who said they were more productive when working from home grew by 50 percent between April and September.

FIGURE 1.1

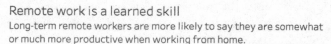

Remote work is a learned skill

Long-term remote workers are more likely to say they are somewhat or much more productive when working from home.

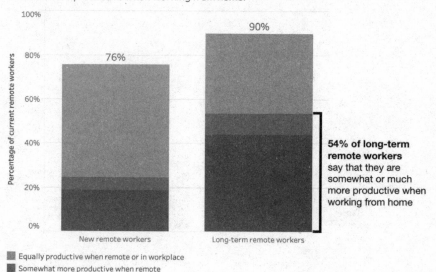

54% of long-term remote workers say that they are somewhat or much more productive when working from home

Autonomy Helps Workers Learn
to Be Productive at Home

Second, if remote productivity is a learned skill, then autonomy is key to that learning process. You can see this result most clearly by looking at figure 1.2: Among new remote workers who have a moderate or high level of autonomy, the vast majority—80 percent—say that they're at least as productive at home as they were at the office. Among low-autonomy remote workers, who report less control over the way they approach their work, barely half feel like they are keeping pace with what they accomplished in the office. Without the latitude to develop a remote-friendly approach to productivity, these low-autonomy workers experience all the drawbacks of remote work, and none of its advantages.

To understand the impact of autonomy on remote productivity, let's zoom in on a single, pivotal indicator: The extent to which remote workers agree with the statement "As long as I get my work done, I have a lot of control

FIGURE 1.2

Remote productivity by level of autonomy
Percentage of new remote workers who say they are equally, somewhat, or much
more productive when working from home.

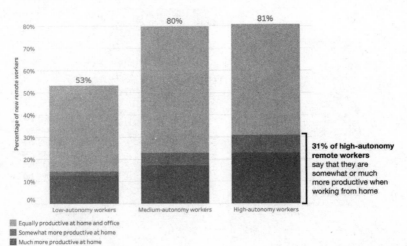

over how and when to do it." Workers who strongly agree with this statement are nearly twice as likely to say they're more productive when working from home, compared with workers who disagree with it (see figure 1.3).

This reflects the productivity impact of measuring results instead of hours. Remote workers who are still being measured by the hour do not have a lot of control over how and when they do their work; by contrast, those who are measured by results enjoy more control. As you can see from figure 1.3, workers who are able to focus on results, and who have the autonomy to figure out the how and when for getting to those results, are much more likely to say they are somewhat or much more productive when working from home.

This data should be encouraging to anyone who is new to remote work, as well as to organizations that worry about the productivity of their newly distributed teams. Yes, the move to a remote workforce may involve some loss of oversight, but that doesn't have to be bad news for employers or employees. On the contrary: once they have the autonomy to work in a way that brings out

FIGURE 1.3

Control over how and when to work makes remote workers more productive

Percentage of remote workers who say they are more productive working from home, by level of agreement with the statement: "As long as I get my work done, I have a lot of control over how and when I do it."

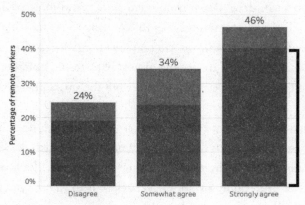

40% of remote workers who say they have a lot of control over how and when to do their work say that they are much more productive when working from home

Somewhat more productive at home
Much more productive at home

their best, workers quickly learn to get even *more* done when they're working from home.

The Business of One model is the way employees and employers can embrace that kind of autonomy. By learning to think like *Remote, Inc.*, each and every remote worker gets the mindset, strategies, and skills they need to work productively in this more autonomous mode. It just requires some patience and guidance on how to adapt to remote work—guidance you will find in this book.

FROM A REMOTE WORKER

Huw Evans, director of growth for management consulting firm Point B, has long operated as a Business of One, with a high degree of autonomy and great results for his firm.

My primary role is as a revenue generator, knocking on doors at companies like Facebook or Google to land our initial project. If you're good in sales, part of the magic is in meeting in person. You're sitting down with the CXO of a big company every quarter, and you know he looks forward to that meeting. I need to be able to do those meetings in person.

Normally I spend about 30 percent of my time in front of customers, clustering my meetings so I can drive down from home and spend most of the day in Silicon Valley. The rest of my time goes into getting those meetings, or staying on top of industry news and working on my energy levels. I'm by myself two days a week, but I spend those days almost back-to-back on internal calls to get prepped for client meetings and figure out the smart questions to ask.

Getting my headspace in the right zone for work is really difficult if you're in a shoebox with noise and trash in the street. My new home north of San Francisco gives me more space. Where I'm living now is a lot like the town where I grew up, outside of London. I want to get back to being a bit more in nature, and cities appeal less as you get older.

Before Covid, our Bay Area team would get together in a shared space on

Fridays, but it didn't bring any value for me. All that water-cooler, casual collision stuff—none of that really moves my needle. I need time to focus on my individual contribution to the firm, because I am a bit of a lone ranger.

That doesn't mean I'm a loner, though. I'm actually an extrovert—I get energy from other people and their ideas. When we're not in lockdown, I sometimes drive to a coffee shop first thing and chat with a stranger. That's enough for me to get my dopamine hit, so that I'm energized for the day. It's like a human experiment: How much interaction do I need to thrive and not go insane during the day?

Now, because of Covid, I have no in-person meetings: everything is by video call and phone. And when you do get a meeting, the fact that it's video or phone means you don't have any of that X factor, that energy in your being, where a customer wants to work with you. It's like you've lost your magic.

To make up for that, I take risks that I might not have taken previously, and really try to connect on a human, personal level. Clients are more accessible and more vulnerable, too, because we all have this common experience through Covid.

I expect that all these video calls are going to be the new norm, even after Covid. In that world, people like me are going to try every trick in the book to convert a video call to an in-person meeting. The whole question is, How are we going to get that in-person meeting, so we can get that X factor working for us?

I have an insatiable appetite for my craft, so I just keep looking for new tips and tricks on how to engage with customers remotely. People don't really appreciate or understand the nuance of sales and relationship development and landing new clients. But if you're doing it well, you're earning more than the CEO.

TAKEAWAYS

1. Productivity is usually defined in terms of what you get done in a day, but it's not clear what counts as a workday once you're working remotely.

2. Measuring productivity in terms of the billable hour, the eight-hour workday, or the forty-hour workweek is an obsolete leftover from the industrial era—which doesn't make sense when you're a knowledge worker.

3. Organizations cling to the billable hour and the eight-hour workday because they are trying to ensure employee accountability, maximize productivity, and measure output. Thinking like a Business of One offers a better way to achieve these objectives.

4. When you think of remote work like you're a Business of One, you can focus on outcomes instead of hours. Think of your boss as a client you want to wow by delivering work that meets their objectives.

5. Clarify objectives with your boss, and negotiate success metrics. How you get there is then up to you.

6. In a survey of more than a thousand remote workers, people with the autonomy to function like a Business of One were happier working remotely, and were faster to adapt their productivity habits to working from home.

7. Employees who have more control over how and when they work are more likely to enjoy a productivity boost when working from home.

CHAPTER 2

MAKING THE NEW MODEL WORK

When you think of yourself as *Remote, Inc.*, you'll be more productive and effective when working remotely. But how can you think like a Business of One when you're working as part of a larger team or organization?

In this chapter, we will map out the specific challenges that you need to address in order to function as a Business of One. We will look at how the structure of your employment and your market power affect your ability to carve out the autonomy and flexibility you need to do your best. We'll help you organize your work around a cadence of "punctuated collaboration" so that you can be a team player and still function as *Remote, Inc.* Finally, we'll talk about specific strategies for managing your boss (if you're an employee) or wowing your client (if you're self-employed) so that you get the benefits of independence and security.

CAN I REALLY OPERATE LIKE A BUSINESS OF ONE?

Thinking and working like a Business of One is an adjustment—especially if you're used to working in a big organization. While some organizations are very successful at structuring themselves as a distributed team, others expect their remote workers to function as if they're still at the office. But that is not a very useful approach for either employers or employees, which is why we want to help you create the autonomy to organize your professional life in a way that maximizes the benefits of remote work and limits its drawbacks.

Depending on your employment structure and your market power, you may find that autonomy easier or harder to achieve. We observe very different experiences and strategies for remote work depending on where people sit in this chart:

TABLE 2.1

		EMPLOYEE	SELF-EMPLOYED
MARKET POWER	HIGH	Irreplaceable employees • C-suite executives • Senior managers • Celebrity employees • Rainmakers • Scarce specialists	Rockstar freelancers • Renowned consultants • Partner-level professionals • Business owners • High-profile creatives
	LOW/ MODERATE	Developing employees • Midlevel employees • Steady performers • New hires • Junior employees	Standard freelancers • Gig workers • Freelancers with easy-to-find skills • Up-and-coming creatives

Let's look at each of these quadrants in turn, and what they imply for the way you will function as a Business of One.

Irreplaceable Employees

Professionals who command a lot of respect within their organizations may still be employees, but they are well positioned to function like a Business of One. If you regularly get approached by recruiters, offered lots of stock options in return for continued service, or get large cash bonuses that reflect outstanding performance, you can be confident you have a high degree of market power and qualify as an *irreplaceable employee.*

Employees in this category include the C-level and senior executives who command a lot of clout within the organization, the top-performing salespeople or partners who bring in substantial revenue, and professionals with skills that are in great demand: PhD-level data scientists, skilled engineers, actual rocket scientists. The harder you are to replace, the more freedom you have to define the terms of your employment.

The biggest challenge for irreplaceable employees is that they face many demands on their time, which they may not always be able to delegate. The way they handle all these demands while working remotely often sets the tone for the rest of the organization: If the CEO keeps erratic hours, the employees of the company may see this as license to be similarly unpredictable. (Or, conversely, they may resent a manager who breaks the rules she expects the team to follow.)

If you're in a high-power position within your own organization, you should certainly use that power to get the autonomy you need to perform well while working remotely. Indeed, as a high-value asset, it's your duty to do what you need to do in order to maximize your performance. Use the Business of One framework to get crystal clear about any conflicts between organizational norms and what you need to do your best work. For example, as the CEO of a five-hundred-person company, you may deliver your best days of video meetings and decision-making when you start out with a ten-mile run. If so, you should tell your client—the board—that you won't be taking calls before 8 a.m.

As much as possible, try to create flexibility for your Business of One in a way that helps build a culture of autonomy for remote workers throughout the organization. That means advocating for remote-friendly policies rather than individual exceptions. If you find that your organization's structure and expectations for remote work prevent you from maximizing your own productivity, use your authority or influence to change that structure so that everyone in the organization can do their best work while working remotely. For managers and leaders, a key deliverable of your Business of One is the remote work culture that helps everyone else do their best, too.

Developing Employees

Most remote workers are *developing employees* who do not have the market power to dictate their conditions for remote work, even if they are dedicated, talented, and valuable to their organizations. These are the folks who keep an organization running, even if they never come into the office. But not every organization offers them the autonomy and flexibility to excel.

That's exactly where the *Remote, Inc.* model comes in handy. You're a developing employee if you are in a professional role that delivers value but does not make you irreplaceable. This is likely your situation if you are in a junior or midlevel role, without any advanced degrees or hard-to-find skills, in a field where there is no particular shortage of qualified candidates. Recognizing the limits on your market power is not a comment on your worth as a human being; it's an essential first step toward operating like *Remote, Inc.*

If you're a developing employee, your ability to function like a Business of One will depend significantly on your role, manager, and organization. Some organizations and leaders recognize the value of giving their team members a lot of latitude, particularly when they're working remotely; others are still trying to operate like a conventional workplace, and rely on constant meetings and surveillance to ensure each employee is putting in a day's work. If you're in that latter kind of organization, especially if you're in a role that requires constant responsiveness to your manager, it will take some work and patience to get the autonomy you need to thrive while working remotely. But don't worry: you can get there!

There are two basic strategies that can help developing employees earn the freedom to operate like a Business of One. First, you can demonstrate that you deliver consistent, timely, and excellent results while working from home: a good manager will give you more latitude once she sees that you can work hard and produce good outcomes without constant oversight. This is likely to be a gradual process: as you deliver better and better work, you will earn more and more discretion over exactly how and when you work.

Second, you can build the market power that makes you harder to replace, so that your manager is eager to accommodate your requests for flexibility. Pursue projects, experiences, and credentials that build up your knowledge, skills, and relationships; better yet, develop an unusual combination of skills that puts you in a category all your own. Consider building a public profile through social media or presentations, so that your employer values you for your reputation as well as your contributions.

Remember, it's not all or nothing: You may be accountable to your boss on a daily basis and still find ways to make better use of your time. Adopting the *Remote, Inc.* mindset will help you create a virtuous circle: by implementing the strategies and tactics in this book, you will deliver stronger results, which will win you more latitude to do your best work. Keep at it, and you will find yourself working more and more like a Business of One.

Rockstar Freelancers

People who are self-employed and have significant market power enjoy a lot of freedom in how they structure their work and their lives. Some of the folks in this category include successful business owners (when you're the boss, you call the shots); others are solo artists or consultants, with enough star power to attract and retain clients or sales; still others are embedded in a firm (like partner-level lawyers or accountants) but run their own independent practice within the firm, and thus structure their own hours and deliverables.

If you are essentially a free agent, and you're also highly skilled or recognized in your field, you are a *rockstar freelancer.* A good measure of your market power is the degree to which you already pick and choose your opportunities: if you regularly turn away potential clients or customers because the rate, hours, or project are just not a fit, and yet you still have enough work and income, then you can be pretty confident you have a high degree of market power.

But even rockstar freelancers have less than absolute freedom. You still need to earn a living, which means that you need clients, customers, or buyers: keeping these folks happy may sometimes require adjusting your hours or deliverables. If you have a team of support staff and collaborators, you also need to establish an appropriate pace and structure for their remote work.

The Business of One model should feel very intuitive to business owners or self-employed folks with a lot of market power, because they're already functioning as a remote business. Yet it's sometimes the people who are literally organized as a Business of One who need this mindset the most. Using this explicit framework will help you bring structure to the way you approach your work in order to be maximally effective—as a partner in a firm, or as the actual owner of a small business.

Standard Freelancers

Not everyone who is self-employed enjoys a high degree of autonomy to function as a Business of One. These days, a great many "independent contractors" are functionally equivalent to employees—so much so that we see more and more laws that require organizations to provide employee status, or some benefits, to their recurring contractors.[1] Even if you are a true freelancer with multiple clients, you may not have much room to dictate the circumstances in which you work: freelancers who work for on-demand services like Fiverr, Upwork, or TaskRabbit may be constrained by the app's terms or rating system, and even true freelancers may find themselves treated as commodities if their skills are not particularly hard to find.

You are in the world of the *standard freelancer* if you are self-employed or a small business owner, but have to compete with other freelancers and businesses on price. If your clients or customers would find it relatively easy to replace you with another supplier, or if raising your rates would make a significant portion of your business head elsewhere, then you know you have only a modest level of market power. Depending on the demands of your clients and field, you may still have quite a lot more latitude than you'd enjoy as an employee—or you may be a Business of One in name only, and functionally constrained by the expectations of your customers.

If you're a standard freelancer, you may aim to increase your market power by wowing clients, acquiring some additional skills or credentials, or building a professional reputation that differentiates you from other people in your field. Like many developing employees, however, you may be happier staying out of the rat race, and instead approaching your freelance practice as a lifestyle business that gives you a nice balance of income and flexibility.

How much flexibility you have will be determined by how effectively you work as a Business of One: Even if you're structurally self-employed, you can easily lose your freedom or productivity to the demands of a client who expects you to keep long hours or work in a specific way. So use the Business of One framework to underline your autonomy in all your client interactions: whenever you see us reminding employees to treat their boss like a client, remind yourself to avoid the trap of treating your client like she's your boss.

Embracing the skills and approaches in this book will help you consolidate your approach as a Business of One, so that remote work gives you the freedom that is the very best part of a freelance career.

DOING YOUR BEST WORK AS A BUSINESS OF ONE

If you experience remote work as an endless series of Zoom calls, email messages, and Slack notifications, it may be very hard for you to deliver great results. Your aim is to find the sweet spot between structure and flexibility that allows you to . . .

- Work during the times when you're most productive
- Collaborate effectively with teammates
- Deliver good results to your boss, customers, or clients
- Regularly relax and regenerate—not only so that you can work productively, but also because you deserve to have a life!

For many remote workers, and especially for developing employees, it can be hard to find this kind of balance. That's because many remote teams operate the way they would at the office, treating meetings as the default form of collaboration, and collaboration as the norm for how work gets done. But these are the very assumptions we need to change when we start working remotely.

The focus on real-time collaboration through meetings made a lot of sense fifty years ago, when it was the most efficient way to exchange ideas. Just think about the alternative: Sit down at your IBM Selectric typewriter (or ask your secretary to type up your notes); Wite-Out your errors; distribute carbon copies or photocopies. Put it in the *mail* and then wait a week to hear back, in the form of someone else's typed-up, Wited-Out, carbon-copied document. What a nightmare!

Seriously, how did anyone do anything back then? Well, through meetings, of course: just get everyone in a room, hash things through, and then it takes only one secretary and one typewriter to get to a final document.

Thankfully those days are now behind us. And yet we often work as if we face the same constraints—even though electronic communication means we can now collaborate across distances, and revise or iterate in close to real time.

Punctuated Collaboration

A smarter model is what we call "punctuated collaboration": an approach that finds a middle ground between the efficiency of solo work and the many benefits of collaboration. Working as a team engages diversity of perspectives and knowledge, builds trust and relationship among colleagues, and builds consensus and buy-in around the outcome. Even if you *could* write a better report entirely on your own, collaboration is the best way to rally your teammates around the result.

The secret is to make collaboration specific, focused, and time-limited, rather than accepting it as our default mode for getting work done.[2] When you work in an office, collaboration may indeed be the most effective option, but in part that's because it's so hard to do focused work when you're constantly interrupted. Once you shift to working from home, you can make the most of solo time, and then use focused check-ins to advance your project or deliverable to the next stage.

You will be most effective at shifting the balance of work from collaboration to solo work if you can propose specific plans that get your team to the finish line with fewer meetings and better results. Here are some common scenarios in which distributed teams default to meetings, but where you can suggest punctuated collaboration: that is, distributing tasks among the team so that people can get more done on their own, with check-ins at specific intervals and with clear success metrics.

INSTEAD OF DAILY MEETINGS TO PLAN YOUR CORPORATE RETREAT . . .

1. Start by creating a project plan that delineates all the tasks involved in organizing the retreat; then group these based on roles or where different people excel.

2. Next, use an online project dashboard to assign tasks and request regular updates on progress toward each task.

3. Ask each person to maintain a separate list of questions/items for discussion by the whole team.

4. Assign a project manager to track progress on each task against deadline and collect questions for team discussion as the basis for meeting agendas. Any questions that require input from only one or two people go to those people via message or email.

5. Post updates on the project dashboard so everyone can see status and key info in one place.

6. Reserve weekly calls for discussing items that actually require group input or decision-making.

INSTEAD OF A SERIES OF CALLS TO BRAINSTORM NEW PRODUCT OR CAMPAIGN IDEAS . . .

1. Set up a standing suggestion box (for example, an online form, Google Doc, or wiki) where team members can collect ideas for the next product or campaign, with every idea attributed to its source. (Credit is one reason people save their ideas for meetings.) An online suggestion box also creates room for less vocal employees.

2. Dig into the suggestion box when it's time to start a new initiative: the project lead collects existing ideas or solicits new ones, which they compile or categorize in an online document (like a Google Doc or spreadsheet).

3. Invite team members to comment on the ideas in the initial brainstorming file, and add other ideas that are inspired by the starting point.

4. Review the document to identify the most promising ideas, and then convene the team to review the top ideas and arrive at a list of top options over the course of two or three virtual meetings.

INSTEAD OF DAILY WORK SPRINTS AS A TEAM . . .

1. Set team goals for the week, month, or product cycle.

2. Schedule manager check-ins at key points in the process—with deadlines and decision points for each meeting.

3. Set up a drop-in virtual meeting room, coworking message channel, phone call, or playlist for team members who like the feeling of ambient collegiality—but make this optional, so people drop in to the coworking space only if they actively want to be there.

4. Empower individual team members to work in pairs or small groups as needed, rather than convening the entire team.

In some organizations, these strategies of punctuated collaboration are already the norm. But there are many teams that spend the majority of their day on video calls, just because they're in the habit of managing by meeting; such meetings often include many agenda items that don't actually require every single person on the call. These are the teams that need to adapt their remote work strategies so that people mainly work solo or in pairs, and group or team calls are scheduled only when they're really necessary.

MAKING THE CASE FOR *REMOTE, INC.*

Encouraging Punctuated Collaboration

It can be very hard to avoid the expectations of your boss or colleagues that you will participate in many online meetings, even though they are probably feeling overloaded by meetings themselves. So you need to model the idea of punctuated collaboration in your own projects, and make a point of explicitly reflecting on its benefits.

At the start of a project where you are the team leader or project manager, use the kick-off meeting to assign initial tasks, and let the team know you'll aim to minimize meetings by asking each person to get more done on their own. Introduce them to the project dashboard and be religious about keeping it up-to-date. At the beginning and end of your (less frequent) project meetings, note that you were able to keep this meeting short (or skip the previous week's meeting) because everyone has been making such good use of punctuated collaboration.

This strategy can work even if you're very junior: Just pick a small "project" where you can replace meeting time with email or messaging. For example, instead of taking up meeting time by getting ideas for the group social you need to organize, let everyone know that you'd like to give them back the next thirty minutes by getting suggestions through email instead; then you'll present a short list of options next week.

Once you shift the balance of your workday to involve less collaboration and more solo work, you'll have a lot more control over your schedule and activities. You'll be able to focus on results instead of hours worked, and concentrate your efforts on the work that matters most.

WORKING WITH YOUR BOSS (OR CLIENT) IN A REMOTE RELATIONSHIP

A successful relationship with your manager or client creates a virtuous circle: The more efficiently and effectively you work, the more they will trust you to manage your own tasks and schedule. And the more latitude you have to organize your own schedule and tasks, the more productive you'll be, and the better your outcomes.

That's why it's so crucial to build a trusting relationship with your boss or important clients: Trust is the key to achieving the flexibility and working conditions that allow you to achieve your best result. Your boss or client should be able to trust you to work hard, show up for the team, and support her in your conversations with other members of the team or organization. You should be able to trust your boss to deliver the resources and information you need to work effectively, provide guidance and troubleshooting, and speak with you directly when she is either disappointed or thrilled with your work.

But that kind of trust can be hard to build when you rarely see each other in person. This is where it pays to think like a Business of One: By thinking of your boss as a client you need to both manage and amaze, you're much more likely to exceed her expectations while also pursuing your own goals. This comes down to three main practices: setting expectations, improving communication, and documenting performance.

Set Clear Expectations

When you deliver consistent results on the timeline your boss is expecting, you make her life easier and the whole team more effective. The essential word there is "expecting": it's your job to get on the same page as your boss from the get-go, so she knows what she can expect from you, and you are absolutely clear on those expectations.

Clear expectations begin with clear success metrics: key performance indicators that you and your boss both use to assess whether you're meeting your agreed-upon objectives. (This is at least as important when you're a freelancer working with an actual client.) Any major initiative should have a clear plan for how you're going to measure success, and any ongoing areas of responsibility should have equally clear metrics, whether they consist of leads generated, revenue earned, or calls answered.

Beyond the expectations you set in the form of success metrics, you can also help set clear expectations in other ways:

- THINK PROACTIVELY. Don't wait for your boss to give you marching orders. Help define the agenda by identifying the projects or tasks you can take on successfully, and then get your boss to sign off on your plan. In some instances, you may be able to wow your "client" by simply taking care of something before your boss even asks, then letting her know what you did.

- SET MEETING WINDOWS. Reach an explicit understanding on how much time you'll spend in meetings, and when you need meeting-free time to get your work done. If you want to work something other than a standard eight-hour day, this is the chance to make a business case for your preferred schedule: "I'd like to be online and available for calls or meetings from 8 a.m. to noon, and then I'd like to block off two hours in the middle of the day so I can get myself fed and exercised so that I return to my desk and my focused work with improved concentration from 2 p.m. to 6 p.m."

  Depending on your role and relationship you may even be able to get more flexibility: "I would love to keep my calendar booked off from 1 p.m. to 5 p.m. so I can do focused work at the times when I'm most productive." As long as you make it clear that you'll be accommodating when it's a matter of booking a hard-to-coordinate meeting or dealing with a crisis, you may be able to carve out a fair degree of scheduling flexibility.

- SPELL OUT TRADE-OFFS. If your boss is asking you to attend so many meetings that it crowds out your ability to complete other kinds of work (or to just take the midday breaks that keep you sane), you may have a hard time turning down these meeting invitations. But you can spell out specific trade-offs and ask for direction from your boss: "Would you like me to delay the delivery date on our client report so I can attend these three meetings, or is it better for me to get the report done before we book those meetings?"

- SET EXPECTATIONS AROUND YOUR OWN AVAILABILITY AND DOWNTIMES. Remote work makes it very hard to set boundaries between work and personal time, especially if you have a boss who sends emails and messages around the clock. That's why it's important to clarify whether and when your boss expects a quick response outside of business hours, and also to be clear about your own boundaries: "I'm happy to answer email in the evening, but I'm offline 5:30 to 7:30 p.m. to spend time with family. And unless we're under the gun on a major deadline, I don't check email after 10 p.m. or on weekends."

This is a practice that helps your manager, too, because now he knows the best times to reach you, and won't find himself waiting around for a response at a moment when he could tackle another priority. If you indicate that you're willing to put in the extra time in a crunch, and do a mid-evening check-in before going dark, your boss may be more relaxed about you disappearing from email or messaging here and there during the workday.

CONVINCING YOUR BOSS TO LET YOU WORK REMOTELY

If you would like to maintain or increase the amount of time you spend working remotely, but your boss or organization insists on you working full-time in the office, here's what to do:

- FIND OUT WHY YOUR BOSS WANTS YOU IN THE OFFICE. Is it to monitor your performance? Support collaboration? Optics? The more you understand her motivations, the more likely you are to come up with the right strategy.
- EXPLAIN THE PERFORMANCE OR BUDGET BENEFITS OF YOUR REMOTE WORK PLAN. Let your boss know how remote work boosts your productivity or contributions, so he can see what's in it for him. Do you spend what would be commuting time on extra work? Are you more focused in the quiet of your home office? Can you put off that raise in return for more time at home?
- OFFER A TRIAL-BASIS ARRANGEMENT. Agree on a period of time when you will work remotely according to your preferences, with clear success metrics.
- COMPROMISE. Remote work isn't all or nothing. Even if all you can get is one remote day every couple of weeks, that's your chance to

demonstrate how effective you are when working remotely . . . so you can build your case for more time outside the office.

Communicate Effectively with Your "Client"

Communicate clearly and frequently with your boss, and you will have a lot more latitude to get your work done. Here are the best practices to follow:

- GET CLEAR ON HOW YOUR "CLIENT" WANTS TO HEAR FROM YOU. When you start a new job or major new project, or shift the amount of time you spend working remotely, find out how your boss or client prefers to hear from you. Some people like daily or weekly updates; some want to be consulted before decisions are made; some like to hear the plan you'll proceed with unless they say otherwise; others just want to hear from you if there's an obstacle you need help surmounting.

  Be sure to ask specifically about frequency (daily, weekly, or just at major milestones?), process (wait for feedback, or go ahead unless they say stop?) and preferred communications channels (email, messaging, or text). Find out how your boss defines an "emergency" and how she wants to hear from you if one arises. Finally, be sure to talk about how quickly she expects a response to her own messages, and whether that expectation is any different during evenings or weekends.
- SET UP REGULAR CHECK-INS. Even if you have a boss or client who is relatively hands off, make sure you have regular check-ins. At the very least that should include a weekly email update where you summarize your accomplishments in the past seven days and your plan for the week ahead. Ideally you will also have a phone or video call every week or two, so that you stay connected: even if this is just a thirty-minute call, it helps you maintain your relationship and see if there are other opportunities for you to be helpful.
- LET YOUR BOSS KNOW HOW TO HELP YOU DO YOUR BEST WORK. Communication is a two-way street, so it's perfectly appropriate for you to let

your boss know how she can help you succeed. If you find it hard
to make sense of a string of text messages, it's OK to ask your boss
if you can get guidance in the form of a call or single email. If you're
motivated by praise and appreciation, let your boss know you need
to hear when you're doing well; conversely, be candid if what you
really want is a running list of ways to improve.

- **OFFER RECOMMENDATIONS WITH ALTERNATIVE SOLUTIONS.** Whenever you
  need to ask your boss or client for a decision, try to offer her options
  and a recommendation. This is even more important if you're asking for her help in overcoming a roadblock. For example, instead of
  saying "We can't find a conference venue in our budget, what should
  I do?", tell your boss: "There is no conference venue available for
  our budget, event dates, and audience size. I recommend reducing
  our planned invitation list by 20 percent so we can go with venue X,
  which is big enough for all our customers (though not our partners
  and suppliers). However we also have the option of going with venue
  Y (if we can increase our budget by 50k) or venue Z (if we can push
  our date back by a month)."

- **WHEN IN DOUBT, OVERCOMMUNICATE.** It's better to communicate too much
  than too little, but aim for a high signal-to-noise ratio: get straight to
  the point when you're emailing or messaging, and provide any additional context in a form that lets your boss decide how deep to dive
  in to the details of your project or question. (Chapter 13, on email,
  will show you how to do this.)

- **GET AHEAD OF PROBLEMS.** The overcommunication rule is especially
  important if you're having any trouble with a project, colleague, or
  customer: It's much better to ask for help early on, and make it clear
  where you're hoping your boss can advise or run interference, than
  to wait until you've got a major issue for them to unsnarl. The same
  principle applies if you're behind on a deadline: If your "client"
  is expecting a deliverable or update that you won't have ready on
  time, let them know *before* the deadline arrives, and provide an updated ETA. If the deadline slip is because you're waiting for someone or something else, you can share that information as context,

particularly if your boss can help clear the logjam: just make an effort to take as much responsibility as you can, so it doesn't seem like you're passing the buck.

Build a Performance File

When you are working remotely, part of your job is to make your manager's work easier—which includes making it easier for them to evaluate you. The best way to do that is by building and maintaining a performance file: a representative cross section of your best work, and a log of your major challenges and areas of growth. This isn't a matter of papering over your mistakes: it's a way of tracking your work so that you and your boss can learn from your successes, and collaboratively strategize on how to continually improve your performance.

Your performance file is something that can help you in your long-run career advancement, by making it easier to update your LinkedIn profile or résumé so that it reflects concrete accomplishments. But do remember that if you're keeping your notes on a company computer or server, your notes may not be just for your eyes alone; even if it's hard to imagine a scenario where someone will pore over your notes, you should keep your own performance notes as if that *could* happen.

This file may help you with future job hunts or promotions, but it's also an asset in your day-to-day, year-to-year relationship with your boss. Before each performance review, look over your performance file and pull out some examples of emails or work you can share with your boss; jot down your particular accomplishments this quarter; and try to anticipate any concerns your boss is likely to raise, so you can make a plan for how you'll address them.

In between your performance reviews, don't be shy about using your performance file to blow your own horn or ask for specific assignments. There's nothing presumptuous about forwarding two or three client emails with a cover note like "I just noticed that three separate clients have sent me emails about the sales decks I've prepared, and it's made me wonder if I could take on more of a leadership role in our client-facing presentations."

While expectation-setting, careful communication, and a performance file can all help you manage your "client," remember that the point is not to wriggle free of their oversight. Rather, your aim is to build the trusting relationship that will help them to help you—which is what effective managers do. At the end of the day, you should both be after the same thing: making sure you can deliver your very best work as a Business of One.

FROM A REMOTE WORKER

Maggie Crowley Sheehan is a product marketing manager at software company Unbounce, where she has used a strategy of punctuated collaboration to turn her remote location into an asset for the whole team.

I worked in the Unbounce office for almost two years, until my husband got a job in the Bahamas, and we moved. Luckily, my supervisor wanted to keep me, so I became a bit of a guinea pig for how the company would handle remote work.

When I moved here, I was suddenly three hours ahead of the team, but I decided to work nine to five in my local time zone. When I started work in the morning, if I didn't have something to work on, I was just waiting for my team, and that left me stressed and feeling like I wasn't doing my part.

We came up with processes that made our time zone differences into an asset. Let's say we're launching an email campaign to get people to use a new feature of the software. Once the copywriter drafts copy, it's my job to review their work, come up with improvements, and maybe mock it up as a website. But if I don't know what stage the work is at, I don't know whether to jump in. So now, when there is an update in their work, the folks in our West Coast HQ leave an update in our internal wiki, saying where the work is at and giving me my next steps.

I see people struggling to create the process that I had to figure out when I went remote. I started using Slack, our team messaging system, a lot more, and taking more notes and being more organized about getting all my materials together.

For example, last week I worked on a positioning document for this new feature we're releasing. So I looked in Slack for a relevant conversation I'd had; I found a related presentation, and went looking for a recording about the feature. Then I centralized all the resources so *anybody* can find all the materials they need just as easily.

Before I went remote I never used a project management tool. Now I rely heavily on it. There is a lot of beauty in breaking down big projects into tasks, and being very clear on what expectations are and when we need to meet again. That gives people more confidence over what parts of the project they need help on, and it makes better use of our collective time.

It's all about being very clear about steps and tasks. Once you break it into these tiny little tasks, you're doing less group meetings and group work. Instead it's "I'll do this, this, and this part, and then we can come together."

When I went remote, I was worried about not being able to do my job and contribute to the team. Instead I became more productive and more efficient. So much so that when the rest of the company went remote during Covid, one guy said "We're all going to become 80 percent more productive now—just look at what happened with Maggie!"

TAKEAWAYS

1. Your ability to function as a Business of One is constrained by your employment structure (self-employed people have more freedom than employees) and your market power (senior employees and people with rare skills are in a stronger position to negotiate some flexibility).

2. Working as a Business of One is most challenging for junior or mid-level employees who need clear strategies for achieving more freedom and flexibility in their remote work arrangements.

3. You will be more productive and flexible as a remote worker if you can tip the balance of your work to favor solitary rather than

collaborative work, since solo work is where remote work offers real advantages over what you can get done at the office.

4. The best way to balance solo and group work is with punctuated collaboration: divide up tasks so that people can proceed with solo work, but check in regularly to share ideas and make decisions that require group consultation.

5. Build trust and earn some freedom from daily oversight by setting clear expectations with your boss, and spelling out the trade-offs between 24/7 availability and your ability to deliver results.

6. Wow your "client" (even if it's your boss) by communicating in a clear and timely way, in a form that reflects their preferences.

7. Err on the side of overcommunicating with your boss or client, and get ahead of any looming issues—no one likes to be surprised with problems.

8. Maintain a performance file that reflects your best work and your notes on lessons learned, both to inform your performance reviews and to help you in future job searches or promotions.

CHAPTER 3

MANAGING A REMOTE TEAM

There's a reason people talk about the "art" of management. It's never easy, but managing a remote team makes it even more complicated. Being an effective manager means knowing how to delegate, how to foster team collaboration, and how to motivate individual employees. Managing all of that for a distributed team makes you Ginger Rogers to the conventional workplace's Fred Astaire: you're doing everything he does, except backward and in high heels.

If you can pull off that fancy footwork, however, you may find management more satisfying than ever. The productivity gains that people can make when they're working remotely are gains that can go toward your projects, and to your team's overall performance. Helping your team members find their remote path gives you the joy of seeing people you've mentored, and people you care about, thrive in a whole new way. And the more successful they are at working remotely, the more freedom and flexibility you will have yourself.

As you will see in this chapter, the Business of One model is the foundation for this bright picture. It's the model you will share with your direct reports in order to move them to a more results-oriented approach: that's where the chapter begins. Next, you will use the model to guide the way you manage your team at all three stages of any given project, where you will function as a coach to each team member's Business of One. Finally, you will embrace several tools that provide a foundation and guideposts for your remote reports: ground rules, team meetings, one-on-ones, and performance reviews.

THE RESULTS-ORIENTED MODEL OF MANAGEMENT

Even before Covid, the command-and-control model of management was on the decline, as highly skilled workers demanded more say on what work they were assigned and how they'd get it done.

The surge in remote work sounded the death knell for this management model. Without an actual office, the boss could not stand at the podium of power and issue orders from on high. Indeed, with a remote workforce, the boss no longer knew where her team members were located or when they were carrying out their assignments.

But we're not saying that managers should just sit back and let their remote teams sink or swim in their home offices. Quite the contrary: the Business of One model depends on great managers who can help remote employees harness the benefits of their newfound autonomy to the goals of the larger organization.

As a manager, you have a broader perspective on what the organization needs and how your team's agenda fits into the organization's overall strategy. That means it's your job to take the lead in proposing objectives for each Business of One that reports to you, and making sure each of those objectives has a clear deadline.

In keeping with the Business of One model, however, you need to rethink how you get your employees to pursue these objectives. Instead of issuing edicts to underlings, think in terms of winning the trust of quasi-autonomous suppliers: You need to motivate and inspire their best effort by explaining how it matters to the larger mission. Follow the example of the CEO of Copper Mobile, a mobile app developer, who obtained widespread support among his employees for a large software project by explaining in great detail (including financial projections) why it was critical to the company's future.[1]

And just as you would with a supplier, you need to agree on clear metrics that let both you and your team know whether they've hit the mark. By all means, collaborate on setting metrics so you get employee buy-in. But once you're all on the same page, follow up with a written list of deliverables and timelines—ideally in a form that can be shared with the whole team. That way, you don't risk the kind of communication problems that can easily arise when people are working remotely, and if anyone has concerns about the list, you can negotiate modifications.

Once you have agreed on deliverables and deadlines, there's no reason you should be calling or emailing for daily check-ins, any more than you would place daily calls to a vendor to see how your project is progressing. Define your success metrics, and then let your team members figure out how to deliver on them.

THE MANAGER'S ROLE AT THREE STAGES

Once you have assigned a project or task to your team members, you need to do your job in setting them up for success. Here's how to think of your role at each stage of a project or mission.

Resourcing Your Team

If a project is large or complex, your team may need more resources, like more money or more team members, to get it done well and on time. Sometimes they may just need your help to deal with a bottleneck, so make it clear that you are ready to help them get what they need from other departments or other organizations. Your relative seniority makes you the helper-in-chief: You're in a better position to get calls returned, emails answered, or disputes resolved. For example, if your team needs to hire an additional salesperson, but HR policy is blocking the salary approval, you are the person in the best position to call HR and get a policy change or waiver.

If there are times when you can't deliver the resources or decisions your team needs to move forward, revise the objectives or deliverables to match what's actually feasible. You don't want to set up your team to fail.

Supporting the Process

Your team needs your brain as well as your troubleshooting skills. Be prepared to help them resolve tough issues that invariably come up in the course of a project.

After the team has a chance to dig in to the project, you should conduct a series of what we call midflight reviews: regularly scheduled videoconferences with your team on the progress they are making and the hurdles they are facing. (See chapter 5, "Focus on the Final Product," for details on midflight reviews.)

Approach midflight reviews like an air traffic controller: You should check that the flight is on track, but it's not your job to land the plane. All too often, managers start out with the wise intention of delegating significant work to their team members, only to end up micromanaging as soon as problems arise. Instead of asserting your power or issuing detailed orders, try to understand the problem and help generate alternative solutions. Let the team go forward and evaluate these solutions as well as other approaches.

Remember, you're trying to help each of your remote employees function well independently. Think of yourself as the business coach who is there to help them find their own approach to delivering great results.

Learning from Results

When a project wraps, it's your job to help your team learn from the results. When a project goes well, there's no such thing as too much positive feedback, especially when it's meaningful and sincere. If a project runs into trouble, it's up to you to surface any bright spots and ensure your team learns from what went wrong.

That's particularly true when you're all working remotely. Your beaming smile and warm glow of appreciation are largely lost through online communication, even if you're speaking by video call. So turn up the volume on your positive feedback, and make an effort to be as concrete as possible: don't settle for a "great job on the Acme project" when you could say "Your problem-solving skills made all the difference on the Acme project, and the client was just thrilled by how quickly you came up with the workaround they needed."

The converse is not true, however. Far from dulling the knife of criticism, suggestions for improvement can come through as doubly harsh when they're communicated virtually, and especially, via text or email. That doesn't mean you can let a disappointing result slide: If a project fails to deliver on its objectives, as measured by the success metrics you established at the outset, you should try to understand the causes of the shortfalls and prevent them from happening again. Your goal as a manager should be to create a "teachable" moment, designed to improve the team's performance in the future.

SPECIFIC MANAGEMENT TECHNIQUES FOR REMOTE TEAMS

Even experienced managers face new challenges when they first start managing an all or partially remote team. You need to ensure your team gets its work done, but you also need to put some extra thought and TLC into managing the issues that crop up for remote workers, like personal isolation and trouble communicating with colleagues.[2]

Your four key tools for handling these issues are ground rules, team meetings, one-on-ones, and performance reviews.

Ground Rules

While remote workers are most effective when they have the autonomy to determine how and when to get their work done, they need ground rules if they are part of a team. An effective manager should establish common baseline expectations that will help the whole team get clear on what you'll all do the same way, and where you can each do what suits you best.

MAKING THE CASE FOR *REMOTE, INC.*

Articulating Ground Rules

Ground rules work best when they're established by a team manager or for the entire organization. But if you work in an organization that has yet to establish guidelines for remote hours, meetings, email, and messaging, you can still help to move the process along.

Take the initiative by drafting a document that reflects your best understanding of current policies and expectations, and leave blanks for any expectations that remain undefined. (Use our checklist, below, as a starting point.) Then share that document with your boss, and ask him if you can help him turn this into a shared set of guidelines for the whole team.

Explain that you will be more productive if you know when and how to coordinate with your colleagues, and that you expect they might find guidelines helpful, too. Then point out the ways that shared guidelines will simplify his work: he'll know when and how to reach everyone, and he won't get pestered to clear communication bottlenecks, because everyone on the team will be clear on expectations.

Here is a unified checklist of the most crucial expectations you will need to set, along with the chapters where you will find relevant guidance.

HOURS AND CONTACTS (SEE CHAPTER 7)
- The common working hours when everyone is expected to be available
- Each individual team member's work hours and contact information
- How and when to reach you or other colleagues in an emergency (and what counts as an emergency)

MEETINGS (SEE CHAPTER 10)
- How long, how many, how often, and how long a break there should be in between
- How to structure and circulate meeting agendas and follow-up notes

- When to turn on your video and when it's OK to go audio only
- Rules for multitasking or backchannel chats during team calls

EMAIL AND MESSAGING (SEE CHAPTER 13)
- When to include people in an email thread
- Shared structure or shorthand for subject lines (like including "URGENT")
- How quickly team members need to reply to email or team messages
- Whether, when, and how often team members should check or reply to messages outside of business hours
- Whether it's OK to email/message/call after hours
- When to email, when to Slack, when to text, and when to call

ONBOARDING A REMOTE TEAM MEMBER

When you do a great job of welcoming a new hire to the team or organization, it boosts productivity and lowers turnover. But how can you onboard a new team member you don't actually meet—because everyone's working remotely? Here are four key steps.

1. Give your newbie a digital welcome pack that includes ground rules for the team and the contact information for all their new colleagues, ideally including each person's preferred contact channels. Consider sending, by mail, a remote welcome basket, like an assortment of tea and coffee along with a mug bearing your organization's logo.

2. Help your new hire settle in by setting up informal, virtual one-on-ones with each of the colleagues they'll be working with closely, plus other key contacts like HR, IT, and Finance.

3. Plan on checking in via phone and video more frequently than you do with your other direct reports, for at least their first three to six months on the job.

4. If at all possible, arrange for some kind of in-person time to help your new hire get a feel for the firm's culture. The best-case scenario is for them to do a few weeks or months at the office either full- or part-time, but if that's not possible, aim to meet up for a walk, a team picnic, or (if all else fails) some just-for-fun team hangouts online.

Team Meetings

Weekly meetings are essential to the effectiveness and camaraderie of any team, but especially a team that includes remote workers. These team meetings help ensure everyone is up-to-date on key organizational news, provide a chance for team members to share their upcoming work, promote the exchange of useful knowledge, and build social bonds among team members.

In addition to whatever meetings your team sets up to tackle particular projects or challenges, you should have a standing weekly meeting that lasts less than than an hour. Hold them at the same time every week in order to create a routine, and make them video calls (with a cameras-on rule) so that everybody can read nonverbal cues and actually see one another at least once a week.

Start with some kind of icebreaker, followed by no more than ten or fifteen minutes of updates on key company news or policies. Then move on to the team updates that are the heart of the meeting: Invite each team member to share what they have on their plate for the coming week, and to ask for any input or support they'd like from the rest of the team—whether that's suggested contacts or suggested approaches to a problem. Set the expectation that these briefings will be forward-looking with lots of discussion; ask everyone to share a summary report of past activities beforehand, by email, so the conversation at the weekly meeting can focus on what's ahead.

Last but not least, make sure there is enough slack time for a little casual chitchat. Leave some time before and after team meetings for informal conversation, and signal that it's OK to use that time by showing up early. (And stick around yourself: otherwise your staff may worry that hanging out and chatting makes them look less productive.) Even if it's just ten or fifteen minutes, this time helps team members to get to know one another better and build stronger relationships.

Besides your weekly meetings, organize regular bonding opportunities for the team, calibrated to engage people with different tastes and schedules. Lack of team bonding is a major obstacle to the success of virtual teams, according to a survey of HR managers.[3] Your bonding activities could be as simple as picking a day or two each week when you'll all have your morning coffee together, over video, or it could take a more elaborate form like an online game night or a virtual cocktail party. The point is to create contexts where people can have fun together, and connect at a human level.

REINFORCING COMPANY CULTURE

Fostering and transmitting a healthy organizational culture are crucial parts of any manager's job, and when you're leading a remote team, meetings become an especially important channel for demonstrating and conveying your company's particular values and traditions. To ensure your virtual meetings reflect and reinforce your corporate culture, identify the key aspects of your organization's culture and translate them into your approach to online meetings.

The *Harvard Business Review* offers a useful survey, "What's Your Organization's Cultural Profile?", based on a typology of eight different cultural styles developed by Groysberg et al.[4] To translate these styles into your meetings, you might . . .

- Reinforce a caring culture with icebreakers that ask people to share personal news or self-reflection.
- Strengthen a purpose-driven culture by underlying the big-picture vision behind each project or major news update you tackle in a meeting.
- Reflect a culture of authority by actively chairing every meeting and ensuring you are the person running the agenda.

> • Underline a results-focused culture by beginning and ending
> every meeting with a shout-out applauding an individual or team
> achievement.
>
> Online meetings can't do all the work of transmitting corporate
> culture to a remote team, which is one reason we support a hybrid
> model where people spend at least some time in the office (see chap-
> ter 16). With a little bit of thought and intention, however, your vir-
> tual meetings can be an integral part of your role as a custodian of
> organizational culture.

One-on-Ones

Maybe you could get away with a quarterly check-in when you were all in the office, but once you're working remotely, you need regular one-on-ones with each direct report. Since these one-on-ones have to cover any gaps left by the loss of in-person interaction, you want them to be as long and as frequent as you can possibly manage: ideally you would spend forty-five to fifty minutes with each direct report every single week, though you could get by with thirty minutes a week plus longer monthly meetings. Book your one-on-ones as in-person meetings, if possible; this is a good use of any time you spend on-site at the office. Otherwise, set up weekly videoconferences, and be absolutely religious about following through on every single appointment: cancellations send a really bad message.

To ensure your one-on-ones have maximum impact, try to structure them so that they come across as helpful rather than as micromanagement. Don't use them to check in on a team project—that's what the midflight reviews are for. The one-on-ones are safe zones where you provide support and guidance, where each one of your direct reports can have your undivided attention to help them address whatever is at the top of their agenda.

Set up a separate standing agenda for each team member, in a form you can amend or update each week; this becomes a running record that you can reflect on together. (A Google Doc is an easy way to do this.) Encourage each person to update the agenda every week with their current concerns, and make sure you look at the notes from the previous meeting to see if there are follow-up items from prior meetings.

When it comes time to start your conversation, don't get straight to business: Spend the first five or ten minutes checking in personally, particularly if you know your employee is struggling with the logistics or stress of remote work. Follow your employee's lead on how personal they want to get.

Next, move on to talking about their productivity, and about how they're working with the team. This is where you step into the role of coach and mentor for their Business of One; even if you have no more experience with remote work than your employee does, your seniority means you have organizational context and knowledge that can be helpful to their development.

If all this checking in and catching up seems like a big investment of your time, it is! But it's the single best use of your time as a manager. If you can improve the performance of every person on a ten-person team by setting aside one day of your week for one-on-ones, both you and your team will become dramatically more effective.

SIX SAMPLE QUESTIONS TO ASK IN A ONE-ON-ONE WITH A REMOTE EMPLOYEE

1. How does your current living arrangement or workspace help or hinder you in doing your best work?

2. What are you doing to keep active and connected while you're working from home?

3. Where have you been able to find some productivity wins from working remotely?

4. Is there anything about your current working arrangement that has been holding you back from doing your best work?

5. What have been the biggest time-wasters in your past week or so?

6. Do you feel like you're getting enough connection and collaboration with the team, or is there any place we need to improve how we're working together?

Performance Reviews

At least every quarter, or at the end of a large project, you should replace each of your usual one-on-one meetings with an in-depth performance review. Feedback at frequent intervals is much more effective than the typical annual performance review, especially for remote workers who feel they don't have enough visibility with their bosses: research shows that fully remote workers receive a lot less feedback or praise than employees who spend several days a week in the office.[5]

Before each performance review, send your direct report a calendar invitation for an in-person or video meeting, and an agenda: This is no time for surprises. Send them a few questions or a self-assessment form they can use to provide their own self-report, in advance of the meeting, so you can see whether you share the same view of how things are going; some people are their own toughest critics, while others may fail to see their own shortcomings.

Start the meeting by going over the performance objectives and success metrics from your past review, which you should both have on file. Lead by noting the places they are doing well, and be effusive and specific with your praise. Make sure to take particular note of anyplace you see significant growth or effort relative to the issues or goals you set out in your previous review.

If you have concerns to raise, frame them as areas where you need to see improvement, and if necessary, clarify the impact that their underperformance has had on their work or the team. "You're a terrible problem-solver" is a discouraging, unactionable criticism. It's much more constructive to hear "We need to work on your problem-solving skills so that we don't have situations where a client request goes unaddressed for a whole week." Someone can learn new work processes or techniques, but they can't get a new personality or brain.

Once you've covered the areas where your team member is excelling and the areas where they need to grow, you should collaborate to draw up an action plan with revised objectives and metrics. Put these in writing so they can be the starting point for the next review. Make it clear how you will help this person achieve the results you're aiming for—for example, by suggesting people to contact, technologies to adopt, or strategies to pursue. Then follow through on those offers of support in your regular one-on-ones.

During at least some of these performance reviews, you should also ask for feedback on your own leadership, particularly as it affects their job satisfaction and performance. Ask what you've been doing that best supports their productivity, as well as what you could do to enhance their performance.

Once or twice a year, each team member should have a performance review where you talk about their broader career path. Ask about their long-term goals, the growth opportunities they would like to see, or the kinds of projects they would like to take on.

TEN QUESTIONS TO ASK IN A PERFORMANCE REVIEW

The questions you discuss in a performance review should be tied to the specific circumstances of your employee. Here are ten questions you can use as inspiration.

1. What have I been doing right that is most helpful in supporting your productivity?

2. What could I be doing better to improve your ability to perform well at work?

3. Should I be communicating more or less often with you and the team?

4. Would you like me to provide more or less guidance to you and the team?

5. What are the most important gaps or risks that I am not addressing?

In the occasional performance reviews where you discuss career plans, you may also ask:

6. What activities are you doing now that are most in line with your long-term goals?

7. Is there a project in the larger organization where you would like to contribute?

8. What factors or people are keeping you from fulfilling your full potential?

9. How can we give you an opportunity to grow your career in the right direction?

10. If you were to create an ideal job in the future, what would it be?

FROM A REMOTE WORKER

Adin Miller is the executive director of the Los Altos Community Foundation, where his own remote experience helped him coach his team through the adjustment to remote work.

I became executive director after serving on the board. I had only seven weeks to get a sense of the organization from a staff perspective before we closed our offices for lockdown.

I like to be surrounded by smart, capable staff who really shine in their own work. That has never been dependent on a schedule: when you're in the office, or when you're not in the office. I've always been more interested in: Do you do your work well, do you do it on time, do you advance the mission of the organization?

Before Covid, the office itself was seven people in one building, a converted house. People would schmooze a little bit and then go back to work. If they had a question, they might go off into a corner to talk about it together, and then the group met once a week for a staff meeting.

When we shifted to remote work, there was no space for that informal water-cooler conversation on Zoom. So I proposed that we take a coffee break once a day, for half an hour. We call it a kaffeeklatsch. People will start either raising personal conversations, like their anxieties with what is happening in the world. Or they raise work issues and then say, Let's take this one offline and meet separately.

We still have our staff meetings, and we actually dedicate a bit more time to them. That's when we deal with the formal business of the organization. The rest of the time, people make sure that as they hear about different projects, they come into one another's worlds and home in on project details. My team is empowered enough to do that on their own, without me needing to ask them to go do it.

We had a real hiccup around donor thank-yous: You can't sign and mail physical letters when you're working in remote locations or worried someone's germs are going to be on an envelope. The staff took it upon themselves to figure that one out.

They knew the end point was, Let's attach a digital signature to the letter. But we had to ensure we had the right details, the right data points, the messaging we wanted to convey. We talked about what the challenge was, but I didn't get into the weeds with them. They sat down and figured it out, and then they cleaned up the huge backlog of acknowledgments to donations for our Covid response.

I don't track what time somebody is getting online; it doesn't matter to me. It doesn't matter when they clock out, either, mentally or physically. I do expect them to come to our kaffeeklatsches and our staff meetings, and if you're not coming, let me know. But that's it.

My spouse has told me, you set the tone: if they see you on email at 7 p.m. they will think it's expected. So I don't send emails late at night; instead, I schedule my messages to go out the next morning, after 8 a.m.

Eventually we'll be back in a physical space. Many of the staff will want that proximity to the team, and a little break from being inside the house all the time. I'd like to just come in and have our check-ins in person, instead of online. And then I want to be able to go back home, and finish up my own work.

TAKEAWAYS

1. Managing a remote team is more complicated than conventional management, but potentially more satisfying.

2. To manage a remote team member most effectively, think of your-self as the coach for her Business of One.

3. After setting the team's objectives, agree with the team on success metrics: a concrete set of deliverables with specific time targets.

4. Your job is to provide your team with the resources, troubleshoot-ing, and other support it needs.

5. Conduct midflight reviews of each project to help your team refine strategies and overcome bottlenecks, but don't micromanage.

6. At the end of a project, you should celebrate if the team meets the success metrics, and make changes to prevent failures from happening again.

7. You should establish ground rules for your team on core working hours, online meetings, and communications channels.

8. You should hold weekly team videoconferences to facilitate com-munication, promote knowledge sharing, and build connections within the team.

9. You should hold one-on-one meetings with each team member every week, which sometimes should be structured as perfor-mance reviews.

10. Once or twice a year, help each team member think about their long-term career path, including their plans for remote work.

PART II

THREE KEY STRATEGIES FOR REMOTE WORKERS

I magine you are advising a valuable company that is renowned for all the products it makes from one particular resource—a resource that only this company possesses. However, you discover that the company is squandering its one unique resource on things that never make it to market; indeed, so much of this resource is being wasted on irrelevant activities that the company can't meet all the demand for its terrific products. What would you recommend?

Thinking like *Remote, Inc.* means recognizing that *you* are the unique resource that only your Business of One possesses. Yet many professionals end up wasting a big chunk of this precious resource, simply because they haven't aligned their time with their priorities. To make the most of your Business of One—to make the most productive use of yourself—you need to spend the majority of your time working toward the goals that really matter.

This part of the book is dedicated to the three foundational productivity strategies that ensure you are spending your time on what really matters to your Business of One.

In chapter 4, we will look at how to set goals in a way that reflects the sometimes competing objectives of your boss or clients, your own professional goals, and your family or personal priorities. We will show you how to factor all three dimensions into your prioritization process, and then use these priorities to shape your task list and schedule.

In chapter 5, we will look at how to focus on the final product. This one crucial strategy can accelerate your progress on key projects—because you're starting from the end point, generating rebuttable hypotheses that steer your work, and conducting midflight reviews to refine your tentative conclusions. Together these steps keep you from wasting time, and lead you to better outcomes.

In chapter 6, we will show you how to follow a crucial principle: Don't sweat the small stuff. Yes, it may seem simple, but it's hard to put into practice. That's why we help you mitigate two of the most common behaviors that get people bogged down in small distractions when they should be focusing on their top priorities: procrastination and perfectionism. We also help you implement two key practices that can get you through the unavoidable small stuff more quickly: multitasking and OHIO (Only Handle It Once).

CHAPTER 4

PRIORITIZE YOUR GOALS

When you shift your focus from hours to results, you need to decide which results you're working toward. That means setting and prioritizing your goals so you spend your hours and days on what really matters to your Business of One.

The prioritization principle applies to every kind of work, in the office or outside of it. Take the case of the doctors Bob mentors, as part of his work with a large hospital. One doctor complained that she was overwhelmed by the combination of managing her division, conducting cutting-edge research, leading surgical teams several days a week, and teaching younger staff to write winning grant proposals.

With Bob's help, she got all of her varied responsibilities down on paper, and set about prioritizing each one based on her ultimate goals. She quickly realized that her two highest priorities were undertaking research and managing her division; she was less devoted to her time in the operating room or her role of shepherding younger staff through the granting process. Thanks to this prioritization process, she chose to reduce her operating room time to one day of surgery a week, and asked her deputy to introduce a monthly seminar on grant writing. These two crucial changes not only created more time for the work of managing her division, but also allowed her to publish more research.

Prioritizing your goals is not easy. When you're working from home, you may well lose sight of your key priorities in a sea of Zoom calls, cats on keyboards, and disruptive toddlers. All those distractions can divert you from what's really crucial to your career or organization. But working from home can be a benefit, too: when your personal life is all around you, it's easier to keep your personal goals in the foreground, alongside your professional priorities.

If that sounds like a juggling act, you're right! You'll need to make steady, meaningful progress on your job-related goals, which means prioritizing the tasks and deliverables that your boss cares about. Since your Business of One is likely based out of your home, you will also want to be responsive to what matters to your family or your partner. And you should absolutely have your own personal goals—learning guitar or becoming a Zen master—that put you on the path to becoming a more fulfilled human being.

This chapter will give you a three-step process to identify, prioritize, and synthesize all these competing goals into a Business of One. First, you identify the full range of your objectives—for your boss or client, for your professional development, and for your personal and family life. Second, you prioritize these objectives by thinking about what matters to you on a given time horizon, whether it's the next week or the next decade. Third, you write down all of your projects and tasks, and tie them back to your objectives so you know what to prioritize. When you've completed all three steps, you can take a clear-eyed look at how you spend your time, assess whether any meeting or task really fits your priorities, and fix any mismatches.

GOALS, OBJECTIVES, PRIORITIES, TASKS, AND PROJECTS

Let's start with some definitions:

1. **GOALS** or **OBJECTIVES** are what you're working toward: the big-picture, possibly long-term vision of what you want to achieve at work or in life. We use the words "goal" and "objective" interchangeably.

2. **PRIORITIES** are the goals you've decided are most important. Priority-setting is the work of deciding what is a high-, medium-, or low-priority goal.

3. **TASKS** are what you spend your time working on: the discrete items you can tackle in minutes or hours.

4. **PROJECTS** are the big items on your to-do list that might take days, weeks, or months to complete. A project is made up of many tasks, so prioritizing a single project translates into prioritizing a whole sequence of tasks.

STEP 1: IDENTIFY YOUR OBJECTIVES

What are you trying to accomplish in the next year or two?

Yes, it's a huge question, but unless your priority-setting starts with a systematic review of your most important objectives, you have no way of aligning your time with your goals. What do you want in each area of your life—for your boss or client, your professional growth, and your own relationships or family? For each area, list a few key objectives.

As you start to list your objectives, be sure you're clear on what your boss expects you to accomplish, because that's how you'll align your efforts with the mission of the larger organization. As we explained in chapter 3, "Managing a Remote Team," your boss is in a better position to identify your business objectives because she is more tuned in to the direction of the organization. Particularly when you're working remotely, it's easy to get out of sync with the big picture.

List all your boss's objectives for you in the next month, quarter, or year. Be sure to identify success metrics for each one: What are the accomplishments that will show your boss that you're working toward the objectives she's set, and making progress within a specific time period? If you're in marketing, perhaps your boss expects you to increase sales of a lagging product by 10 percent within a year. If you're in human resources, maybe it's your responsibility to formulate a new diversity policy within the next quarter. If you're in systems development, the boss could expect you to clean up all the bugs in your latest software release within the next month.

If you are self-employed or run your own company, you may have several clients—or if you're a consumer-facing business, many customers. So you'll need to list the objectives of all your current clients (or different types of customers). If you're thinking about the objectives for a one-time client who's retained you for a specific project, just list the goals for that project, like "launch new lead-generating website by end of Q2." If you're thinking about an ongoing client, list the objectives that recur from one engagement or cycle to the next, like "complete quarterly financial audits."

Next, think about your own professional goals. Where would you like to be in this organization at the end of the year? Do you want a promotion, perhaps to a role where you take on managerial responsibilities—or if you're already a manager, to a role where you manage a larger team? Or you might focus on developing skills and contacts that could open the door to other jobs or industries—perhaps by undertaking an executive MBA.

If you run your own freelance practice or small business, think about your goals for this company. Could you add a few new clients in the next six months, so that you're less dependent on the one big contract that's been keeping you afloat? Alternatively, you could work on building your name recognition, with an eye to attracting at least one speaking invitation each month; double your revenues, so you can afford to hire more staff and expand your business; or pursue meetings with at least ten senior executives, with the goal of getting offered a full-time job.

In addition, you should consider your personal objectives. You may want to carve out time to play regular gigs with your garage band, plant a vegetable garden, or learn to ski. At the very least, these passions lend balance to your working life; for some people, creating time and money for personal hobbies is the greatest reward of a successful career. And when you're working remotely, you may find it easier to incorporate some of these into your day—for example, in the time you previously spent commuting.

This process of figuring out your objectives should not focus on you alone, but should also extend to your family and friends. If you've got a partner, kids, close friends, or other family members you love and support, think about how you want to show up for them. If you have a friend who is critically ill or going through a difficult divorce, perhaps you want to work from their house one or two afternoons a week so that you can help out with their household chores or give them other assistance. This isn't something you can decide on your own: make time for a serious discussion about what the people you love want and need from you, so they can see that you're listening.

STEP 2: SET YOUR PRIORITIES

Once you've made a list of all your boss, client, professional, and personal objectives, you're ready to start prioritizing: to rank each item on your list as low, medium, or high priority, and to identify any objectives that overlap—so that one set of tasks can advance multiple objectives at once.

There's an infinite number of ways your priorities might play out, so let's look at an example: Daniela, who works remotely as a regulatory specialist at a biotech firm, has a mix of professional and personal goals, as well as goals from her boss, so she starts by marking each item on her list as low, medium, or high priority, and then sorts her list based on this categorization. Here is what she might include in her list of objectives, each with a priority level:

BOSS

1. Get regulatory approval for new drug (high)

2. Ensure that we are sharing and obtaining information as needed to work effectively with other teams (medium)

3. Provide updates, feedback, and contributions during weekly meetings to ensure all projects are on track to meet regulatory obligations (low)

PROFESSIONAL

1. Get a pay raise (high)

2. Expand industry contacts so that I have more professional opportunities in the future (medium)

3. Take biochem course to improve my scientific literacy so it's easier for me to understand our researchers' work (low)

PERSONAL

1. Carve out the time to personally take Louise to her music group on Tuesday and Thursday a.m. so it's a bonding activity (high)

2. Exercise every morning so I feel calm and energized at work and relaxed on the weekend (medium)

3. Learn to play golf (low)

How can Daniela juggle all these different objectives? By looking for places where her objectives overlap, and making some hard choices about what to cut.

For example, Daniela's company needs to obtain regulatory approval to launch a new drug next year. And Daniela has her sights set on a raise. She can meet both these objectives by obtaining regulatory approval for the drug (and then asking for a raise), so that becomes Daniela's highest-priority objective.

On the personal side, Daniela wants to have some bonding time with her daughter, so she should aim to reserve Tuesdays and Thursdays as meeting-free mornings. While she can accomplish her exercise goal by doing a virtual fitness class nearly every morning, she will skip that on Tuesdays and Thursdays, in order to look at any urgent emails before she goes offline.

What doesn't make the cut? Lower-priority goals like taking that biochem class, or learning to play golf. Providing team updates during weekly meetings may still stay on the list, however, if her boss feels this is an essential part of Daniela's duties.

The process might look a little different if you're a freelancer. For example, a famous TV producer might have a big network client who wants him to sign another long-term contract to create more hit comedies. But let's say the producer has objectives that include getting into TV dramas, spending more time with his family, and taking longer summer vacations. His compromise is to sign a long-term contract that includes an option for him to create dramas, as long as he continues to create one comedy per year—plus an agreement that he can spend several months of the year working far from the studio lot, at his family's vacation home.

The difference between these two examples is not primarily due to the fact that Daniela is an employee while the TV producer is a contractor; the difference is that a famous producer has a lot more market power, putting him in a good position to negotiate for personal priorities like family and vacation time. Unless she's entertaining other job offers, Daniela does not have much market power as a midlevel employee. That means her boss's top priority—obtaining regulatory approval for that new drug—also needs to be Daniela's top priority, especially if Daniela has her heart set on that pay raise. And if she's going to ask her boss for two meeting-free mornings a week (so she can do a music class with her toddler), that will use up just about all her wiggle room with the boss and limit her use of free time to pursue her lower-priority objectives.

In either case, the outcome of this process is a single list of prioritized objectives. You don't need to have a perfectly ranked list, but you should have all your objectives rated as low, medium, or high priority. Whether you focus just on your high-priority items, or also have room for pursuing some of your medium-priority objectives, depends on many factors—like your market power, the number of objectives you are pursuing, and how much time your top priorities will consume.

STEP 3: LINK YOUR TASKS AND PROJECTS TO YOUR PRIORITIZED OBJECTIVES

The list of priorities you created in steps 1 and 2 serves as the foundation for what comes next: prioritizing specific tasks and projects. In this third step, you take the list of all the tasks and projects currently on your plate and think about whether and how they line up with priorities you have identified for your work and life.

This is a crucial step precisely because you may not have the time to tackle everything on your task list. That's why you need to review your task list side by side with your prioritized objectives, so that you can determine what you're going to fit into your schedule, and what you're going to let go (at least for now). Most people should take this step once a month. If you have highly seasonal or project-driven work, however, you may find it makes more sense to take this step when you move from one set of big projects to the next.

List All Your Tasks and Projects

Start by listing all your tasks and projects for the next month, quarter, and year. Don't worry about making your lists too long: You'll have a chance to cull when we sort everything into categories. But that will be easier if you capture all your tasks and projects in a spreadsheet or task management app. (You will find some suggested apps in chapter 8.)

Link Enabling Tasks and Projects

Your next step is to link your lists of tasks and projects to the objectives they further—what we call "enabling" tasks and projects.

Suppose you are a senior member of the marketing team for a consumer packaged goods company, and one of your high-priority goals is to increase sales revenues from the company's cleaning products. You might see a lot of tasks on your to-do list that relate to this goal: brainstorming new marketing ideas, analyzing customer surveys, testing out new pricing models. And perhaps you have some project responsibilities that advance that top priority, too: creating a social media campaign, launching a new website for one of your product lines, and developing improved packaging for another.

But your task list includes a bunch of other items that have no relation to the goal of boosting cleaning product revenue: introducing a lunch-and-learn program for junior members of the marketing team, running a market research study on your paper products line, and launching a social responsibility blog. Nor are these tasks tied to any of your other high-priority objectives.

Stop and ask: Did I leave any significant objective off my list? Yes, you omitted the goal of improving retention on your team; that's why you wanted the lunch-and-learns. So you add staff retention to your medium-priority list, and keep the lunch-and-learns on your task list.

If you can't tie a task or project to any of your high- or medium-priority objectives, you should presumptively cut it from your schedule. In this example, the market research study and the blog aren't related to any of your high- or medium- priorities for this month or quarter, so you'd like to set them aside for now. Before you do that, however, you should make sure that these tasks are not vital to your boss, even if she has not explicitly assigned them to you. So in your next one-on-one, talk this through with your boss, and explain you'd like to back-burner these tasks so that you can focus on the projects that advance her key objective of boosting cleaning product revenue.

Assess Assigned Tasks and Projects

By this point, your task list will include a number of tasks or projects that are linked to high-priority objectives. You may also have tasks and projects that your boss has assigned to you, but which aren't related to any high priorities. In these situations, you may need to negotiate with your boss. You could point out that your assignment to write a report on the significant accounting policies of your competitors does not actually advance any of her highest priorities for this quarter, whereas you could more effectively support her goal of reducing the turnaround time on your annual financial reports if you reallocated that time toward your evaluation and implementation of a new reporting platform.

As this suggests, your goal is to shift your time toward tasks that advance the top priorities you and your boss have identified. For example, if your boss has you putting together a slide deck for her monthly internal meetings, you might convince her that this is not the best use of your time because the participants at these meetings hardly look at the slides. Instead you might suggest that your time is better spent writing a monthly article for her to place in an industry publication. That article would advance your goal of honing your writing skills, while serving her goal of increasing inbound sales leads.

Match Your Time to Your Priorities

After you've linked your tasks and projects to your objectives, you'll be ready to determine how well your day-to-day schedule lines up with your high-priority goals. This step is absolutely essential, because it's the moment of truth that will help you find the capacity to tackle the key tasks and projects that will advance your most important priorities—especially if those are the projects that keep getting crowded out by the other tasks on your plate.

A small number of professionals may find that their list of tasks and projects related to their high-priority objectives is much too long: Even if they spent all their waking hours on these tasks and projects, they could not possibly finish them. If that sounds like your situation, you need to get a lot tougher about which objectives you consider a high priority. It's far better to make this decision deliberately, even if it's painful, than to end up dropping high-priority items on the fly simply because you didn't have time to get to everything.

For the vast majority of people, however, the problem is different: a weak alignment between their top goals and their use of time. In a survey of nearly 1,500 senior executives by McKinsey, the consulting firm found that only 9 percent said they were "very satisfied" with the match between how they used their time and what they hoped to accomplish. Almost one-third said they were dissatisfied to some extent. Further, only half of the survey's respondents felt that their time allocations were aligned to a great extent with the strategic priorities of their organizations.[1]

This kind of mismatch is highly perilous for remote workers, especially if you've succeeded in getting yourself evaluated based on success metrics rather than hours worked. Then all those misspent hours represent effort you *could* have devoted to something that actually mattered to your success metrics, but instead wasted on a less important (and quite possibly invisible) task.

But you won't know if you're wasting your time on unimportant work unless you know where your time goes. Most professionals have a much better grasp of how they spend their money than their time. If you won $100,000 on a game show, a year later you'd be able to recount the vacation you took, the debts you retired, and the taxes you paid. Could you offer the same level of clarity on how you spent your time during the past year? If you earn $100,000 per year, where did that $100,000 in time really go?

To get a good grasp of how you actually spend your time, look at your calendar or (even better) the logs generated by your time-tracking software (see chapter 8 for how to set that up). Then answer these three questions:

1. On average, how many hours do you spend at work versus other activities each week? (Your time-tracking software can answer this for you if you have your time categories set up to track work versus personal activities.)

2. At work, what are the three main activities on which you spend the most time? (Your time-tracking software can help you see this by project or by type of work: for example, how much time you spend on writing versus Web searching versus email versus spreadsheets.)

3. How many hours each week do you spend on work-related meetings and emails? (Use your calendar to total up your video call time, and use either your time-tracking software or a time tracker specific to your email client.)

Now take your record of how you've spent your time, and compare it with the goals you articulated and prioritized earlier in this chapter. (Again, use your time-tracking software to help you answer the questions below.)

1. What percentage of your working time do you spend on activities that support your top-priority goals?

2. What percentage of your working time do you spend on activities that support your medium-priority goals?

3. What percentage of your working time do you spend on activities that support your low-priority goals, or that do not further any of your listed objectives? (This would be what's left after you totaled up your answers to questions 1 and 2.)

This is the moment when a lot of readers may feel a sense of horror set in. Oh my goodness, you might be thinking, I spent forty-five hours last month on meetings and calls that were entirely unrelated to my objectives of boosting leads, increasing my close rate, and building more industry contacts. Why did I waste all that time?

Wasting time is unfortunately all too common, especially when you're first adjusting to remote work. In the effort to demonstrate that you're responsive and available (and not sneaking off to the driving range), you can get sucked into spending time on all kinds of activities that are about other people's priorities, instead of focusing on your own goals or the goals that matter to your boss. As a result, you may find that you're not really productive, in the most fundamental sense—because productivity is all about ensuring you can deliver on the projects and priorities that are most important.

But here's the good news: all that "wasted" time actually represents potential capacity that you can now reallocate to the tasks and projects that actually do advance the goals of your Business of One. In the next two chapters, we'll look at how you can make the most of that capacity: first by learning how to efficiently complete your largest, high-priority projects, and then by learning how to clear away all the low-priority clutter as quickly as possible.

FROM A REMOTE WORKER

Simone Alexander is a project manager with Chrome Enterprise, where her ability to prioritize has helped her focus during the pandemic, just as it previously allowed her to launch an entrepreneurship program.

Oleada is a pilot program in entrepreneurship that is 100 percent self-funded. It brought refugee and immigrant women in Barcelona together for one month to learn basic skills, with the goal of being self-sustaining.

The idea came out of a combination of past experiences: working with TED, working with another global program for entrepreneurs in developing regions, and taking projects from startup to successful exits. I love supporting women, taking care of women, empowering women, so I knew I wanted to do something that would support women in that way.

I had visited Barcelona a couple of times before, and met with interesting, influential folks. I realized that Barcelona is a community in beta: they are open to testing new ideas, and even though I was not connected to an organization, they were able to meet me, hear me out, and support me in various ways.

I made the program happen because I was able to prioritize my time. I was working remotely for a team that was mostly in London, one hour behind me. I could wake up at 5:30 a.m., work for a couple of hours, then send things off to London before the beginning of their day. From 9 a.m. to 3 p.m., I was running the Oleada program. Then from 3 to 9 p.m., I would go back to client work, and stay up later to talk to team members in California. Then I would sleep from 9 p.m. until 5:30 a.m.: I'm a big believer in sleep.

Until a few months before Covid, I'd been working remotely like that for five years. Then there was a health crisis in my family, and I needed stability, so I took a job at Google. The first three months of Covid were really scary in New York, and I struggled when I went back to working from home. Working remotely during a pandemic isn't like normal remote work: It comes with an emotional, physical, and mental tax. When you are confined to your home, there is no work/home separation.

Part of it was the racial uprising in the United States: I am a Black woman, people in my family are Black people, and the people who were dying more from this disease happened to be Black and Latino. It took a toll on me, but there was so much work going on that I didn't have time to process my emotions.

It forced me to have a very clear routine: waking up, having my coffee, doing meditation, doing yoga, having a set time for talking to my therapist. I function better on that routine.

Every second of my day is scheduled in my calendar because of my events background, where you have to be sharp with time. I start at 9 or 9:30, and I allow myself an hour to get caught up over email. Then there is a fifteen-minute break for my morning smoothie. I come back and I jot things down based on priority, and put that in my calendar.

I can't function if I'm at the computer like a regular nine-to-five day. I do what I need to accomplish; I get that done.

TAKEAWAYS

1. To move from hours worked to results accomplished, you need to think carefully about your objectives and priorities. That way you can get really clear on what you want to achieve.

2. Begin by listing all your goals in several categories: what your boss or client expects from you, what you as a professional want for your career, and what you need for yourself and your family or friends.

3. Next, assign a priority to each of the objectives on your list. These should be grouped into high-, medium-, and low-priority objectives. Take particular note of any goals that overlap, so that one set of tasks can advance multiple priorities.

4. Once your goals are clear, move on to making a list of all of your tasks and projects over the next month, quarter, and year. Try to connect all these tasks and projects to a specific objective.

5. If a task is not connected to an objective that is at least medium priority, try to drop it, or negotiate with your boss to determine what can be taken off your to-do list so that you have time to focus on her key priorities.

6. Go through your calendar or time tracker to assess how your time allocation matches up to your top objectives. You should aim to spend a majority of your time on tasks and projects related to your highest-priority goals.

7. As you identify any mismatch between where you spend your time and what's at the top of your priority list, take note of the amount of capacity this represents—because that will help you refocus your time on what really matters.

CHAPTER 5

FOCUS ON THE FINAL PRODUCT

When Bob was working remotely in the spring of 2020, he was asked to give a talk on how boards of directors should respond to the pandemic. So Bob asked a smart researcher to put together materials on this subject. Working from home, the researcher scoured the Internet to find a myriad of articles and studies on what makes an effective board of directors. After a few weeks, he presented Bob with a long memo on all these sources. However, this memo wasn't useful because most of these sources dealt with the effective operations of boards of directors in normal times, not in pandemics.

Bob then asked his researcher to write down a list of the issues that might be most important to a board of directors during the pandemic. The researcher immediately identified several key topics: how to maintain enough liquidity to get through the crisis, which safety measures are needed to keep employees healthy, and how to rethink supply lines in the event of any international trade restrictions. With this outline in hand, the researcher was able to focus the findings and quickly put together an excellent summary of the key issues for boards of directors to address during the pandemic.

This story illustrates our second big strategy for increasing personal productivity: focusing early on the final product. This strategy is essential to efficiently completing your high-priority projects, which may often be broad ("look at our entire sales pipeline") and complex (". . . and figure out which sales practices are most effective across different regions").

Focusing on the final product is especially important when you are working remotely and operating like a Business of One. Your goal is to produce great "deliverables" for your "client"—aka your boss. That means keeping a sharp focus on what is going to impress your client; that is, what is going to lead to an outcome that meets all the success metrics you've defined together. When you keep your eye on the final product, you concentrate your efforts on what really matters to the ultimate success of your project.

The best place to start any big or complex project is at the end, so we will show you how to quickly formulate a set of tentative conclusions that will guide your work. The crucial word here is "tentative": Throughout your project, you should periodically step back to think about what you've learned so far, and revise your tentative conclusions accordingly. These moments of stepping back are what we call midflight reviews, and they're particularly important for remote workers.

But those midflight reviews aren't enough: As you approach the finish line on your project, you need to try out your conclusions by running a series of pilots or beta tests. It's hard to know whether your conclusions will hold up unless you try them out on the relevant audience.

START AT THE END

The best place to start any large project is by thinking about the *end* point: If you were walking into a boardroom right now to deliver your report, what are the critical issues you would expect to address? How are those issues likely to be resolved?

All too often, professionals do the opposite: They begin a big project by researching comparable projects or case studies, or collecting a big pile of customer or industry data, just because that seems like the obvious place to start. A few hours of gathering background information can easily turn into days or even weeks when you're working remotely, separated from your colleagues and team: without their reality check or curious glances, you can get lost down a rabbit hole.

In fact, extensive and meandering research is a very inefficient way to get going on a big project. Thanks to the volume of information now available online, and the ease of searching through it, there is no end to the number of related facts you could gather for your project. But do you really want to collect all of them? No, because most of them won't be significant to your conclusions, and many won't even make it into your report.

Instead allow yourself no more than one or two days of information gathering before you force yourself to sit down and write some tentative conclusions for the project. Think of these conclusions as rebuttable hypotheses that can be revised as the project progresses. You might even have to scrap your tentative conclusions completely as you learn new facts and gain new insights. That's fine: These conclusions are only trial balloons that you can pop and then discard if they turn out to be wrong. You can even posit several alternative conclusions, and aim at discovering which one is closest to the truth.

For example, if you've been asked to develop a guide to onboarding employees that works even for distributed teams, your rebuttable hypothesis might be "All employees should spend two weeks of onboarding on-site before they start working remotely," or conversely, "All employees should spend two to four weeks working remotely and getting their basic systems in place, after which they should spend one week in the office meeting team members and getting other basic orientation."

This approach of generating tentative conclusions early on has two big advantages over gathering lots of facts and then waiting until the end of your project to knit them all together. First, the tentative conclusions provide a guide to your information gathering as the project goes along. Without this guide, you will probably gather lots of information you don't need, while failing to gather the data points necessary to support final recommendations. In our example above, your tentative conclusions would lead you to focus on research that compares on-site onboarding with off-site onboarding.

Second, the tentative conclusions force you to come to grips with the tough analytic issues that arise in almost any major project—so the earlier you tackle them the better. Without this prodding, you may not have enough time or facts to resolve these analytic issues as you rush to make your final presentation. For example, suppose you were asked to do research on whether a company in Los Angeles should move to a hybrid plan in which some of its employees work from home, while others work in the office. Instead of just gathering reams of data, you should focus on the key questions such as: What are the commuting times of your employees, what are the office costs for your employer, and what would be the challenges in managing a hybrid team?

Tentative conclusions are especially useful when you're working remotely, because they help avoid some of the communication problems that can arise when you don't see each other in person. For example, say your boss asked you to come up with a retail launch plan for a new luxury product; after some initial research, you come back with some tentative conclusions. When your boss sees them, he realizes you missed part of the brief: because you've never seen the physical product, you assumed the packaging was already designed, when that is actually part of your assignment. By starting with early, tentative conclusions you've avoided wasting weeks of work due to the kind of misunderstanding that often crops up when communicating by phone or videoconference.

This approach can make any interview- or survey-driven project go faster. For instance, Bob once asked a skilled researcher to interview the executives of charitable foundations that had made mission-related investments in private firms, like a cancer foundation buying stock in a biotech company. The researcher initially made a list of standard questions that would have yielded lots of interesting information . . . without actually getting at the issues that prevent many foundations from investing in for-profit companies. So she generated some rebuttable hypotheses that focused on the likely constraints that limited mission-related investments, like legal risks or reputational concerns; these hypotheses then helped her generate specific questions that got to the heart of the problem.

We strongly recommend this approach to large projects in academia, nonprofits, and government, as well as in business. Give yourself a very strict time limit—no more than two days—to do some initial digging. Then no matter how little you think you know, force yourself to write down some tentative conclusions. They simply need to be plausible enough to steer your continued work, because you'll be able to revise these conclusions as you progress. Those revisions will occur in the midflight reviews, discussed below.

If you can create some success metrics—not only for what it means to deliver on time and on budget, but also for how you'll assess whether your conclusions are correct—that will help you stick with your approach. These metrics will reinforce the discipline of keeping focused and avoiding a thousand research tangents, while establishing explicit standards for assessing your results (like "our recommendation must be backed by at least three credible case studies or academic articles").

THE MIDFLIGHT REVIEW

If you're flying a plane from New York to Paris, it's a good idea to check your bearings while you're crossing the Atlantic Ocean, just to make sure you're still pointed toward Europe rather than the North Pole. For the same reason, you should plan on midflight reviews throughout any major project, to look at your tentative conclusions and make revisions in light of what you've learned so far.

In other words, you need to start with a set of rebuttable hypotheses to guide your research, but you should not wait until the end to evaluate them. By pausing and reflecting on what you've learned so far, you will be able to refine your thinking and guide the remainder of your research with a new and improved set of tentative conclusions. In a large project, you may need several such midflight reviews, so that you can pause and examine your work every few weeks.

The midflight review is even more important when you're working remotely. You can't get a quick reality check from your colleagues the way you might by sticking your head through a coworker's door, or talking through your ideas in the office kitchen. Instead you need to make a plan for reviewing your conclusions solo—or even better, through a one-on-one phone call with a colleague who will listen to your rebuttable hypotheses and challenge you in ways that will help you make any necessary adjustments.

Let's go back to the example of the researcher who helped Bob look into foundations buying stock in mission-related private companies. By generating rebuttable hypotheses at the start of the project, she was able to design questionnaires aimed at what she believed was the most critical issue: the legal risks of mission-related investing. After conducting a few interviews,

however, she found that trustees faced a bigger challenge: recruiting and paying talented professionals to make these investments. So she formulated new
interview questions to explore these problems. In other words, she revised
her rebuttable hypotheses so they were better aimed at the critical issues that
emerged through her initial work.

PILOTS AND BETA TESTS

How do you know when you are ready to make your tentative conclusions de-
finitive? If you've been conducting regular midflight reviews throughout the
project, you should be seeing smaller and smaller course corrections, until
you approach the point where you're reasonably confident you have reached
the right conclusions (or as close as you're going to get in the available time).

Just before you get to the final product, however, you should do a pilot
or beta test of your conclusions to see if they are appropriate and effective.
In our experience, this is a necessary step before finalizing any product or
service. No matter how hard you try to gather the right data and do the right
analysis, you don't know how customers will react to a new product or service
until they try it out. You may find a small tweak that will turn a dud into a big
winner.

If the large project involves analyzing an issue or recommending a decision, you should try out a draft of your conclusions on the appropriate audience before you finalize them. This might mean sending a draft of your report
with recommendations to experts outside of the organization or a few of the
relevant staff members inside the organization. If you can get feedback on a
draft before you finalize, you can avoid factual mistakes or political mine-
fields.

By starting from the end, generating some rebuttable hypotheses, and
testing your tentative conclusions with midflight reviews at various points in
your progress, you should arrive at this moment of truth in far less time than
if you followed the common path of spending weeks on unfocused research
and trying to synthesize your findings near the end of a project. Even more
important, the efficiency of your approach is certain to lead to better results,

because you've spent your time and attention on what really matters to your project's outcomes, and continually refined your thinking and approach. And those outcomes are the ultimate measure of your Business of One.

FROM A REMOTE WORKER

Amy Lightholder uses Agile—a specific software development methodology—to ensure a team is constantly learning and adjusting its progress toward the final product.

I'm an Agile coach and scrum master (the "process" role for an Agile software development team). When companies began hiring overseas engineers, translating what used to be in-person processes to remote work became part of my job.

As early as 2011, my entire team was remote. After a few months of getting to know the management and design team, so was I. I even worked from Vegas a few times. I find gambling both nerve-racking and tedious but my wife is very fond of it, so I would just hang out in the hotel and work there.

In Agile projects, there's little requirements analysis because often you can't know what those will turn out to be. Instead the focus is on being very clear on what you need to achieve.

We once made an educational app that provided lessons, assessments, and a record of student progress. That meant an account for each user, a list of classes, recorded lessons for each class, etc. The team figured out how to achieve that and created a "project backlog" of all the "stories" (pieces of work) that are needed to produce the final project.

We worked in two-week increments (called "sprints"), selecting the most important and urgent work for a smaller "sprint backlog." We'd work on those stories until two weeks were up, then present the results to the client for feedback. The client's feedback (which often included new work) and any other learnings would be integrated into the project backlog and the planning for the next sprint. This cycle repeated until the project was finished.

It was absolutely essential to have a functional product at the end of every sprint. Without a working product, you can't get real feedback. Also, should the project be interrupted at any point, the work you've invested up until then is not wasted. This is a game-changing difference from pre-2010 methodologies, when aborted software projects often meant a total loss.

A similar approach ("lean startup") is used for Agile entrepreneurship: you identify a need and a market, then create the simplest offering possible ("minimum viable product") to verify whether your proposed solution is something those customers will pay for. (MVPs are often ridiculously simple. One famous example is Zappos: the founder would take pictures of shoes in local stores, create a website with the photos, and fulfill each shoe order by hand as they came in.) Only after verifying that you have the right solution for the right people (known as "product/market fit") do you invest the time and effort into making a better version. And you make many, many "better" versions, improving your solution incrementally and verifying your customers' enthusiasm in each iteration.

This iterative, empirical approach to business mitigates one of the largest entrepreneurial risks: sinking enormous amounts of time and money into a product that cannot be sold.

The applications of Agile methodology are literally endless, and most Agilists I know incorporate this approach in many ways . . . including their personal lives. One of the most valuable things it's taught me is an awareness of my own capacity. You'd be surprised at how terrible the average person is at predicting how long any given task will take, and this is entirely due to the lack of reflection that careful measuring in repeated cycles provides.

TAKEAWAYS

1. Start at the end: force yourself to write down some tentative conclusions early, after no more than a day or two of research.

2. Structure your tentative conclusions in the form of rebuttable hypotheses, which you should expect to change as you gather new evidence and insights.

3. Periodically during your project, undertake a midflight review, in which you revise your tentative conclusions in light of what you've learned so far in terms of new data and deeper analysis.

4. A large or extended project may require several midflight reviews, in which your course corrections get smaller and smaller.

5. If a big project involves analyzing an issue or recommending a decision, get feedback from inside or outside experts on a draft of your conclusions before going final.

6. If you are designing a new product or service, try it out on a few customers or users. Their feedback can avoid serious problems before a broad launch.

CHAPTER 6

DON'T SWEAT THE SMALL STUFF

Alex was in her final months of graduate school, finishing her dissertation, when her husband went on the road for five weeks as the speechwriter for a national political campaign. All of which would have been just fine . . . except that Alex had an eight-month-old baby.

But Alex was determined to finish her PhD, baby and all—and she wasn't going to let anything else slide in the process. She kept on pitching freelance stories and making dinner and preparing academic job talks. She even took on the challenge of assembling a new desk so that she and her husband would have separate workspaces when he returned.

That's how she found herself in the garage, looking for a toolbox. As she searched frantically through the chaos, she had a sudden burst of clarity: She did not need to be building a desk seven weeks before her complete dissertation was due. She did not need to be preparing job talks or pitching freelance stories. She didn't even need to keep making dinner. All she needed to do was write her dissertation and look after her baby: everything else was small stuff that she had to let go.

It's easy to get bogged down in small stuff when you're working from home. On top of all the trivial stuff that comes up at the office—the pro forma meeting invitations, the dozens of pointless cc's, and the expense reports—you are never more than a few feet away from the trivia of household life: the laundry, the home repairs, and the dinner vegetables that need chopping.

But you can't tackle your top priorities and focus on your important projects if you're constantly sucked into all the little details and personal tasks that can easily occupy every minute of your day. You may *feel* productive when you cross fifty tiny things off your to-do list, but it's usually better to put that time toward your big, high-priority projects.

That's why you need to embrace this life-saving mantra: Don't sweat the small stuff. Yes, easier said than done! We know that a lot of the small stuff is dumped in your lap by other people—which is why this book spends later chapters tackling two of the biggest culprits, meetings and email.

But a lot of the time, that small stuff comes from within, from the part of ourselves that feels a great deal of anxiety about letting *anything* go. In this chapter, we look at two of the biggest internal constraints on your productivity—procrastination and perfectionism—and offer tactics to overcome them. We then look at two tactics that can help you with the small stuff that comes from other people: multitasking and the OHIO rule (Only Handle It Once).

PROCRASTINATION

If you are working remotely, you are almost always using a computer that offers you a veritable smorgasbord of distraction: At any given moment you could be checking your email, catching up on your Slack messages, or reading the industry news on LinkedIn—all of which are less important than the big project that is due on Friday. You could also be watching a YouTube video, playing a video game, or reading an 8,100-word history of the children's TV show *Wishbone*—which are all less important than looking at your list of must-do tasks for the day.

But there's no shame in this struggle. The habit of procrastination is driven by what behavioral economists call "hyperbolic discounting": the tendency to give much less weight to future rewards than current ones.[1] Most people will choose to do something pleasurable now and put off whatever takes effort.

Plenty of people are moderate procrastinators: When they're faced with something that's boring or time-consuming, they'd rather put off the boring thing and do something pleasurable instead. These folks can often tame their habit with mini-deadlines: interim dates for completing specific stages of a project.[2] Reinforce these deadlines by adding them to your calendar or project management app so you can see where you intend to be by a specific date, and tie each one to a personal reward for completing the task. If Bob grades another five essay exams, he rewards himself with a dish of ice cream; for ten exams, he rewards himself by watching a TV show.

There are lots of other tactics that can help remote workers with a moderate procrastination habit. Set a time when you will get to your desk every day, even if it's just to play solitaire: Simply getting to your computer is half the battle. Position your chair so that you can't see the unwashed dishes or the messy living room, thereby reducing the temptation to tackle housework instead of job work. Promise yourself a small reward when you complete the first paragraph, the first phone call, or the first chart: whatever small task gets the ball rolling so that you don't put off the challenge of getting started.

Some moderate procrastinators may find their problem gets a lot worse when they're working from home: there's always some household chore you can use to put off your work. It pays to nip this tendency in the bud, because chronic procrastinators pay a high personal price for their dysfunctional habit. They are very anxious in the early days of a project, but may not accomplish anything except avoiding work. As the deadline nears, they go into panic mode: they eliminate all aspects of their lives and do all-nighters in the final days before the deadline. This roller-coaster rhythm not only compromises the quality of their work, but can also wreak havoc with friends and family when the procrastinator disappears overnight to meet a deadline.

Here are some tactics that can help chronic procrastinators:

- BREAK IT DOWN. When you're having trouble getting started because you're overwhelmed by the size or complexity of a project, break it into smaller pieces. If there is a piece that feels easy to start on—or better yet, actually fun!—then get underway with that piece, even if it's not the logical starting place. Once you get started, it will become much easier for you to continue.
- DECLUTTER. If you are easily distracted and constantly find other things to do, take a look at how you can declutter your work environment— both your physical space and your digital space. Close browser tabs and open applications, block social media (or possibly turn off your Internet connection altogether), throw all the clutter on your desk

into a big box with a lid (so you don't look at it), and put your phone on "do not disturb."

- SET INTERIM DEADLINES. If you need the adrenaline rush of a pressing deadline to get you into gear, create a series of firm deadlines, each with a reward, for completing each stage in the process. Maybe you save your favorite chocolate bar for the day when you write your initial set of tentative conclusions in a large project; maybe you promise yourself a little online shopping spree once you finish your first three hours of work.
- MAKE YOURSELF ACCOUNTABLE. Create some form of accountability—to your boss, or to a colleague whose work is connected to yours. Give your boss or colleague a list of mini-deadlines and commit in writing to meeting them. If that feels too daunting (or if this strategy has backfired in the past, because you *still* don't live up to your commitments), try finding a friend who can be your accountability partner.
- DIG INTO YOUR REASONS FOR PROCRASTINATING. If you are a severe or chronic procrastinator, try to understand the source of your problems. Instead of just telling the procrastinator in your head to shut up already, try to listen to it: What are you avoiding? What are you afraid of? You may suffer from a deep-seated fear of failure, or you may feel that you are not good enough to have this job.[3] If you've never really dug into the underlying reasons for your procrastination, consider working with a psychotherapist to figure out the source of your habit as well as potential solutions.

PERFECTIONISM

Perfectionism is another habit that can interfere with your productivity—if it means that you obsess over correcting every tiny detail on every project, regardless of whether it's a high or low priority. Psychologists characterize perfectionism as a personality trait that makes an individual strive for flawlessness.[4] It can be manifested as an impossibly high performance standard, intense self-criticism, or a preoccupation with how others will evaluate you.

It's easy to paint perfectionism as a superficial flaw, the kind of thing you mention when you're asked about your weaknesses in a job interview. But perfectionism is a genuine obstacle to productivity: While perfectionists may be bright and hardworking, they have a difficult time letting go of projects, delegating to others, and knowing when enough is enough. All of that means they end up spending too much time on the wrong things—the small stuff—instead of focusing on the final product and aligning their time with their top priorities.

Here are two examples of what that kind of perfectionism looks like in practice . . . and why it's so damaging:

- Each week, a midlevel employee spends over an hour double-checking the accuracy of her weekly timesheet, which is read by no one . . . when she could use that time to participate in the company's mentorship program and get valuable coaching.
- An IT director responds personally to every email asking for a software recommendation with a detailed, two- or three-page message explaining all the available options . . . when he could write a single sentence suggesting his preferred tool, and then use the time to create a software selection guide for the whole company.

Why do workers become perfectionists? Some say that their parents or teachers inculcated them with this habit. Others admit that they are perfectionists because they are control freaks, or they have a deep-seated fear of disapproval.[5] Still others have long been operating in roles or professions that demand great attention to detail, such as project management, law, or engineering.

Are you *literally* a brain surgeon? Are you *literally* a rocket scientist? Are you in some other field where a tiny mistake could kill one person—or thousands? Nuclear reactor managers, air traffic controllers, civil engineers: Please keep up your perfectionism. We really appreciate it every time our reactors don't explode and our bridges don't collapse.

Everybody else: Stand down. Your lack of perfection is not going to kill anyone. It just keeps you so overwhelmed completing low-value tasks that you never have time to really dive into your top goals, and you never get assigned to the big projects that could truly advance your career.

One of Bob's business colleagues used to spend days, and sometimes weeks, perfecting policy manuals on minor subjects. He took great care to address every conceivable contingency and cover every nuance, no matter how esoteric. By the end of the process, the policies were jam-packed with footnotes and definitions . . . even though there was no need for these details, and very little risk in the areas he was documenting. The amount of time this professional spent on every minor project meant the boss was wary of handing him any big or complex assignments.

Overcoming perfectionism is critical to becoming more efficient at work. When you spend a lot of time on a specific task, you typically run into diminishing returns. It can take you a few hours to write a rough draft of a memorandum, and weeks or months to write a polished final product. So you should spend that extra time only if that project is one of your high-priority goals—or a high-priority goal for your boss. If you are not sure how important a project is to your boss, ask her. Most bosses will want to help you avoid spending a lot of time and energy on low-priority projects.

To tackle your perfectionism problem, adopt some or all of the following tactics:

- SET YOURSELF A HARD DEADLINE, AND MEET IT—without working extra hours or sacrificing sleep. Your challenge is to get the task done in a fixed amount of time, even if it's not perfect.
- INTENTIONALLY DELIVER LESS-THAN-PERFECT WORK WHEN YOU'RE TACKLING A LOW-PRIORITY ASSIGNMENT. Your goal is to deliver B-level work, so if you turn in an A+ product, you fail. Although this may take practice, it will help train you out of your perfectionism habit.
- USE YOUR PRIORITY-SETTING REVIEWS TO TAKE A HARD LOOK AT THE HIGH-PRIORITY PROJECTS YOU DID NOT HAVE TIME TO PURSUE. Make a list of these priorities and place them somewhere visible in your office, as a reminder of what you're trying to gain time for by obsessing over low-priority details a little less.
- LET YOURSELF CATASTROPHIZE. If you really dropped the ball on this project, what would happen: Would anyone die or lose their house

if you left a couple of typos in that report? Would your job really be at risk? Letting yourself imagine the worst-case scenario can be a useful way of sapping the power of your vague but unarticulated fears.

MAKING THE CASE FOR *REMOTE, INC.*

Delivering Less-than-Perfect Work

Worried your boss won't let you stop sweating the small stuff? Then it's time to draw her attention to what you can accomplish when you keep your eye on the prize.

When you deliver a piece of work that's important, and that delighted your boss, make a point of sharing how you made time to achieve this great result: "I'm glad you're so pleased with the slide deck for the board of directors. I was able to put extra time into getting the deck just right once I realized you'd be OK using a prefab template for our holiday party poster."

Beyond overcoming the negative constraints of procrastination and perfectionism, you can adopt a couple of positive practices that can have a big impact on the extent to which small stuff gets in your way: multitasking and OHIO.

MULTITASKING

A lot of busy people multitask on a regular basis. CEOs may make phone calls while they're in a car, getting driven to a presentation. A VP of marketing may write a short memo while keeping half an ear on a competitor's webinar. And lots of professionals may discreetly check their email while suffering through a long, boring meeting.

There are even more opportunities to multitask when you work from home. You can watch TV while checking email, pedal an exercise bike while reading the latest industry news, or fold the laundry while listening to a business podcast.

It's easier to multitask during meetings, too, since so many take place via video or phone call. As long as you mute your microphone and keep your camera off, nobody will know what you're doing while you're on that call. Indeed, the more people work from home, the less secretive remote workers are about their multitasking: it's increasingly common for someone to admit that they're joining the call while walking the dog, or turning aside from the meeting in order to give a child a little homework help.

Nevertheless, multitasking has a bad reputation in academic circles. Lots of studies have found that multitasking results in lower-quality work and decreased productivity. Most people simply can't focus on more than one task at a time, so they're not really multitasking: they're just switching back and forth between different tasks—and paying a price every time, because their brain has to restart and refocus, wasting time and energy. Researchers point out that it would actually be more efficient to do one critically important task at a time, rather than incur these switching costs.[6]

When people multitask, however, they're rarely trying to juggle two genuinely critical tasks. Rather, they multitask by eating a sandwich while listening to a long conference call, or checking the weather while sitting through a boring meeting. The key here is that neither activity requires your full attention: You're not trying to absorb and analyze all the information you receive. Instead you're monitoring one activity and waiting for cues that you should switch your attention to the other. This kind of multitasking can be a terrific method of accomplishing low-priority tasks in an efficient manner.

And yes, there *is* research to support this approach to multitasking. For instance, multitasking may not be a problem when you're doing tasks that use different parts of your brain.[7] People can do two different tasks at once if they don't directly conflict with each other, especially if they've simultaneously practiced the tasks in question before.[8]

So when you're deciding whether to multitask, think about the relative importance of each task and how much brainpower it requires; don't try to do two important tasks at once. Consider planning your multitasking in advance:

rather than allowing a second task to semidistract you from that meeting or call, deliberately choose a second activity that uses a different kind of thinking (or very little thinking at all).

Sometimes you may find yourself in situations where you feel eminently capable of handling a second, low-demand task, but where you need to refrain for diplomatic reasons. You should generally not multitask when dealing with customers or potential customers; they may see it as a sign that you are not really interested in their business. Don't multitask when you are meeting with people who wield power over your business life, such as your boss or a regulator, because you can't afford to offend them.

If you're in a situation in which multitasking may or may not be socially acceptable, consider taking the direct approach, and just ask: "I have a feeling you are going to need me for only a couple of key points in this meeting, so is it OK if I check my team messages during this videoconference?" If you let your colleagues know that you're working on something that's related to your shared work, and you don't attempt to hide your slight distraction, they're a lot more likely to respond positively to your two-track mind. Indeed, they may well appreciate the license to do a little multitasking themselves.

OHIO (ONLY HANDLE IT ONCE)

Whenever Bob speaks at conferences, readers of *Extreme Productivity* introduce themselves to say how much more productive they are, thanks to OHIO. No, we're not talking about the Buckeye State: we're using the acronym for Only Handle It Once.

In other words, respond immediately (if feasible) whenever you receive an email, call, or message that is important—that is, associated with a person or goal that is important to you. Deferring a response for later just means that you have to think about it a second time (or a third, or a fourth), using up time and energy on each occasion, and accumulating anxiety in the interim.

Think about how this practice could transform your own daily life. Every day you receive a barrage of requests for your time and knowledge: from your coworkers, your family, and your friends. You may also get requests from people you don't know, like salespeople or fundraisers. When you work from home, you may be susceptible to a broader range of inquiries: the door-to-door canvasser, the friend calling to catch up, the kid asking for a snack.

When you get a request, decide right away whether you're going to respond to it or ignore it—permanently. As a general rule, we recommend ignoring 50 to 75 percent of your inbound requests, whether that's spam from advertisers, daily reports from national groups where you have minimal connections, and even irrelevant emails from inside your own organization. You need to be ruthless in discarding these low-priority messages so you can spend more time and effort on your high-priority goals. (In chapter 13, we will show you how to set up filters to automatically discard these low-priority emails and texts, so you don't have to see them even once.)

If you tend to avoid requests that will require you to (uncomfortably) decline, consider shoring up your willpower by drafting a few all-purpose "no thank you" emails, and saving them as email signatures or text snippets. Now you won't have to deal with the friction of figuring out how to say no; you'll just use one of your prefab messages.

On the other hand, from time to time you will receive an important request; in that case, you should usually respond immediately. Suppose you get a notice from the Internal Revenue Service advising that you have an outstanding tax bill. If the amount is small and you have a lot on your plate, it's tempting to put the notice aside—after all, who wants to think about the IRS? But a week later, when you have time to pay the bill, you now have to hunt for it: the half hour you spend searching through your piles of paper is time you could have spent working or relaxing, if you'd just paid the small tax bill when it first arrived. Alternatively, you might forget to respond at all, and the IRS will garnish your wages!

Remember that waiting for a day or a week to respond to an important request may double or triple the time involved. For instance, suppose you receive an email invitation to attend a conference on a subject directly relevant to your work; it's a good fit, because one of the top-priority goals for your Business of One is to expand your industry contacts. Following the OHIO rule, you immediately look at the date and location of the conference to see if it fits in your schedule; you also do a gut check to see if you feel eager to accept the invitation, or have some form of hesitation that signals that more investigation is needed. Assuming that your gut check yields an enthusiastic yes, you should immediately accept the invitation and put it in your online calendar.

But let's say the invitation lands in your inbox at a moment when your calendar is in flux. You take a brief glance at your calendar to see if the date is free, but then set the invitation aside with the intention of returning to it later that day. Instead you forget about it until a few days later, when you suddenly remember that you didn't respond. Although you know it's in your inbox somewhere, you can't remember exactly when you received it, or the exact name of the event, so you can't just search for it in your inbox: You have to go paging through until you find the message. Finally you find it, read it, and cross-check your calendar again. You've just spent almost fifteen minutes on this invitation when it would have taken less than five minutes to just accept or refuse it in the first place—by following the OHIO principle.

Sure, you've wasted only ten extra minutes—what's the big deal? But now multiply that ten minutes by every single email, every single phone call, and every single memo you handle more than once. That's a lot of minutes you could be devoting to your high-priority goals. Beyond helping you get those minutes back, the OHIO principle will strengthen your relationships with all the important people in your professional and personal life, because everyone appreciates a prompt reply.

WHEN TO HANDLE IT LATER

There are times when the best decision is *not* to provide an immediate response: Perhaps you need to gather some information or give the matter some thought. In that case, let the other person know when you'll get back to them with an answer; then put a reminder in your calendar for a day or two ahead of that time, or use an email add-on like Boomerang to return the message to your inbox at the specified time. If you're going to need information from someone else in order to provide your answer, get that information request underway immediately. All of this ensures that the important request does not get lost in the shuffle, while providing the courtesy of a timely initial response.

Beating procrastination and perfectionism may be the big wins here, but multitasking and OHIO will help you accumulate a lot of small wins, too. Together, all that recovered time amounts to a potentially transformative increase in your professional capacity: capacity you can commit to the most important work of your Business of One.

FROM A REMOTE WORKER

Katrina Marshall's freelance experience has helped her approach her remote job as a local government communications officer in England by cutting through irrelevant rules and bureaucratic minutiae.

When I started this job a few months ago I thought, Katrina, you've never done local government before, you need to be humble. But the entire system is set up for bums in seats, and productivity is sometimes sacrificed for bureaucracy.

So much of what I do is working around systems that were built for in-person work. When I was onboarding, I was asked to print my documents and post them to the office so someone could sign and stamp them and then send them back; I could accomplish the same thing if I could take a high-res photo and email it. And I've been reminded I need to do a health and safety training for the office—but it's obsolete, because I'm not in the office.

When I worked as a freelancer, I learned to underpromise and overdeliver. I never ignore calls; I always have my phone on; if I can action an email I do; and if I hit a road bump, I say it loudly and often. I just have no time for purveyors of presenteeism, who have this need for systems to measure everything from how often you sit at your desk to your keystrokes.

Managers could just say "My team is not working well having to check in every five minutes." That degree of presenteeism does very little for productivity because your interest is in showing up, not in delivering.

I start as I mean to go on: I don't chime in with "good mornings" and "good afternoons" in the staff WhatsApp chat group. When everyone else is creating a digital timestamp of their movements, I don't. As long as my work gets done, I don't feel like I'm under the same pressure as government "lifers" to be present. But I learned really quickly that sometimes the performance of productivity is as important as the productivity itself.

I'm a plain speaker even for typically blunt Barbadians. I'm sometimes like the court jester; jokes are one of many tools in my arsenal. They help me build relationships with all the people I have to work with, and I don't worry if silently they're thinking it's not professional to be a bit of a jokester. Professionalism is about appropriateness, not a static framework of behaviors.

I once worked with a production company whose definition of professionalism was: Show up! They didn't care if your jeans were torn, if you were eating instant noodles out of a bag, if you had your pet turtle in a camera bag downstairs. Nobody cared! Professionalism was showing up and doing what you say you're going to do.

Now I am working with a group of people who are genuinely a team; they are not out to get you, and I don't feel like I'm always avoiding a gotcha. But it's really different from my years as a freelancer, because when you're on a contract, you're not there to blend with the team: you're there to do a specific task, get it done, and then spend two weeks on the beach before the next project starts.

When I'm trapped on a call reprimanding me for not filling out a timesheet—a timesheet that does not affect my paycheck or my annual leave—I know it's just a tracking system to make sure a line manager can say their team is not overworked. If you're putting in eight hours, does it matter how?

TAKEAWAYS

1. We all have a tendency to procrastinate when faced with tedious or boring tasks, especially if you are working at home with an extra layer of distractions.

2. For moderate procrastinators, create mini-deadlines for each step of a large project, and give yourself rewards for successfully meeting each of these mini-deadlines.

3. For severe procrastinators, get started with an easy first step, or dig into the reasons that you tend to procrastinate in the first place.

4. Perfectionism wastes your time on excessive attention to detail on small tasks, preventing you from tackling the work that is higher priority.

5. Do B-quality work for tasks and projects that do not serve your high-priority goals or those of your boss, so you can do A-quality work that furthers either set of goals.

6. Multitasking is a good way of accomplishing low-priority tasks efficiently as long as you combine two compatible tasks and pay careful attention to circumstances in which multitasking is not socially appropriate.

7. Don't try to multitask if both of the activities are mentally demanding. The rapid switching between tasks takes too much time and uses up too much mental energy.

8. Under the principle of OHIO (Only Handle It Once), you should try to skip over the majority of your messages and requests.

9. Try to respond immediately to any message or request from a person who is important to you or that furthers one of your high-priority goals.

PART III

GETTING ORGANIZED AS A REMOTE WORKER

To translate into action the fundamental productivity principles we've just covered, you need to get organized—and that looks completely different when you're working remotely. This is especially true if you're used to depending on the workplace routine to pace your day, or on the IT team to keep you up and running, or on face-to-face interactions with your colleagues for human connection.

How you spend your time determines whether you're living like a lonely echo of the nine-to-five office drone, or seizing the flexibility of home-based work to get great work done on your own schedule. Chapter 7 helps you manage your time as a remote worker so that you get the most from each day, while taking care of your own health and well-being.

How you manage your technology affects whether your day is a series of tech-related frustrations, or whether your digital tools keep you connected to your colleagues and effective in your own work. Chapter 8 will give you a complete picture of the time management, collaboration, productivity apps, and tech gear you need for your Business of One.

How you set up your workspace has a huge impact on your ability to put some boundaries around your work—both to keep work from encroaching on personal time, and to keep your mischievous kitten from encroaching on that all-important client call. Chapter 9 will advise you on how to set up your home office and choose your home wardrobe, and how to think creatively about options for workspaces to enhance your effectiveness.

CHAPTER 7

ORGANIZING YOUR TIME

Time is a remote worker's best friend—and greatest foe. If you try to sustain a nine-to-five workday the way you might at the office, you'll burn out fast. Your eight hours at the office includes all kinds of little breaks, from the chitchat as a meeting begins to the twenty-minute hallway catch-up on your way back from the bathroom. Put in a nine-to-five day at your home office desk, and initially you may get twice as much done. But eventually you'll likely feel isolated and unhealthy as your productivity declines significantly.

That's why you need to organize your time as a remote worker so that you tap in to the productivity that comes from solitude and the lack of interruption—and then cash in on all those missing break times by going for a long walk with a friend or stepping away from your desk to make dinner. The right time management system aligns every day of your week with your key priorities, and gives you control over the pace of your day.

If your goal is to deliver the best possible results to your client or boss, then you need to do your deep thinking or creative work at the times when you're really switched on, and handle less demanding work at the times you're unlikely to have a burst of genius. That's why people who have more control over their schedules are more likely to say they're most productive at home.

This chapter will walk you through the key components of a daily routine that is effective, sustainable, and regenerative. We'll start by reframing the way you look at time as a remote worker, so that you can truly free yourself from the tyranny of the nine-to-five office regime and instead focus on the results that matter to your Business of One. Next, we'll show you a time management system that will keep you on track with daily and weekly reviews. Finally, we'll help you establish routines to keep you happy and healthy when you're based at home.

RETHINKING TIME AS A REMOTE WORKER

If you look at your calendar and see a nonstop series of colored boxes representing your wall-to-wall schedule of meetings, you're undercutting your own productivity. The widespread shift to remote work has made it a lot more common to have that kind of packed agenda. Yet long-term remote workers will tell you that the real magic of remote work lies in having long, uninterrupted blocks of time when you can think deeply about your projects and strategically about your job. It's that big-picture vision that separates someone who's just crossing off tasks and doing their job, from someone who is taking true ownership of their Business of One.

Creating some slack in your day is also the secret to handling the unexpected: Nobody wants to tell their boss that they are too busy to handle a sudden emergency, and professional life is just full of these kinds of surprises. If you're a developer who writes enterprise-grade software, are you going to tell your largest customer that their security breach will just have to wait until tomorrow for a patch, because you're booked solid? If you get a call from a reporter about your company's bid on a big government contract, are you going to offer "no comment" just because you don't have time to get them accurate facts and your company's position?

When you work from home, you're likely to experience a whole other set of emergencies, too: Maybe you can ignore the broken dishwasher or the beeping smoke alarm for an hour. Unless you call the plumber or change the battery, however, you're going to end the day with a backlog of unsolved problems. Part of the joy of working from home is being able to attend to these matters in a timely way.

To handle crises large and small, you should keep at least one hour open every morning, and one hour every afternoon. But if you have work that requires deep concentration, that may not be enough: programmers, writers, architects, designers, and other people responsible for preparing complex documents or products may need much bigger chunks of time to get into a groove.

Besides keeping time open for focused work, you may find you are most productive if you rethink when or how much you work, period. As you reclaim your time from unproductive meetings (something we cover more deeply in chapter 10), you may find that you can get *much* more accomplished in a day at home than you did at an office. Once you dispense with the time you spend answering the questions of the junior colleague who just popped his head into the office, and once you replace the thirty-minute outing to the nearest lunch place with a two-minute trip to the kitchen, you can get a lot more done.

But that doesn't mean you can live without the physical movement and social interaction that you got from those outings and interruptions. If you are conscientious about evaluating your work based on outcomes rather than time, you may be able to reclaim some of the hours between nine and five so that you can meet up with a friend or go for a walk—consciously reallocating some of the time you would have "wasted" on office chitchat.

Keeping that kind of time open can be very challenging if you work in an organization where people can just book themselves into any open slot in your calendar; or if your calendar is managed by an assistant who is charged with fitting meetings and calls into your day. So book your reserved times into your calendar, just as if they were appointments—because they are! They're appointments you make with yourself, and, therefore, the most important appointments in your schedule. By blocking them off, you avoid having your colleagues book themselves into your calendar at the times you need to get your own work done.

Yet keeping that time open is utterly pointless unless you're using a good part of it to tackle what's really important—that is, the work that will truly advance your goals and priorities. In the next section, we'll look at how to set up a system that makes the best use of both your booked and unbooked time.

YOUR TIME MANAGEMENT SYSTEM

Your time management system is how you ensure that every day and week at work focuses on the tasks and projects that advance your key objectives. The goal-prioritization process we outlined in chapter 4 will help you identify those tasks and projects on a yearly, quarterly, or monthly basis. But it takes weekly and daily discipline to follow through on those priorities.

There are two components to this system. In your weekly review, you look ahead and identify your top-priority tasks for the week, as well as when you will get to each one. In your daily review, you look back on the day and ahead to the next, to ensure you're sticking to your plan, or adjusting it as needed.

Your Weekly Review

Once a week, you should look at your list of key tasks and projects, and identify what you need to move ahead in the next seven days. Set aside about an hour for this process every Friday afternoon, or at some point over the weekend: if you wait until Monday morning, you're starting the week already behind.

As you review your big-picture projects and priorities, jot down the specific tasks you will undertake to advance each one. Then, when you sit down to do your weekly review, start by looking at the list of tasks you set out the week before. Did you accomplish everything on the list? If not, transfer any relevant remaining tasks to the coming week's list, and retire anything that no longer needs to be addressed. If your team uses a project management platform to assign tasks, take a look and see if there are any tasks that have been assigned to you, but which aren't yet on your radar screen or personal task list.

You can compile your task list for the week on a piece of paper (Bob's approach), in a fresh note within a digital notebook labeled "Tasks" (Alex's approach), or in a task management app (which may just be a matter of assigning a specific date to a task you had already captured). Any of these can be effective as long as it gives you an easily accessible, at-a-glance view of your top priorities for the week ahead.

Once you've jotted down your top-priority tasks for the week, you need to think about when you'll tackle each one. On the days that are jam-packed with meetings, perhaps you'll have time for only two or three small items, or for organizational tasks (like filing) that you can do while you're on a call. If you have more demanding work that requires intense concentration, pencil those tasks in for the days where you have wide-open blocks (and consider booking it into your calendar so the time stays open). If you have more high-priority tasks than blocks of time in which to tackle them, look at whether you can decline any of the meeting invitations that are currently filling up your schedule.

To the extent that you have some choices or flexibility about what you tackle in the week ahead, think about how to mix and schedule your activities so that you make the most of remote work, and limit its downsides. Is there a day when you'll have the house to yourself? Consider excusing yourself from one or two less-than-essential meetings, and reserving that day of quiet for the deep, focused work you need to do on an upcoming presentation. Worried you'll get restless after those five hours of back-to-back Wednesday calls? Organize your scheduled catch-up with a colleague as a Wednesday afternoon walking date. (If you can't meet up in person, you can have a virtual walking date if you simply connect by phone instead of video.)

As a final step in your weekly review, you should look back on the previous week's calendar, as well as at the logs from your daily time-tracking software (we'll cover that in the next chapter) so that you can see where your time went. Were there any calls or meetings that felt like a waste of time? Take mental or literal note of them, so you can develop a strategy for sidestepping similar invitations in future. Did you spend more time surfing news, shopping sites, or social media than you intended? Think about how you can limit or pace your check-ins so that you don't lose track of time. Although this weekly review process takes only a few minutes, it's how you become smarter and more effective in how you use your time.

Note that you don't need to move forward on each one of your projects every week. For example, imagine you're an insurance broker, and one of your goals is to increase your residential property insurance revenue by 20 percent over the course of this year. You may have identified some big-picture projects or recurring tasks that advance that goal ("develop a local ad campaign to promote our residential insurance business" or "attend networking events where I can meet real estate agents.") Because the first week of every month is when your commercial clients have all received their tenants' rent checks, you know that's a good time to collect outstanding payments or look for upsell opportunities. So you leave your residential insurance tasks off your agenda on those weeks, in order to schedule more calls with your commercial customers.

Your Daily Review

Your day is not a magic box that expands to fit as many tasks and meetings as you care to dump into it. That's why it's so crucial to look at each and every day's agenda, and determine what does or doesn't make the cut. This is the point of the daily review.

You can do your daily review at the very end of your workday, so you're ready to hit the ground running the next day, or you can do it first thing in the morning—at least half an hour before your first call. Either way, you'll use this time for three purposes: to identify a few top tasks for the day, write down your goals for each appointment, and assess your progress on the previous day's goals and tasks.

Start by reviewing the tasks you'd planned for this day when you did your weekly review, as well as scanning the rest of your weekly list: Not everything looks as urgent on Wednesday as it did on Sunday, and new things might appear that you need to address. So you do need to make a daily decision about the three or four tasks that are most crucial for you to complete each day, either because they're time-sensitive or because they're really important. If you can cross other items off your list in the course of the day, great! But the key is to put these three or four crucial tasks front and center, so you can be sure you address them.

Next, it's time to think about your goals for each appointment or meeting. The best way to do this is with a two-sided schedule—or the closest you can get with your particular calendar app. In a two-sided schedule, you can see not only the who, what, and when of each appointment, but also the why: your goal for that particular meeting. Without the goals side of the schedule, you may find yourself thirty-six minutes into a forty-five-minute videoconference, realizing that there is *nothing* on this call that moves any of your own work forward. In fact, that's the case with a lot of what fills up our calendars: all those meetings and calls are often just based on someone else's priorities, which you are implicitly accepting when you accept the meeting invitation.

With a two-sided schedule, you note your objective for each and every item you book into your calendar, other than recurring items like exercise or catching up on email. Yes, we really mean every one! After all, if you don't know your reason for attending, why are you in the meeting? (Though sometimes your goal will simply be "Show Joan I'm a team player by chiming in on this brainstorming session.")

Here's what a two-sided schedule would look like if you printed out your daily agenda and noted your goals for each meeting on the printout. In this case, it's a two-sided schedule for the chief technology officer of a midsize software company.

TABLE 7.1

START TIME	APPOINTMENT	GOALS
8:00 AM	EXERCISE	
9:00 AM	STRATEGY CALL WITH SENIOR MANAGEMENT	IDENTIFY Q2 BUDGET PARAMETERS
9:45 AM	SCAN TWITTER AND LINKEDIN	REPLY TO ANY TWEETS/POSTS ABOUT MY TUESDAY BLOG POST
10:00 AM	MEET WITH DEV TEAM	GET ETA ON COMPLIANCE IMPLEMENTATION FOR FIN TECH
11:00 AM	OPEN	
12:00 PM	ONLINE LUNCH WITH RECRUIT	SEAL THE DEAL WITH SENIOR PROGRAMMER
1:15 PM	MEET WITH BOSS	RE-EVALUATE PRIORITIES
2:30 PM	READ STAFF REPORT	ASSESS UX FEEDBACK ON A/B TEST FOR NEW LOAD EXPERIENCE
3:30 PM	WRITE MEMO TO CEO	HOW RESPONDING TO NEW COMPETITION
4:30 PM	OPEN	
5:30 PM	PHONE CALL WITH VP OF SALES & MKTG	PROMOTE NEW FEATURE IN BETA TESTING
7:00 PM	FAMILY DINNER	CELEBRATE DESHA'S DEBATE TEAM WIN

Across from the CTO's entry for a meeting with the developer team, for example, is her objective of identifying the estimated completion date for a crucial new feature that the company's financial technology customers require in order to meet their compliance obligations. That note reminds her that she needs to figure out the right approach to the related interface changes they'll need to implement, so she adds a note to the time she's set aside to read the latest staff report, reminding herself to look specifically at the interface issues. And when she gets to the time for family dinner, she notes that they're celebrating her daughter Desha's debate-team win; this ensures she'll remember to order a celebratory cake so it's delivered in time for dinner.

You might prefer to capture these goals electronically, but this is where things get tricky: Most calendaring apps include only a standard "notes" field, which is shared with everyone else on that meeting invitation. This is why we recommend looking for a calendaring app that includes a private notes field that is visible only to you, though you may have to do a little digging to find a calendaring tool with this feature, like BusyCal or Woven. Alternatively, you can import, paste, or type your next-day calendar into a document or spreadsheet every night, and add your goals there.

You can start the work of building your two-sided schedule when you do your weekly review: Just note the goals for any meeting that's already in your calendar, and consider extricating yourself from any meeting you don't have a reason to attend. But you'll still need to do this goal-setting as part of your daily review, because most remote workers have new events and invitations pop up in their calendars every day.

The final part of your daily review is to study the list of tasks and goals from the day you've just completed. It's actually best to start your daily review with this part of the process; we've put it last only because we needed to explain the idea of mapping out your tasks and your goals for each appointment.

Picture the process like this: You get to the end of your workday (or the beginning of a new one), and you start by reviewing the list of goals and tasks you set up the evening before. You cross out the tasks you accomplished, add anything new, and maybe switch around the priorities based on what's happened in the past twenty-four hours. Then you pick out the three or four tasks you're going to prioritize in the day ahead, and fill in the goals you have for each call or meeting.

It might sound like a lot of work. However, once you get the hang of it, it is more like a fifteen-minute ritual that will save you many hours of time, and better align your time allocation with your actual priorities. It's the ritual that will help optimize the efficiency of your remote working life, so it doesn't displace your family or personal priorities. And it's the ritual that will get you thinking like a true Business of One, taking charge of your most precious resource: your own time.

YOUR DAILY ROUTINE:
THE IMPORTANCE OF SELF-CARE

The whole idea of work-life balance implies a zero-sum game in which your work is somehow in opposition to your actual life. But the real joy of remote work comes from removing that friction, and instead shaping your work and your workday so that they are fully integrated with the life you want to live. If you can find a rhythm that makes your day feel like a naturally unfolding sequence, rather than a constant struggle to pull your attention back to your work, you will be much happier and more effective. The right routines will also ensure you eat, sleep, and exercise in a way that supports your productivity, health, and happiness.

Establishing some fundamental routines—what Charles Duhigg calls "keystone habits"—can foster this kind of rhythm.[1] For example, if you make a point of getting up and exercising first thing every morning, this will lead to a cascading series of subsequent choices: Your workout leaves you sweaty, so you shower and dress. It leaves you hungry, so you prepare breakfast and make coffee. Now you've got a coffee in your hand, you're fully dressed and camera ready, and you're in the calm, energized post-exercise mental state that helps you do your best work. You're ready to start your workday, and it all flowed naturally from that one commitment to a morning workout.

Smaller routines can be helpful, too. Every remote worker makes literally thousands of little decisions each day, both personal (What should I have for lunch?) and professional (When should I send a message to my colleague?). Conserve your brainpower by turning these decisions into daily routines that are as simple and automatic as possible. The more boring and repetitive you are when it comes to the little things, the more inspiration and creativity you'll have for thinking about the big things! For example, plan on eating the same thing for breakfast every day (you can eat something simple, or cook a week's worth of breakfast in advance); wear the same "uniform" every day; or commit to a specific time every day when you will tidy the house while listening to your favorite business podcast.

In establishing routines to serve as the foundation of your day, be sure to build in regular breaks from sitting through audio and video conferences. Most people can work productively only so long; unless you're the Terminator, your attention will start to wane after about seventy-five or ninety minutes.

At that point, the best thing you can do for your productivity is to take a break! Get up and move to a different room, do the dishes, or go for a walk around the block. A good break is about twenty to thirty minutes: long enough to allow human brains to consolidate their learning, and human bodies to re-energize. And no matter how busy you are, try not to skip your lunch break.

THE POMODORO TECHNIQUE

Not everyone enjoys working for ninety minutes at a stretch. If that feels like too long a period for tackling a focused, challenging task, try the Pomodoro technique.[2] In this approach, you set a timer for twenty-five minutes, and work until the timer goes off. Then you take a three-to-five-minute break, reset your timer, and go back to work. After three or four of these cycles (one and a half to two hours) take a proper twenty- or thirty-minute break.

Until we build our army of remote working killer robots, most remote workers will continue to be actual human beings with a need for food, sleep, and exercise. Think of yourself as an Olympic athlete, in training for the Remote Work Event. Just like an athlete, you need to take care of your instrument—your body—so that you can perform at your best in running your Business of One.

Every sleep study will tell you that if you don't sleep seven or eight hours per night, you will be much less effective at doing anything more complex than hitting "send" on a previously drafted email. Take the example from one study at the University of Pennsylvania: six-hour sleepers performed much worse than those who enjoyed a full eight hours per night, but had no idea of how their sleep deprivation was affecting their performance.[3] While remote work might give you the luxury of keeping your own hours, you'll do best if you sleep the same hours each night (for example, from 11 p.m. to 7 a.m.); this routine will help you develop a sleep rhythm.

TAKE A NAP

Napping is one of the great joys of remote work. And science says napping works! People who nap are consistently shown to be more alert and productive.[4]

To become a napper, you should develop a regular routine, like putting your feet up on your desk and taking off your shoes. But don't let yourself sleep for more than thirty minutes, since longer naps can leave people feeling foggy or disoriented once they wake up.[5] So set an alarm at the end of twenty-five minutes; after a few weeks of these alarms, you will tend to wake up just as the alarm is going off.

Eating habits can get better or worse with remote work, depending on whether you use your at-home status to do some healthy meal prep, or work until you're too starved and tired to do anything other than order a pizza. Establish regular times for three meals a day, which you should eat in a pleasant kitchen or dining area, away from your desk or computer. Try to eat only when you're hungry and not just to take a break. Keep a supply of healthy snacks on hand, and think of your workday meal and snacks as fuel rather than treats—that means eating plenty of protein and fresh produce, and going easy on the carbs that can give you a blood sugar spike and crash.

Physical exercise is essential to the health and productivity of your Business of One. One study showed that exercise not only enhances workers' personal health but also significantly improves their workplace performance on days when they exercised.[6] The most crucial thing is to build a regular exercise plan into your calendar: Although you don't always need a huge workout, you should aim for some physical movement every single day—a short walk, a few minutes of dancing, or even some active housework. Choose a time of day that works for you, and that helps lend structure to your schedule—whether that's a morning workout to get your day started, a midday walk with a coworker, or an afternoon bike ride with your kids. If you find remote life lonely, a running or cycling group will help you get regular exercise and give you some social interaction.

Just remember: Remote work is a marathon—not a sprint. When you're eating, sleeping, and exercising like an Olympic athlete, you're not doing all that self-care just so that you can shine for a single event, or even a single year: you're building a self-care routine that will sustain your Business of One for the long haul.

FROM A REMOTE WORKER

Corey Branstrom, a freelance tech consultant, scales
his Business of One up and down depending on
his family commitments and sleep rhythms.

I do WordPress, server, and network support and maintenance. I'm not a developer; I'm that computer guy you want to call. Wouldn't you rather call me than some anonymous person in a big company? Do you want to call the Geek Squad, or do you want to just call Corey?

I shifted to full-time freelance work three years ago. When we moved to Portland, my wife became the primary breadwinner. I looked after our two-year-old during the day, and updated WordPress sites at night.

Then I got a part-time gig at a midwifery school, and I worked there for a decade. I did my freelance work once my kid went to bed—working about twenty hours a week between 8 p.m. and 2 a.m. I'm a night person, and I'm not usually in bed before midnight, so it didn't seem like a big deal when it was two nights a week and I could roll in a little later at the midwifery school.

But then my freelance hours started to increase, so that I was working not just twenty but thirty hours a week at night. And when my first marriage split up, and I was doing the single-dad thing with a second grader, it just didn't work: I was too stressed juggling the midwifery school and my freelance work. Besides, I charge a lot more for my hourly rate than I made at the school, so it made more sense to go freelance full-time.

Last month, I billed nineteen different clients. I pick and choose which clients to take on, but mostly it's based on skill; if someone sends something my way that is not my thing, I don't try to do it. I can't think of when I last flat turned down a client even when I could do what they needed. This would be my hobby anyway, so if someone calls me with some weird problem, I'm a sucker for that.

There are days where my brain is just not engaging, so I spend the day playing a video game like *Breath of the Wild* instead of working. Then there are days when I can do eight or ten or twelve hours wall to wall. Days like that, I will literally work all day, do dinner, then after my kid's bedtime I'm back to work for three or four hours.

Once I got a taste for it, I just didn't want to work in an office anymore. Knowing what I'm worth now, I wouldn't want to go to meetings and report to people. I've worked in a big tech company and I've worked in a small tech company, but I like that I get to pick my own clients now. If I can make it work, I never want to go back.

TAKEAWAYS

1. Your daily agenda should not be booked solid: you need free time to think, and deal with business and personal emergencies.

2. Conduct a weekly review before the start of each week, when you identify how you will advance your key priorities with specific tasks, and where these tasks will fit into your schedule.

3. Review how you spent your time each week so you can identify opportunities for improvement, as well as meetings and activities that were a poor use of time.

4. Conduct a daily review in which you go over the results of the previous day and identify the three or four key tasks that are crucial to complete that day.

5. Put together a two-sided daily schedule, with a note to yourself about what you want to get accomplished in every meeting or call.

6. Transform repetitive tasks into automatic routines that use less energy and cue productive choices.

7. After concentrated work for at most ninety minutes, take a break to consolidate your learning.

8. Sleep at least seven hours per night to avoid lower performance on complex tasks.

9. Eat three regular meals a day, and keep healthy food on hand for snacks.

10. Follow a regular exercise regime, with help from colleagues and friends.

CHAPTER 8

ORGANIZING YOUR TECH

When you're working remotely, your computer and phone aren't just the tools you use to get your work done: they're the pipelines that keep you connected to your boss, clients, and colleagues.

This chapter walks you through the four main pieces of the tech toolkit for your Business of One. We start with the physical infrastructure that will make your remote work easier and more comfortable. Next, we look at the core of your software toolkit: the calendar, task list, and time tracker that you can use to organize your time. Then, we turn to the collaboration tools that will keep you connected to your boss, clients, and colleagues—which will mostly be dictated by the platforms *they* choose. Finally, we look at the productivity apps that are essential to your toolkit, but which you get to choose for yourself.

MEET THE TECH DEEP DIVE

The rest of this chapter covers the tech essentials for any remote worker, as well as some "Tech Deep Dives" that offer additional options for people who enjoy tinkering with their tech, or who need a solution to a specific tech problem. Here is how to use the Tech Deep Dives in this chapter and throughout the book:

- IF YOU'RE SOMEONE WHO ENJOYS TINKERING WITH YOUR TECH TOOLS . . . treat this as a checklist and inspiration file. Keep your eye out for the Tech Deep Dive features throughout the book, because they are included just for you!

- IF YOU'RE HAPPY WITH YOUR CURRENT SYSTEM AND TOOLS, WHETHER THEY'RE PAPER OR ELECTRONIC OR SOME MIX OF THE TWO . . . treat this as a quick tech audit. Skim through this section to see if it can solve any particular problems or introduce you to a new tool that could improve your efficiency.
- IF YOU'RE STRUGGLING WITH THE TECH YOU USE IN YOUR WORKING LIFE . . . read this entire chapter, but skip the Tech Deep Dive features. You can glance at them throughout the book, but don't read them unless they solve a specific problem for you.

INFRASTRUCTURE ESSENTIALS

Most remote workers will find the following devices and services absolutely essential:

- A LAPTOP THAT IS GENUINELY A PLEASURE TO USE. There's no bigger choke point than a computer that is slow or crashing constantly, so press your employer to keep yours up to date, or consider buying your own.
- GOOD NOISE-CANCELING BLUETOOTH HEADPHONES WITH A BUILT-IN MICRO-PHONE. They'll give you some privacy and focus when you're on a call, and you can use them to block out the kids or other distractions with music or white noise when you're trying to concentrate.
- A WEBCAM COVER. For $2 to $5 you can get a tiny stick-on sliding door that hides or covers your laptop's webcam. It's a comforting way to ensure that you really are off camera if you need to step away during a call.
- RELIABLE HIGH-SPEED INTERNET SERVICE. Ensure you have a strong signal in any room where you do work; consider investing in network extenders until you have solid coverage.
- A MOBILE PHONE THAT CAN TETHER. Your phone needs to be new enough to sync flawlessly to the same apps and services you use on your laptop, with a plan that allows you to "tether": that way, if the Internet goes out at home, you can use your phone as an emergency backup connection.

- A BULLETPROOF BACKUP PLAN. Ideally you will keep almost all your data in the cloud, and back up your apps, settings, and any highly sensitive data to a local hard drive. The key question you have to answer: If your computer died right now, how many workdays would it take you to get back up and running, with all your work restored to the point you're at right now? If the answer is more than one, you need a better backup plan.

YOUR TIME MANAGEMENT DASHBOARD

Your time management dashboard is made up of the two applications you will look at over and over again, every day (your task list and your calendar) as well as one you will review every week (your time tracker). Think of the relationship between these applications the way you'd think of your bills, your bank account, and your bank records. Your task list is what you have to budget for, your calendar is what you have to work with (your time), and your time tracker is like your bank records: it tells you where your time actually went, so you know whether you stuck to your budget.

While you can keep your task list in one section of a digital notebook, most people who keep an electronic task list prefer a dedicated task management app. (And yes, it's fine to use paper if that's what you prefer.) You can use the task manager that's built into Microsoft Outlook, or the Reminders app that comes with every Mac and iPhone. However, if those annoy you or you have trouble sticking with them, experiment with task management apps that are designed to be more visual (Trello uses a Post-it Notes metaphor), offer more categorization options (like TickTick, Things, or Todoist) or turn task management into a game (like Habitica).

A calendar that works smoothly with your organization's calendaring system allows you and your colleagues to see one another's availability, so you can book meetings without a string of emails: this is why, even if you're a paper person, you *must* keep your calendar in digital form.

Whenever you are adding a meeting or appointment to your calendar, use the invitation function to invite anyone else who is participating, even if it's just a coworker you are meeting at the coffee shop. Calendar invitations are the best way to avoid miscommunication about your meeting time and call mechanics (Who's phoning whom? Which videoconferencing link will you use?), and to ensure there's no confusion about call times for people in different time zones. Include your mobile phone number in the notes field so your fellow attendees know how to reach you if you have any trouble connecting.

TECH DEEP DIVE

Five Things to Look for in a Calendar App

You can ask for more from your calendar than a date and time. Look for a calendaring tool that offers all five of these valuable features, or add them to your existing calendar app through optional extensions or add-ons you can download to extend the functionality of most major calendaring solutions.

1. **VIDEOCONFERENCING INTEGRATION.** It's a pain to manually set up a conference link or call-in number for each virtual meeting, so look for a calendar that lets you set up those details at the time you create your calendar invitation. Google Calendar automatically gives you the option to add Google Meet videoconferencing to any event, and you can add other videoconferencing services to major calendar apps like Apple's Calendar or Outlook, either natively or with a plug-in.

2. **AVAILABILITY POLLING.** When you're setting up an internal meeting, you can look at your colleagues' calendars to find a time that works for everyone. When you're booking a meeting that includes people outside your organization, whose calendars you can't see, you need a scheduling poll: a way to ask people about the dates and times they are available. You can do this with a service like Doodle, an add-on like FindTime (for Outlook) or with a calendar app that has built-in polling, like Woven.

3. **APPOINTMENT SLOTS.** Reduce the volume of scheduling-related emails by setting up bookable appointment slots so people can add themselves to your calendar. Put the link to your bookable calendar in your signature line or online profiles, or just send it to people when you want to invite them to book a meeting. This is a native feature in Google Calendar (using the "Appointment Slots" feature) and Woven (using "Scheduling Links") or you can use a service like Calendly, which integrates with most major calendaring services.

4. **A PRIVATE NOTES FIELD.** Most calendar apps share your notes with anyone else who is invited into the same meeting. An additional private notes field gives you a place to record your goals for each meeting. (See Chapter 7 for guidance on how to use this feature as part of a two-sided schedule.)

5. **DAILY AGENDA VIEW.** A view that shows you all your appointments in a concise list gives you a handy, at-a-glance view that you can print or copy, and then annotate with your goals for each meeting.

We also recommend using a time tracker: When you're managing a Business of One, your time is the currency you have to spend, so you need to know where it's going. A good time tracker not only acts as your mirror and reality check, but also simplifies the job of filling in timesheets or invoicing for your services. While you can log your time manually, it's far more efficient to use a time-tracking tool that automatically tracks what you're doing on your computer (and possibly also on your phone). For Mac users, the best option is an app called Timing; Windows users can look at options like RescueTime or ManicTime.

PRODUCTIVITY SOFTWARE

The apps you use fall into two big categories: the ones you can choose yourself and the ones you use to collaborate. When it comes to document collaboration, file sharing, team messaging, and project management tools, you should just use whatever your IT department, team, or client uses: the whole point of these tools is to make it easier for people to work together. If you're the person running projects or tech choices for the team, you can also look at building a custom remote work dashboard that exactly suits your needs. (See "Build Your Own Remote Work Dashboard" below.)

TECH DEEP DIVE

Build Your Own Remote Work Dashboard

A new generation of productivity tools makes it possible for remote workers (as well as office workers!) to build the tools they need for their specific work. If you enjoy playing with tech, or get really aggravated by the limitations of off-the-shelf solutions, you might enjoy building your own productivity solution—no coding required! The major options in this field are Coda, Airtable, Notion, and possibly Google Tables (in beta as we write this).

You can use these platforms to build your own calendar and task management system to create specialized Web applications, or to create project management tools for your whole team. Alex uses Coda for about half her work, for example, to create:

- A CUSTOMIZED TRACKER FOR FREELANCE WRITING ASSIGNMENTS. Alex uses Coda to capture all her story ideas, mark them ready to pitch, draft her pitches, and then send them all to Gmail (as a single draft email magically addressed to the right editor). Once she marks a story assigned, the deadline gets added to her deadline calendar.
- A PROJECT DASHBOARD FOR EVERY MAJOR SOLO PROJECT. In her typical setup, one table holds all tasks and timelines, and another section (which functions like a folder) holds all call notes. Other sections might hold working notes and draft documents or pages

of related Web links, shown in teaser form. And for data-driven projects, additional data tables hold the actual data Alex is working on, with as many different "views" as she needs to get the job done.

- A COLLABORATIVE DASHBOARD FOR EACH TEAM PROJECT. On any client or group project, Alex uses Coda to track tasks, share notes, organize data, and exchange drafts in one well-structured location. (We've used a Coda dashboard for *Remote, Inc.*)
- A MASTER PRODUCTIVITY DASHBOARD. This dashboard uses Coda's "Cross-doc" feature to aggregate all of Alex's tasks from across all her project dashboards.

Beyond these collaboration essentials, there are three kinds of applications which not everybody uses—but which can transform your productivity. These are the three tools you can and should pick for yourself, so that you really commit to using them:

- A DIGITAL NOTEBOOK. You can get a huge boost to your productivity from keeping all your digital notes in one dedicated app, rather than scattered across different Word docs, text docs, and sticky notes. Evernote and OneNote are two leading options, but there are many others (including Notion, Google Keep, and Bear). Look for a tool that syncs to your phone, offers a Web clipper (to save Web pages to your notebook), and includes good optical character recognition (OCR) so that you can snap a photo of a sign, document, or even a handwritten note, and make it text-searchable just like any note you jotted down in the app yourself.
- AN EMAIL CLIENT YOU LOVE. An email program that suits your particular needs can make it much easier to stay on top of incoming messages and find old ones. The system that's used to host your email on a server doesn't have to dictate the choice of software you use to access that email on your computer or phone: You can choose an email

"client" with an interface or workflow that you like, and that keeps your email from getting lost in a sea of browser windows. Thunderbird, Mailbird, Mailplane, and Spark are a few of the dedicated email clients that have wooed fans away from the default email apps.

• A PASSWORD MANAGER. Every security expert will tell you to use a dedicated password vault, so that it's easy to follow the crucial practice of using a unique, complex password for each single Web service or site you sign up for. 1Password and Dashlane are the leading options.

TECH DEEP DIVE

Extending Your Software Library

In addition to the software tools that everybody needs, there are many categories of software that can be useful to remote workers. Here are some examples of the kinds of tools that can make your working life dramatically easier, once you know to look for the right tool for the job:

• A text editor that's designed for long-form writing (like Scrivener).
• A mind-mapping tool for brainstorming or mapping out ideas (like MindNode or MindMeister).
• An image editing tool (like Photoshop, Canva, or Pixelmator).
• An integration platform (like Zapier; or If This Then That, also known as IFTTT) that lets you connect other apps together in time-saving automated workflows. The best way to see how these tools can enhance your productivity is to go to the Zapier or IFTTT sites, and browse their lists of how other people are using the tool.
• A screen capture and annotation tool (like Skitch or Greenshot). A quick screenshot, with a note jotted in the margin, is often the easiest way to share an idea or image with your colleagues.

Even if your toolkit already feels complete, consider embracing the practice of upgrading one part of your tech toolkit every month—perhaps not by choosing a new tool, but by learning how to use an untapped feature of a platform you already rely on, or by fine-tuning your setup so that it works more effectively.

By making a habit of upgrading your tech tools or skills on a regular basis, you will continuously improve the efficiency of the online toolkit that is so essential to your productivity as a remote worker. Even more important, you will develop your own ability to learn new tech skills. The more comfortable you are adopting and integrating new tools into your toolkit, the easier it will be for you to grow and evolve as a remote Business of One.

FROM A REMOTE WORKER

Michael Morgenstern, a partner in an investment technology startup, uses tech to work efficiently— whether at the office, at home, or on a beach in Bali.

I've spent most of my career in offices: some fancy offices, some superfancy offices, some warehouses. In 2019 I left New York and bought a one-way ticket to the Philippines. My girlfriend and I got rid of all our stuff, and we combined travel with working as digital nomads, all across Southeast Asia. We spent two months in Bali, and I spent every single day working out of different cafés.

That's when I started Morning Capital; I lined up our first few clients while I was still in Bali. We have a data platform that can match investors to companies, and we sell subscriptions to venture capital firms. But selling investors is a hard sell when you can't meet people.

When we came back to the US, we moved to Austin because it was a very easy landing pad—a city where I could get an apartment with a second bedroom I could turn into an office, all for less than I'd pay for four hundred square feet in Manhattan.

But adjusting to a home office was very difficult. Having a desk that's next to a bed is really different from working on the thirty-second floor of a midtown tower where you get a catered lunch. And video infrastructure still has so many glitches.

I have two partners in LA and New York, and at least three times a week, we have two hours on the calendar to connect by video. I look forward to it, because it's a way for us to share perspectives. We often use Miro, a virtual whiteboard app, to reach an agreement or map our ideas. I love the real-time collaboration—it's almost better than using a real whiteboard, because my handwriting sucks.

I use a lot of different tech tools. I've just switched from Evernote to Notion for my notes, I use Excel for my business analyses, and I use LinkedIn's Sales Navigator for prospecting. I once caught a client's attention using Venmo, which is designed for person-to-person payments. But I found this client's Venmo ID and sent them a note—"My 2¢ on your business"—with a two-cent transfer to their account.

I also use Lunchclub, which automatically matches you for one-on-one video meetings, so you can make new professional connections; I do that over lunch hour twice a week. And to hold myself accountable, I use Focusmate. You log on to the website, you get matched with someone, and you get connected as a video call. At the beginning of the call you state your intention for that hour—for example, I might say that I'm going to call a certain number of people in the next hour, and at the end of the hour, you each say what you've accomplished and you end the call. Having that person watching me really forces me to do the work I need to do.

In the long run, I want us to have space to convene and collaborate in person, though I don't know that it needs to be full-time in the office or at home. But in the VC and private equity world, you need that conference room; you need to stress test your ideas. It's hard for me to see all these investors and do deals over Zoom.

TAKEAWAYS

1. Insist on—or invest in—a great laptop, a mobile phone that lets you "tether," high-speed Internet access, and a bulletproof backup

plan. There's no sense risking your productivity on an Internet outage or data loss.

2. Use the combination of a digital calendar, a task list, and a time-tracking app to drive your daily and weekly review and day-to-day task management.

3. Embrace the collaborative software tools that are used by your entire team, and make the best of them. Don't try to swim against the current.

4. Optimize your productivity by making your own choices when it comes to the software tools you use solo—like a digital notebook, an email client you really love, and a password manager.

5. Extend your software toolkit when there's a recurring task or type of work for which you feel like you're using the wrong tool. There is almost always an option that is the right tool for the job.

CHAPTER 9

ORGANIZING YOUR SPACE

There is nothing like working at home to make you appreciate the organizational miracle that is the modern office. From the HR team that settled you into the office on your first day of work to the custodial staff that empties your recycling bin, the conventional workplace solves a lot of the logistical problems of how to organize your working life. When you switch to working remotely, even part of the time, you need to think through everything—from where you'll work to what you'll wear during the workday.

While running your own Business of One means you now have to take on all this overhead, it also means you get to choose the workspace, infrastructure, and working environment that brings out your best. So think about your office setup and even your dress code the way a good CEO thinks about cultivating a particular kind of work environment: as an investment in worker productivity. Spend money (or time) on the changes that will actually make you more effective. Don't waste it on the stuff that doesn't actually make a difference to your productivity.

In this chapter, we will look at the three essential areas where you need to decide what you want your office to look like: your physical workspace, the gear in that space, and the clothes you wear when you settle down to work.

SETTING UP YOUR WORKSPACE

Just like some people enjoy open office plans while others depend on an office with an actual door they can close, not everyone likes the same setup for their home workspace. There are two basic approaches you can consider:

1. **ONE WORKSPACE TO RULE THEM ALL.** If you take your productivity cues from your immediate environment, need privacy or quiet for all your tasks, and (most important!) have access to a dedicated private workspace that you can use all day, every day, you may be happiest designating one particular room of your home as your home office and doing all your work there. This is how Bob likes to work.

2. **DIFFERENT WORKSPACES FOR DIFFERENT TASKS.** If you benefit from a change of scenery to break up the day, prefer different settings for different kinds of tasks, or have to share your home's one closed-door workspace with a roommate or spouse, you may thrive by relocating from room to room (or even off-site) over the course of the workday or week. This is how Alex likes to work.

Setting Up a Dedicated Workspace

If your home includes a space that you can use exclusively for work, take the time to optimize it—and take a fresh look at the space every time you change your work in some substantial way. (For example, if you move into a role that involves more or fewer daily calls.)

As a Business of One you can make your own rules for what constitutes a "professional" environment, so don't feel like you have to replicate the desk-and-credenza of a traditional workplace: if you're most productive when you sit in a giant easy chair, staring at a wall that's jammed with dozens of photos and art prints, go for it!

For most people, however, a calmer and less chaotic visual environment is more likely to foster productivity. A 2019 study of workplace clutter found that "chaotic and disorderly" workspaces are associated with higher levels of work stress and emotional exhaustion.[1] The ideal workspace includes storage for work tools and papers so that they're not visual distractions; instead, make deliberate choices about where your eye will land when your attention drifts during a call or task. For a visual cue that keeps you focused and energized, consider a bookshelf full of titles that reflect your most important professional influences, art that represents your goals, or a shelf of awards that represent your biggest accomplishments.

Sharing a Workspace

If you are planning to work in a single space that also has to serve other purposes—like a dining room or a bedroom that you use as your office during the day—try to create a defined area for your work, and purchase the furniture or storage system that will make it easy for you to take out your work or put it away. Some good options include:

- A SECRETARY DESK IN THE CORNER OF THE BEDROOM. Fold up the desk at the end of the day and your work is hidden from view.
- A BIG TRAY THAT CONVERTS THE DINING TABLE INTO YOUR DESK FOR THE DAY. At the end of the day, the tray (with all your papers) goes into the buffet or pantry.
- A TOOL CADDY WITH PENS, STAPLER, TAPE, AND OTHER KEY TOOLS. Carry it with you if you change workspaces throughout the day.
- A DESIGNATED SHELF OR CABINET IN THE BEDROOM WHERE YOU WORK. Keep your printer, a paper supply, and your caddy of tools in the closet so it's out of sight once the workday ends. This is particularly helpful if your daytime workroom is someone else's nighttime bedroom.

Of course, buying a cute set of storage boxes or a handsome folding desk is no guarantee your workspace will be magically cleared off every evening—or each morning. Make a plan for both the morning and evening transition, ideally in a form that is actually enjoyable: perhaps your teen gets to blast her favorite band for the ten minutes it takes to clear off her desk for you each morning, or maybe you get an extra five minutes to listen to your favorite sonata while you pack up at the end of the day.

Building a Workspace Rotation

If you're going to rotate among different workspaces, don't just hop from spot to spot: make a plan for what you're going to work on where (and when!). Here's how to think it through:

1. **MAKE A LIST OF ALL THE POTENTIAL WORKSPACES YOU CAN USE.** This might include your bedroom, living room, a kid's room, a nearby coffee shop, your deck, your car (it's a phone booth!), or a patio. Not every workspace needs to have a desk or table: Alex does lots of her work on the sofa, in her favorite easy chair, or even in bed.

2. **MAKE A LIST OF THE DIFFERENT TASK TYPES YOU DO IN A TYPICAL WEEK.** For example, video calls, phone calls, document writing, assembling slide decks, reading and sending email, and filling in timesheets.

3. **CATEGORIZE EACH OF YOUR TASK TYPES BY SPACE REQUIREMENTS.** You might have categories like "quiet/privacy needed," "focused but not silent," "stimulation needed," "large work surface needed," or "flexible." Depending on your personality type and preferences, you may perform at least some kinds of work better in the presence of some kind of stimulation: one study of introverts and extroverts found that introverts worked better in silence, while extroverts performed better while listening to music.[2]

4. **IDENTIFY WHICH OF YOUR POTENTIAL WORKSPACES ARE SUITED TO EACH OF YOUR TASK TYPES.** For example, Alex does her video calls in her bedroom, her writing at a coffee shop or on her front deck, and her email and invoicing work while hanging out with her kids on the living room sofa.

5. **IF NEEDED, MAKE A SCHEDULE.** If you have limited access to spaces that are viable for the tasks that require quiet or privacy (like video calls or focused writing), try to make a schedule that gives you predictable access to the space you need. For example, perhaps you can aim to do all your client calls in the morning, so your spouse can use your shared office to conduct her calls in the afternoon. If you can't make a consistent schedule, book a standing date with your partner or roommates for every week or even every evening, so you can review your respective calendars for the coming week or day, and plan out who will use which space at which time.

Note that if you're sharing space or rotating among different workspaces, your game plan is unlikely to last forever. Reassess your spaces, schedule, and plan when the seasons change, or when anyone in the household changes jobs, roles, or personality. For example, you might be happy using your patio as your personal office—until it starts snowing; or fine using your twelve-year-old's bedroom as an office—until she turns thirteen and needs her bedroom to become an ultra-private sanctuary.

MAKING THE MOST OF COWORKING SPACES

Professionals whose first experience of remote work took place due to Covid missed out on one of the most useful supports for remote workers: coworking spaces. Here's how to make the most of a home away from your home office.

- **CONSIDER DIFFERENT KINDS OF COWORKING SPACE.** You might buy a membership or drop-in privileges at a shared office space that is specifically intended for coworking, or pay to rent part-time office space in a shared office suite. But you can also use coffee shops, restaurants, bars, libraries, or a friend's house as a co-working space: if you're with another remote worker, and you're working, it's a coworking space!
- **KNOW WHAT YOU'RE LOOKING FOR.** If you want an escape from your noisy family or a change of scene, look for a space that offers privacy or thoroughly enforced quiet. If you're looking for net-working, look for coworking locations that cater to people in your industry, host networking events, and/or have a dedicated "visit-ing" area, like the office kitchen.
- **BUDGET FOR YOUR COWORKING COSTS.** Coworking membership and drop-in fees can add up; daily fees may not be worthwhile if you spend only a few hours on-site at a time.
- **BE A REGULAR.** If you find a coffee shop, bar, or restaurant that of-fers a conducive environment for your work, try to stick to it. A

regular spot lets you build friendly relationships with the own-ers, staff, or fellow patrons, providing some of the ambient colle-giality you may miss as a remote worker.

- TIP WELL. If you nurse your coffee for a couple of hours while you work away on your laptop, tip well. You may find that you're wel-come to camp out at a local restaurant and work during the quiet hours between lunch and happy hour . . . if you start by ordering lunch, ask politely about staying longer, and habitually leave a 30 percent tip.
- COWORK QUIETLY. Remember that your favorite coffee shop or co-working space is probably someone else's favorite spot, too. If you're going to take anything longer than a two-minute call, take it outside, so that you don't subject the rest of the room to a dis-tracting one-sided conversation.

EQUIPPING YOUR REMOTE WORKSPACE

Whether you're staying put or moving from room to room, you will want to ensure your workspace(s) addresses a few essential needs:

1. ERGONOMICS. If you're going to sit in one place, your chair should be set up according to the standard ergonomic recommendation of one-quarter of your body height.[3] But you may find it more comfort-able to alternate between a sitting and standing desk, or among alternative chairs (like a kneeling chair or a sofa). Don't forget your feet: if you're used to wearing supportive shoes or orthotics when you're at the office, spending all day padding around in socks or bare feet could throw your knees or back out of whack.

2. VISUAL ENVIRONMENT. Yes, you can import a beautiful landscape back-ground for your video calls, but you still have to live with the mess in your corner of the house. So identify at least one space where you can conduct a professional-looking video call, and arrange

the different places you work so that you are not distracted by clutter.

3. **SOUNDPROOFING.** In a world where more and more of us are working from home, it's OK if your colleagues can occasionally hear a barking dog or a whirring blender. But it's a lot more considerate if you can take your calls in a room that's at least somewhat removed from the action. To get a sense of how much noise is leaking from your calls and video calls, ask someone else to use your usual calling location, and then see how much you can overhear from adjoining rooms.

4. **DOCUMENT PRIVACY.** Even if your work isn't confidential, you don't want your work papers to get relocated, lost, or recycled by your family members. A simple magazine box, accordion file, lockbox, or filing cabinet will keep your work papers in order.

5. **LIGHTING.** The right lighting to do your work is different from what will make you look sharp and professional on camera. To avoid looking like a confidential informant who's trying to elude on-camera identification, you want a light source that's facing you (or at least, no more than 45 degrees off-center).

6. **POWER.** There's nothing worse than hunting for a power cable when you realize your laptop or phone is running out of juice midway through a call. To avoid that terrible fate, put a power bar with USB outlets in every place you regularly work, and get two or three laptop chargers so you don't have to carry the same one from room to room.

7. **DISTRACTION BLOCKERS.** If you're liable to be interrupted by kids, pets, or roommates, build a moat to minimize or address potential interruptions. A door is a good starting point (especially if you can lock it from the inside), or hang a sign to indicate when you can or can't be interrupted.

LITTLE LIFESAVERS FOR MOBILE REMOTE WORKERS

Here's what to keep in your bag or briefcase if you do some of your remote work at coffee shops or coworking spaces.

- A power adapter with a *really* long cable for when you can't get a spot near an outlet
- A pouch of adapters/cables that will let you plug your phone into the wall or your computer if you need to charge
- A backup battery for your phone
- A USB keychain drive: consider a dual USB/USB-C version that works with *everything*
- Wired headphones for phone and/or computer use in case the wireless ones run out of juice
- Mini–dental flossers for after lunch
- An extra pair of socks for when your feet get cold
- A high-protein emergency snack (a pack of almonds or a protein bar)
- A travel power bar that can help persuade a fellow customer to share that last available outlet
- Painkillers
- Hand sanitizer and a face mask

BUILDING YOUR REMOTE WORK WARDROBE

Remote work changes what we wear just as surely as it changes where we work and which technologies we utilize. You should think about how your clothes affect you physically (by making it easy to get out for some exercise, or removing the low-grade discomfort of office wear), mentally (as a way of putting yourself in a workday mindset), and professionally (in terms of how other people perceive you). Unless you're someone who is at their sharpest and most comfortable in a business suit, you will probably have some trade-offs here: the clothes that feel good on your body may not be the clothes that make you feel like a professional powerhouse, and they may not do a lot for your on-screen (or face-to-face) impact.

For that reason, you may find it useful to think of your workday closet as if it contained three separate wardrobes (which you may want to literally separate into different dressers or closets):

1. **WHAT YOU WEAR ON A REMOTE WORKDAY.** Simple clothing that is physically comfortable and makes it easy to stay active. Think in terms of a uniform based around a few basic shapes, colors, and textures, like soft trousers with a simple crewneck, or leggings and a tunic.

2. **WHAT YOU WEAR ON A VIDEO CALL—OR TO THE COFFEE SHOP.** A small collection of polished layers or accessories: a couple of easy jackets or accessories can lift your remote work "uniform" up to a suitable level of professionalism.

3. **WHAT YOU WEAR FOR MEETINGS, PRESENTATIONS, AND OFFICE VISITS.** Suits, dresses, or (in more casual fields) nice shirts, sweaters, blouses, and trousers. If you get a lift from wearing a great outfit (or from the compliments that go with it), don't hesitate to break out the fancy clothes for a morale-boosting day of working at your favorite coffee shop while in glamour mode.

FROM A REMOTE WORKER

Hollis Robbins is dean of the School of Arts and Humanities at Sonoma State University, where she has not only created her own home office, but ensured faculty have the space and equipment to teach from home.

I had been following the virus in Wuhan, because I have friends in China. Once I began to think it would arrive in California, I advocated for making the call to move online quickly so that faculty could use spring break to retool their classes. My department chairs rose to the challenge: we problem-solved together and established chains of command that were sort of loose and that I made explicit.

If faculty needed something, they would go to their departmental chairs, who would come to me and I would see if I could get it—laptop upgrades, access to campus to retrieve books and files, etc. I checked in to see who needed support—who needed Wi-Fi help and who needed better laptop help, who needed access to campus for teaching because of small children at home, who needed to take a leave of absence, who needed to kick roommates out, and who needed to move out of state to live with an elderly parent.

I've spent a good amount of time making sure our faculty have the home office technology they need to teach well. I try to meet with as many faculty members as I can every week; I see who is sharing space with family, who is in the basement or the laundry room, who has dogs, and who keeps a fake background up every time so I have no idea what their home office situation is. We agree that the most important rule is not to apologize for what we can't control (children running in the room) but to focus on what we can control. So we're very present with one another, which is the most important thing!

My own home office is not ideal. I have a treadmill desk but you can't really Zoom while walking because the movement distracts other people. So I have a corner near a bookshelf with pretty good light that I use for Zooming, but it's not terribly comfortable. Sometimes I work at my kitchen counter with my living room behind me but I have to carry notebooks and calendars up and down stairs.

We've been able to focus on the important task at hand, which is teaching students remotely. One exception was the theater department, which was slow to accept the new reality. One particular faculty member kept asking if we could make exceptions for in-person teaching for his fall classes, since "actors really had to interact with each other." No amount of science about aerosol transmission and loud talking could make him understand that of all the courses that we might need to hold in person (chemistry labs, nursing practicums), acting classes were at the bottom of the list. Instead of objecting, he should have been guiding his students toward the challenge of acting for Zoom, acting for the camera.

The point is to plan and adapt. We made an agreement among our chairs not to multitask during chairs meetings, to take Zoom seriously, to be up front about our mental health, to ask for help, to show one another grace, and to trust one another. Our top leadership continues to lament that we aren't "together." But if we adjust to the reality and lean in to it we will be, in fact, together.

TAKEAWAYS

1. Set up your workspace so that it enhances your focus. That means thinking about your visual environment, soundproofing, and distraction-proofing, in addition to basics like ergonomics.

2. If you have a dedicated office, take the time to make an attractive place to work with a comfortable place to sit, good lighting, and artwork you like.

3. If you are working in a multipurpose space, use containers that make it easy to set up and take down at the beginning and the end of the day, and make the turnover process enjoyable.

4. If you move around throughout the day or week, match your work environment to the task at hand by thinking through the types of spaces you have available, and the types of work suited to each one.

5. Build a remote work wardrobe that supports your professional image, as well as your physical and mental well-being. Consider separating it into "home," "video call," and "office" wardrobes.

PART IV

ESSENTIAL SKILLS FOR REMOTE WORKERS

Most professional work consists of some combination of three major activities: meeting, reading, and writing. Musical theater stars are known as a "triple threat" if they excel at singing, dancing, and acting. You can be a triple threat in your own career if you excel at all three of your core activities.

And yes, all three are learned skills that you can develop and master. If you are great at leading online meetings and making the most of the meetings you attend, you'll have stronger relationships, better access to information, and more time available for other work. As a remote worker, reading and writing are your essential tools for communicating with your boss, your clients, and your colleagues. If you are a consistent and efficient reader, that will be a significant comparative advantage for your Business of One—you will stay informed about your organization and field, and develop your own knowledge and expertise. Similarly, your Business of One will be greatly enhanced if you are a clear and compelling writer—you will be more persuasive and influential in your company and beyond.

In this part of the book, each of the three chapters grounds you in a fundamental professional skill, with basic best practices that apply to any context (though we focus on the setting of remote work). Next, we move on to the particular challenges and requirements that emerge when you're working from home.

We then help you adapt your skills to these challenges by looking at meeting tactics that mitigate the problems of Zoom fatigue, a reading system that harnesses the rhythms of the work-from-home day, and writing techniques that tap the power of online collaboration with remote colleagues.

CHAPTER 10

MAKING THE MOST OF MEETINGS

Online meetings can be the best or worst part of your life as a remote worker. At best, they help you stay connected with your colleagues and clients, get your work done, and beat isolation. At worst, they drain your energy, eat up your day, and crowd out more important work. That's why taking charge of your online meetings, and using that time effectively, has such a big impact on the productivity and pace of your Business of One.

The Covid pandemic moved online meetings from a small slice of our lives to the backbone of most business days. Overnight, we heard new terms like "Zoom fatigue," which refers to the unique exhaustion from a day of back-to-back video meetings. Some employers have introduced new policies and tools that aimed to reduce online meeting overload. However, in a lot of cases, it's up to individual employees to free themselves from the prison of nonstop video calls.

While video call overload may be a product of the shift to remote work, meetings have long been one of the biggest drags on personal productivity. Executives, on average, spend over 70 percent of their days attending meetings.[1] Yet few organizations have clamped down on the number and length of meetings; when our work moved home, so did the problem of too many meetings. Unless an organization gives careful attention to its meeting culture, and lays down key principles on the frequency and flow of meetings, it will fall to individual managers and employees to address the problem.

But there is good reason to be hopeful. Precisely because remote work imposes some friction in setting up meetings, it can inspire us to be more intentional and effective in how we make use of our Zoom, Microsoft Teams, or Google meetings. When you can't simply herd people into an empty meeting room, you have to earn the participation and attention of your meeting attendees. Often, the way to do that is with a shorter, more focused meeting—or no meeting at all.

This chapter will explain how you can make effective use of virtual meetings in your Business of One. Our examples focus primarily on group video calls, since those have come to serve as the remote team's replacement for in-person meetings. But many of the strategies apply to other kinds of virtual meetings: the in-person meetings where you're the lone person calling in from another city or a home office; the group meeting where everyone is voice-only, rather than on-screen; and even some of the one-on-one meetings you conduct over phone or video.

To ensure your time is well spent in all these types of virtual meetings, we'll begin by reviewing what you need to do before, during, and after a meeting. Next, we'll look at the specific challenges of online meetings and the phenomenon of "Zoom fatigue." Finally, we'll share the secrets of making online meetings effective, despite these challenges, so that they support your goals and priorities.

THE THREE STAGES OF A MEETING

An effective online meeting is like a good three-course meal: it includes an appetizer, a main course, and a dessert. The actual meeting may be the main event, but your pre-meeting work whets the appetite and provides a solid foundation for what's to come. And the conclusion of the meeting leaves your participants with the sweet feeling that their time has been well used, and the outcomes clear.

For that to happen, everybody at the table has to work together. It's the job of the meeting leader to ensure there's a clear agenda or plan for how to involve your team, to keep conversation flowing and on-topic, and to ensure different voices get heard. It's the job of every meeting participant to listen respectfully and attentively, and to contribute thoughtfully to the conversation without dominating the room. But making that flow happen when the room is strictly virtual is not easy, so you need to think about all three stages in the process: before, during, and after.

Before an Online Meeting

Every meeting requires preparation on the part of both the meeting leader and the participants. A little advance thought and planning will make meeting time more focused and meaningful.

WHEN YOU'RE ORGANIZING THE MEETING . . .

- Every meeting, no matter how informal, needs an agenda that summarizes what is to be discussed; this should be distributed along with the invitation to attend. If you would like meeting attendees to add items to the agenda, put it in the form of an editable Google Doc. For recurring meetings, like a weekly team meeting or a biweekly project update meeting, create a standing agenda that you can use as the basis of each week's meeting, adding additional agenda items as needed. Keep meetings under an hour, if possible. Researchers have found that the attention of meeting participants drops off sharply before the end of one hour.[2]
- Limit invitations to those who truly need to attend, so you can keep meetings smaller.[3] When a meeting gets bigger than ten, it becomes difficult to reach a decision or forge a consensus on significant issues. And participants feel less responsible for making the meeting a success, instead relying on others to lead the discussion and reach group decisions.
- If you're booking an internal meeting with other people in your organization, look for a window that works in everyone's schedule before setting your meeting time and sending invites. If you're organizing a meeting with people outside your organization, or whose schedule you can't access, use a calendar "polling" tool like Doodle, or the scheduling tools built into Outlook, to find a time that works for as many people as possible.
- To have an effective meeting, the participants should receive the materials twenty-four hours in advance of the meeting. Share the materials via Google Docs or another tool that facilitates collaborative annotation before and during the meeting.

- Always include the online meeting link and call-in number (as a backup) in your calendar invitation. The agenda can go in the notes field of your invitation or a separate cover email.

WHEN YOU'RE INVITED TO A MEETING . . .

- If you are asked to attend a meeting, don't just accept the invite. Ask to see the agenda so you can ascertain whether it's a good use of your time. You should think not only about whether the meeting aligns with your objectives, but also about the opportunity costs of attending: Which tasks (or what personal time) will get displaced in order to make room for this in your calendar?
- Declining invitations for meetings from esteemed colleagues will require tact: As much as you want to help your colleague with her interdepartmental project, you won't be able to join her for this meeting because of your pressing client deadline or your boss's directive to complete a special assignment. Just be sure your excuse isn't something that she can address by moving her meeting to suit your availability.
- When you accept a meeting invitation, consider what you will need to do to prepare for the meeting. If you will need to review background materials or pull together some information to share in the meeting, add a task to your task list (and possibly reserve a window in your calendar) so that you make the time to do your prep.

THREE WAYS TO AVOID A MEETING

If you would like to avoid or extract yourself from a meeting called by your boss or another influential colleague, you can often create a situation in which *they* choose to excuse you from attending. Here are three useful tactics:

1. **THE TRADE-OFF.** If your boss invites you to a long and irrelevant meeting, you should identify a trade-off that pits your atten-

dance against some work that your boss prioritizes: "I'd love to join that two-hour Thursday brainstorm meeting about our new mission statement, if you don't mind asking Acme to wait until next week for our consulting report? We promised it by noon on Friday."

2. **THE PREREQUISITE.** Your goal is to identify a relevant step that will require moderate effort on the part of your colleague, which acts as a speed bump: "I'm happy to join if I can be useful, but I'll need to prepare by thinking about the account first. Can you send me their last-quarter billing and a summary of their key concerns?" If your input in the meeting really matters, they'll make the effort to get you the background information. If not, the meeting isn't worth your time.

3. **THE ALTERNATIVE.** If a colleague asks for your participation in a meeting that requires your particular knowledge, insight, or expertise, see if you can offer that in some other form: "I would have to move things around to make that time work, but I can pull together a few of my latest relevant client proposals so that you can use them as a starting point, and send them to you in advance."

During the Meeting

If you've done your homework, the time you spend in the meeting itself should be productive and enjoyable. That doesn't mean every meeting needs to be all business: indeed, you should think of fostering a sense of connection as an unwritten agenda item in every meeting, since building interpersonal trust is crucial to team effectiveness, and particularly challenging when working remotely.

WHEN YOU'RE LEADING THE MEETING . . .

- It's not enough to get butts in chairs: You need to pull your meeting attendees into the conversation by engaging their attention right away, since remote attendees may still be looking at their email or messages even after they switch on their video cameras and notionally join the room. Your best bet is to start the meeting with what facilitator Suzanne Hawkes calls an "arrival practice": "Ask everyone to be sure to close all other tabs; eliminate other distractions if possible, and strive to be fully present."[4] Hawkes suggests a moment or two of silence, a couple of slow breaths as a group, or an invitation to just all look at one another on-screen as ways you can bring everyone's attention into your meeting space. This also has the advantage of getting everyone in the room to make their first contribution to the meeting, which can be a crucial hurdle for reticent participants.

- Once everybody is fully present, kick things off by summarizing the agenda: the key issues to address and the decisions to make. But keep your opening comments to five or ten minutes; if you take up too much of the meeting time, there's no room for discussion and debate. Work from the assumption that participants have read the materials sent out in advance; otherwise no one will read them before the meeting.

- If you work in an organization where everyone is so overbooked that people consistently show up for meetings without reviewing the background materials, consider whether you need to restructure your meetings to reflect this reality. One option is to incorporate a five- or ten-minute briefing presentation into the opening of your meeting. Another is to run your meeting as a "coworking meeting" in which prep time is incorporated into the meeting agenda (see "The Coworking Meeting" feature below).

- If you're trying to generate ideas or ensure you get candid input from your whole team, consider using a rebuttable hypothesis and then inviting participants to push back. For example, you might say "I'm thinking about converting our annual sales conference to a monthly online series instead of one big in-person event. But I'd love to hear your thoughts on the pros and cons of that change, and welcome any other approaches you might suggest."

- Pay close attention to power dynamics within the meeting. Is one person hanging back? Invite their ideas by calling on them by name and letting them know you want to hear their perspective. Is there a participant who interrupts or talks over his colleagues? Don't hesitate to interrupt the interrupter and return the floor to the person who was interrupted.

THE COWORKING MEETING

With more and more people working remotely, some organizations now run meetings in which succinct background materials are shared at the beginning of the meeting, rather than in advance. Participants then sit silently reading the materials at their respective desks before the meeting begins. While this may seem like a poor use of time, it has the benefit of ensuring that everyone starts the conversation fully prepared. For a distributed team, the opportunity to do silent, solitary reading while sharing virtual space can also provide a respite from isolation and Zoom fatigue.

WHEN YOU'RE PARTICIPATING IN THE MEETING . . .

- You can be a good meeting participant by staying on the agenda, offering relevant ideas, and respecting the views expressed by others. Reflect on whether you typically over- or underparticipate and respond accordingly: If you tend to talk only once or twice in a call, push yourself to ramp that up to three or four comments. If you tend to dominate the conversation, set yourself a "budget" of how many comments you'll contribute, and stay within that envelope.
- Show that you are listening as well as speaking by engaging with what other people have already shared. If you're building on the comments of someone else, make a point of acknowledging their contribution; a common concern around gender dynamics in meetings is that women may share ideas that do not get acknowledged until a man repeats the same comment.[5] Pay careful attention to gender

dynamics when it comes to the pace of conversation, too: numerous studies have shown that women are far more frequently interrupted in meetings,[6] so it's up to both the meeting leader and meeting participants to ensure that dynamic doesn't carry over to your online meetings.

- Remember that you are on camera! Your facial reactions are as important as your words, particularly if all people can see is your head and shoulders. To the extent you can stay aware of your own expressions, do not grimace in reaction to someone's ill-informed comment, and try to look like you're actually interested and receptive to what people are saying.

FIVE ALTERNATIVES TO A SLIDE DECK

While a slide deck is the natural way to focus everyone's visual attention around a boardroom table, you may find other approaches more effective when you're working with a distributed team. Here are some approaches and tools to consider:

1. **VIRTUAL WHITEBOARD.** Use a virtual whiteboard like Miro, Mural, or Jamboard to capture and organize ideas during your meeting. You can also use a whiteboard as a sort of icebreaker, perhaps by inviting each person to contribute one image that represents their goals for the project or their mood for the day.

2. **COLLABORATIVE NOTE-TAKING.** Create a Google Doc with the meeting agenda and invite everyone to add notes to the doc as the meeting progresses.

3. **COLLABORATIVE MIND MAP.** Use a tool like MindMeister or Coggle to capture and organize ideas or information in a treelike structure.

4. **PROJECT DASHBOARD.** Assign tasks right on the screen, adjust deadlines, or look at an overview of project timelines.

5. **SPREADSHEET OR DOCUMENT.** If you're brainstorming the content for an upcoming report, write the outline directly into a Google Doc everyone can see or contribute to; if you're figuring out the line items for your corporate retreat budget, put them right into a spreadsheet that everyone can see and edit.

At the End of the Meeting

Many meetings end without a clear understanding of what has been decided at the meeting. If you are sending or receiving post-meeting emails and messages like "Were there any next steps from that meeting that I need to know about?" or "Did I miss something in that conversation, because I am a bit confused about where we landed?," that's a sign your meeting wasn't very effective. This is a particularly big challenge for online meetings because they can end abruptly on the hour, without the opportunity for informal clarifying conversations on the way out the door.

The good news is that many a chaotic meeting has been saved in the final ten minutes if it ends with a tidy set of conclusions and next steps.

WHEN YOU'VE LED THE MEETING . . .

- At least five or ten minutes before the meeting is scheduled to end, switch to wrap-up mode, even if you haven't made it all the way through the agenda. It's better to defer some items to a follow-up meeting or email than to leave people hazy on what you've already covered. If some participants can stay past the appointed end time, you can cover any additional agenda items that don't require the full group.
- Summarize what has been decided and focus on what the next steps should be. Close the conversation by asking three questions: What are the follow-up items from this meeting? Who is going to take responsibility for doing them? And what will be the deadline for delivering these items? Make sure every task or next step has been assigned to someone specific, and that there is a clear deadline for

each item. You will get more buy-in and commitment if you're sum-marizing the collective consensus of the meeting, rather than hand-ing out assignments from on high.

- Both the decisions and the next steps should be recorded in notes or on a project dashboard accessible to everyone in the meeting, as well as anyone else who needs to know the outcome. Even if every-one already has access to this information, send a follow-up email to the whole group that includes links to the relevant notes (perhaps including a few key points in the body of the email) or reminding people where they can find the task list and timeline in your shared dashboard. An organization that consistently follows this practice will also have less meeting overload, since people may be able to attend fewer meetings if they know they can see the notes and tasks emerging out of the meetings they miss.

- Leave the meeting room open even after the agenda wraps up, in case anyone wants to stay online and talk informally.

WHEN YOU'VE ATTENDED A MEETING . . .

- If you are heading into the last ten minutes of a meeting without a clear sense of next steps, you, as a participant, should ask what the group has decided and what you're all going to do as your next steps.

- Before you get up from your computer or check your email at the end of a meeting, make sure you've captured your own tasks or follow-up items. Jot down any personal notes on the meeting that weren't part of the team's collaborative note-taking, and put them in the con-text that will make them useful or actionable (like your task man-agement app).

THE CHALLENGE OF ONLINE MEETINGS

When you're looking around a meeting table, you pick up all kinds of non-verbal cues from the other folks in the room: you can see that someone is disengaged from the way he's leaning back in his chair, or you can register an enthusiastic reaction from the way someone smiles and straightens up in response to a particular idea.

The moment a meeting moves online, however, almost all those signals disappear.[7] Even if you consciously register the idea that an online meeting is going to feel different from an in-person gathering, your brain is going to work away on the job of making this collection of disembodied heads feel like an actual group of live humans. Your subconscious will try to synchronize the nonverbal cues from meeting participants with what they're saying, and predict what is coming next. But the delays and glitches that are an inevitable part of video calls mean these cues won't actually sync up, and your predictions will be less accurate because you can't see anyone's full body language.[8]

Biochemistry plays a role, too. According to psychologist Susan Pinker, face-to-face conversations release neurotransmitters like dopamine—a key enabler of what we call pleasure—as well as the hormone oxytocin, which facilitates interpersonal communication.[9] Without those chemicals, we experience meetings very differently at a physiological level, in ways that can affect both what we accomplish and how we feel during and after a meeting.

All these differences take a toll, and make meetings more exhausting and disorienting, leading to what has become known as "Zoom fatigue."[10] In addition to this psychological and physiological punch, online meetings impose a cognitive and logistical burden. The cognitive load comes from all the distractions and complexity of screen-based communication. Some people find it distracting to see their own faces or cowlicks on-screen, or feel self-conscious about how they appear on camera. Others may be disconcerted by seeing so many faces across the gallery view of a meeting, or get startled when the screen reshuffles and faces move to new locations.

Last but not least are all the logistical hassles that come from a day or week that is packed with video meetings. We've all had calls where the first five or ten minutes are used up getting everyone connected, or where the screen-sharing doesn't work, or calls where the connection breaks down midway. If these video meetings run for the full sixty minutes, there is no time to take a break—to get coffee, check your email, or go to the bathroom.

For all these reasons, even a professional with great meeting skills may find that online meetings end up as a net detractor from their effectiveness as a Business of One. In the final section of this chapter, we'll look at strategies for dealing with the characteristic problems of online meetings.

MAKING ONLINE MEETINGS WORK

Because of the psychological, physiological, cognitive, and logistical challenges of online meetings, we need to minimize their number in any day or week, and make the most of the meetings we lead or attend. "Minimize" is not the same as avoid: It just means that you are going to keep the number of meetings you attend, and the amount of time you spend in them, to the minimum required to be effective in your Business of One. Depending on your role, organization, and the demands of your boss/client, that minimal amount might be six or seven meetings a week . . . or six or seven meetings a day.

Meet Only When Necessary

In the section on "Doing Your Best Work as a Business of One" in chapter 2, you will find suggestions for how to replace or reduce several common types of meetings by shifting toward punctuated collaboration. While it's important to minimize unnecessary meetings, it's just as crucial to know when a meeting is the right way to go. An online meeting is the right choice when you need to . . .

- DISCUSS A CRITICAL DECISION where there is no simple answer: vigorous debate lets you identify and work through all the relevant considerations.
- NEGOTIATE THE FINE POINTS OF AN IMPORTANT AGREEMENT. Otherwise it would take days and weeks of drafts going back and forth, without a clear understanding of the other side's concerns.

- BRAINSTORM NEW IDEAS for a project or initiative. You may need free-style and energetic interaction among creative minds to generate innovative approaches to products or services.
- KICK OFF A NEW CLIENT, SUPPLIER, OR COLLEGIAL RELATIONSHIP—whether you're welcoming a new customer, onboarding a new employee, introducing a new supplier, or convening a new project team, an initial round of introductions and rapport-building lays a solid foundation, after which email and phone communication goes a lot more smoothly.
- ENGAGE YOUR TEAM in a shared mission. From celebrating a big success to introducing a new vision for your organization, there are certain pivotal moments that require everyone in the (virtual) room, both to mark the occasion and build a sense of common purpose.

Make Meetings Shorter

If one hour stretches the limits of human attention when we're all in the same room, it feels even longer on a video call. Plan and structure your meetings so that you get through your agenda quickly, and then do your socializing by staying on the call for an informal chat.

TO MAKE MEETINGS SHORTER . . .

- KEEP ORDINARY MEETINGS TO FORTY-FIVE OR FIFTY MINUTES, instead of one hour. (Or better yet, twenty or twenty-five minutes.) Establishing this norm within your organization means people can count on having a few minutes between calls to go to the bathroom, get a snack, or check their messages.
- IN EXTENDED ONLINE MEETINGS, KEEP EACH SESSION TO A MAXIMUM OF TWO HOURS. When you need to hold an in-depth and longer meeting, like a retreat or strategic planning session, break your agenda into smaller chunks so each chunk is less than two hours, with a fifteen-minute break every hour. Take a longer break (at least thirty to forty-five

minutes) between each two-hour session; if possible, organize your sessions into morning and afternoon blocks so you can have an even longer break.

- BE CLEAR ABOUT THE LENGTH OF BREAKS IN LONGER ONLINE MEETINGS. Announce how long each break will be: let attendees know the exact time when you will resume ("We'll resume at 4:05"), and then follow through on that commitment by resuming promptly.

MAKING THE CASE FOR *REMOTE, INC.*

Winning Shorter Meetings

In an ideal world, your organization or manager will make a policy that keeps ordinary meetings to less than one hour, so people get a break in between. If you're not the one calling the shots, however, you can still help nudge expectations in that direction.

When you schedule a meeting yourself, explicitly note that you are making this a forty-five-minute meeting: yes, that might be obvious from the calendar invitation, but you should underline the point by saying that "we'll end exactly on time so everyone has fifteen minutes before whatever comes next in their day." If you are in a role or relationship that allows it, accept any hour-long meeting invitation with the caveat that you will have to sign off ten minutes early in order to prep for your next call.

If you're rarely the person running the meeting, look for other ways to cue the person in charge: "I notice that the last twenty minutes of next week's marketing meeting are reserved for getting ideas for upcoming blog posts. How about I collect those from folks in advance? Then we need only five minutes to pick the best ones, and can give folks a break before their next call."

• • •

Make Meetings Human

Smaller meetings are more efficient and more engaging. These smaller meetings reduce the psychological and cognitive stress of online meetings because it's easier to track body language with a smaller number of participants. To humanize your meetings . . .

- KEEP YOUR MEETING TO FEWER THAN TEN PARTICIPANTS if it requires meaningful conversation, especially if that conversation is likely to be emotional or controversial. The exact number will depend on the videoconferencing platform you use: Your goal is to limit the size of the meeting to the number of faces you can fit on a computer screen and still see some level of detail; if it gets any bigger, people will need to switch to a view where they see only the person speaking. When your participants can keep everyone in the meeting on their screens the whole time, it allows them to track one another visually, and gauge reactions.
- STEP BACK FROM THE SCREEN and ask participants to do the same, so that you get the full benefit of seeing one another. If you all sit farther back, you can see one another's upper bodies, which lets everyone take in more visual cues and synchronize them with spoken words.

Prepare for Your Meetings

You can reduce the logistical stress of your online meetings (and reduce the frustrations of your colleagues) by getting yourself properly organized beforehand.

- ADD THE VIDEO LINK FOR EACH CALL TO YOUR CALENDAR as part of your daily review. Ideally this information will be included in any calendar invitation you send out or receive. But if it's missing, email the organizer for details.
- IDENTIFY AND DOWNLOAD OR UPDATE YOUR VIDEO CALLING SOFTWARE whenever you see a meeting in your calendar that uses a platform other

than the one(s) you use routinely. As you're reviewing your calendar every day, look at the videoconferencing platform each call will use, and make sure you have the latest version of the software installed; launch it and ensure you know how to log on. If you're going to share your screen, try that out so you can enable any screen-sharing permissions before the call begins, since this often requires you to quit and restart the conferencing application.

- MAKE A PLAN FOR HOW YOU'LL MINIMIZE BACKGROUND NOISE AND INTERRUPTIONS during the call. If you have a reasonably soundproof, private home office, that is great. If not, negotiate with your spouse or roommates to maintain a quiet space for the duration of the meeting.
- LOG ON TO THE CALL A FEW MINUTES BEFORE THE MEETING BEGINS so you have time to troubleshoot any connection issues. Make sure your headphones are working correctly (if you're using them), turn on your camera, and make sure you have your audio turned on. And just in case all of that fails, keep a phone nearby so that you can fall back to the dial-in number if you have any issues with your video connection.
- TURN OFF NOTIFICATIONS ON YOUR COMPUTER and close any browser windows that might play incoming notification sounds (like an open Facebook window). Consider quitting any high-demand applications to improve the performance of your computer and provide a cleaner desktop if you end up sharing your screen. Take particular care to close any email or messaging windows that could accidentally become visible if you share your screen.

Maximize Advantages

So much of this chapter has focused on reducing the footprint of online meetings—how to make them fewer, shorter, smaller—that you may think we're arguing that you shrink your meetings as much as possible. But really, we're just correcting for the widespread overuse of meetings, particularly as they moved online in the early months of the Covid pandemic.

Online meetings can and should be an important part of your working life as a Business of One, since they keep you connected to your clients and colleagues and mitigate that other curse of working life, email and message overload. (Far better to book one twenty-minute meeting than to initiate a chain of twenty emails instead.)

Indeed, there are unique advantages to online meetings (especially relative to their offline predecessors) that you can maximize by making use of the specific features of videoconferencing platforms. Video meetings allow you to . . .

- USE TEXT CHAT TO SUPPORT THE FLOW OF CONVERSATION by directing people to relevant resources and providing a home for less essential comments. If there is a document you're referring to in the conversation, drop a link into the chat so that people don't waste time looking for it. The chat window is also an unobtrusive way to applaud someone's good news, or to announce your own departure from the call, without disrupting the flow of the meeting. If you have a clarifying question, consider posing it by chat: instead of asking the meeting leader to fill you in on an acronym she just used, post your question in the chat window so someone else in the meeting can answer it.
- MUTE WHEN YOU'RE NOT SPEAKING so that you aren't a distraction, and can hear your colleagues more clearly. This not only minimizes background noise but also gives you a little bit of welcome freedom—if, for example, you want to request a coffee refill from a nearby spouse, or yell at the cat jumping onto the kitchen counter.
- USE POLLS TO ENGAGE PEOPLE AT SCALE. A poll lets you quickly get a sense of how meeting participants feel about an important issue, even if you have many people on your call. Bob likes to use polls before and after a major debate to see if the arguments made during the debate changed the opinions of any participants.
- FOSTER DISCUSSION WITH BREAKOUT ROOMS. Particularly when you're running a large meeting, breakouts are a great way to facilitate active discussion by a small group of three or four people for a short period of time. Ask each group to report its findings to the whole group in a debriefing session.

FROM A REMOTE WORKER

*Beth Kanter is a virtual facilitator, trainer, and author
whose three decades of experience as a remote
worker put her in a unique position to address the
post-pandemic transition to remote gatherings.*

I've been remote since 1990. When I first worked from home, it wasn't over the Internet. I was running a marketing strategy firm for arts organizations, consulting to them on-site, mostly locally.

Then the National Endowment for the Arts hired me as a consultant, and sent me all over the country to do evaluations. They gave us these fifty-pound laptops, which we'd hook up to a dial-up modem at night.

When the New York Foundation for the Arts launched an online network called ArtsWire, I didn't even know what the Internet was, but I had a second phone line installed at our house, and that became the help line for their network. ArtsWire was a completely remote team when you didn't even have remote teams.

Now I work with nonprofits and foundations all over the country. I work with a client to design, facilitate, and prep speakers for a large convening every other year; we usually start the planning process with a day of on-site meetings every other month, and then I work with them remotely. But with Covid, we couldn't meet in person, so we started the process by trying to chunk our face-to-face meeting time into shorter online meetings.

It took only a couple of weeks to realize that people were getting overwhelmed, because they have so many more meetings now. In organizations where people are used to being in a physical workspace together, the move to remote work means there is now a lot more need to communicate. Everything is scheduled, and there's an agenda, instead of the serendipity that comes from just being in the office together.

Before the pandemic, we could discuss the conference and make decisions in real time, but with all the other meetings everyone has now, and the overload, we can't do that effectively. So I restructured our meetings so that it was more like a series of smaller deliverables, almost like a college course. I take the next piece of work, and package it up, and email it to my clients so that they can review and prep for our call. Then our video calls are shorter and much more efficient.

I have experimented with silent meetings, where I start by sharing a report with everyone. I give them five minutes to read it, and then I say, OK, here's the Google Doc with the report, please put your comments in. Our meetings go much faster because everyone has given focused thought and our discussion is more productive.

Our collaboration has helped us come up with a really innovative approach to the conference. Instead of a two-day convening with meals and sessions and tons of social interaction, we are going to do one day a month over four months. There will be a ninety-minute morning plenary, and then a long break, and then a ninety-minute breakout in the afternoon.

We're experimenting with a really amazing 3D space for the breakouts that's built to look like the conference center: You get a robot avatar, and your video screen is in the robot's chest. Then you can navigate around the virtual conference space, and when you get nearer to people, they get louder—so that allows for some serendipity in whom you talk to. And then there will be fun breaks in between, because you just can't do Zoom for eight hours!

TAKEAWAYS

1. When you're inviting people to a meeting, include a clear agenda and provide any background materials at least twenty-four hours before the meeting.

2. Only accept meeting invitations that have an agenda, make good use of your time, and advance your priorities, and find ways to politely decline everything else.

3. The meeting leader's job is to bring participants into the room with full attention, move through the agenda, and encourage participation from the full group.

4. Generous meeting participants listen as well as contribute, and acknowledge and build on the contributions of others.

5. The last five or ten minutes of the meeting should be reserved for summarizing decisions, identifying follow-up steps, and assigning responsibilities and deadlines.

6. Online meetings impose unique psychological, physiological, cognitive, and logistical burdens.

7. To mitigate the downsides of online meetings, aim for fewer and shorter meetings with a smaller number of participants.

8. Opt for meetings only when they're necessary—typically because you have a complex or important decision, require group creativity, or need to build group trust.

9. Before an online meeting, test out your equipment, find a separate space that is quiet, and try to minimize the distractions at home.

10. Take advantage of the unique benefits of online meetings, like the ability to use chat, polls, or breakout rooms.

CHAPTER 11

READING ONLINE AND OFFLINE

When you're a working professional in a busy office, you're constantly learning. As a midlevel employee at a big consumer goods company, for example, you might encounter a wall display showcasing your company's latest ads on your way into the office in the morning. You get to your desk and somebody has left an industry newsletter on your chair, with a feature on making a splash at your next trade show. As you're getting your coffee, you overhear a conversation about a TED Talk that gave your colleagues a whole bunch of new ideas for customer service improvements. It's not even ten o'clock in the morning and you're brimming with new information and ideas.

When you're working from home, by contrast, you can't just wait for knowledge to drop into your lap: you need a strategy for reading the right things—and reading them *efficiently*—so that you're continually growing and always well-informed. You may also need to be more deliberate about carving out reading time, especially if you're accustomed to doing your reading on a daily commute.

Think of this as the growth strategy for your Business of One: just as a good employer plans regular staff lunches with guest experts, or organizes professional development events with a deep dive into relevant topics, you need to organize your own ongoing learning strategy. Yes, conferences and webinars can be a part of it, but on a day-to-day basis, reading offers the biggest payoff from the smallest amount of time.

As a remote worker, you're likely to do a lot more of this reading online. Nobody's dropping documents on your chair, and you're unlikely to pass a newsstand as you travel from breakfast in the kitchen to your first meeting at your desk. And unless your employer provides a generous budget for toner and paper, you may find yourself much more reluctant to print out your working documents.

But reading on a screen is very different from reading on paper.[1] Research has found screen reading to be more physically and mentally taxing—causing eyestrain, headaches, and blurred vision. Nick Carr famously argued that hyperlinks interrupt the reader's flow.[2] More recently, a meta-analysis of seventeen studies concluded that paper is better than screen reading for comprehension, though there is no significant difference in speed.[3] In any event, there's no question that much of our on-screen reading is designed to send us skipping from one page to the next: a great many websites depend on clickbait links as a crucial source of income.[4]

It's worth facing these challenges head-on. In a professional context, reading on-screen offers some major advantages over print, including:

- HIGHLIGHTING AND TEXT EXTRACTION. You can extract and store text you've highlighted while reading on-screen.
- REAL-TIME ANNOTATION AND EDITING. You can annotate or edit text live, instead of making your changes later.
- SEARCHABILITY AND REFERENCE. You can find exactly what you're looking for, and mark it for future reference.
- SHARING. You can share key articles or snippets with colleagues and on social media.

To unlock these benefits, this chapter will show you how to master essential reading skills so you can quickly grasp the information you need for your work, resist the online distractions that can interfere with your reading, and build an online reading system that makes it easier to save, clip, and share useful material.

MASTER ESSENTIAL READING SKILLS

Many remote workers are passive readers; they march through all articles and memoranda in much the same fashion. But we want you to become an active reader—thinking in advance about your reading objectives and applying systematic techniques.

If you want to become an effective reader, you need to think hard about your purpose before you pick up that iPad or fire up the news app on your phone. Your reading goals should shape the way you read any given article or book, whether that means concentrating on every word, or just zipping through for a general picture. For example, if you want to . . .

- UNDERSTAND THE MAIN IDEA. Skim the article or memo to get the main points.
- FIND SPECIFIC FACTS. If you're reading on-screen, use search to look for likely keywords that will take you to the exact info you need. If that doesn't work, or you're reading on paper, slow down and do a careful read.
- DISCOVER NEW SOURCES OF INFORMATION. Read quickly through the material until you get to a reference to a data source, a useful-looking hyperlink, or a page full of thoroughly documented footnotes.
- EVALUATE A PROPOSAL. Pay careful attention to the assumptions underlying budget or investment proposals and the quality of their arguments, as well as scrutinizing the numbers.
- GET INSPIRED. If you're looking for fresh energy or ideas, skim until you get to the human or organizational stories that you connect with emotionally.

The Three-Step Reading Process

Once you know your purpose for reading, use a three-part process: wrap your mind around the structure, get the big picture from the introduction and conclusions, and then maybe—if it really looks worthwhile—dig in to the meat of the text.

Grasp the Structure

Stop! Don't read this sentence!

When you start by reading the first sentence of your material, you miss the chance to extract the maximum amount of information in the shortest amount of time. Instead take a few minutes to understand the structure of a document before you plunge in. How does it begin and end? How is it divided into key themes or sections? Look for any headings or subheadings, or a table of contents, so that you can quickly grasp the structure. Once you understand how a document is put together, you can figure out how to read it most efficiently.

Read the Introduction and Conclusion

You can usually count on the introduction to cover the main theme of a piece in a sentence or paragraph. The most useful introductions also tell you how the article or memorandum will be organized.

Even if the introduction has your attention fully engaged, resist the urge to just keep on reading. Instead skip directly from the introduction to the conclusion, which will tell you where the writer ends up. It usually summarizes the main points and suggests key takeaways. Now if you get interrupted while reading, at least you have the big picture.

Dive In to the Full Text

Reading the introduction and conclusion will let you know if this article, memo, or report is really worth reading. Will this case study of a struggling firm actually help you achieve your goal of developing a sales recovery plan? If not, stop right there and go no further.

But if it *is* a fit, then tackle it one paragraph at a time, treating the first sentence of each paragraph as a kind of "sudden death" contest. If the first sentence suggests this will be a useful bit for you to read, keep going. If not, skip to the next paragraph. (This technique will reveal just how much of the world's written work does not warrant close reading.)

As you read an article or memo, constantly ask yourself what you want to remember from it in a few weeks or months, depending on the time frame for your work. In other words, distill what you want to remember into a few key points relevant to your purpose for reading the material. This is what we call active remembering.

You can train yourself to become better at actively remembering by jotting down a few notes at the end of a reading: this is a great use for your digital notebook (like Evernote or OneNote), where you can maintain a "reading notes" folder. Another option is to tweet a few key learnings so that in addition to remembering them for yourself, you're sharing them with others. By jotting down a few notes, you will substantially increase the likelihood that you will remember the key points most relevant to your reading purpose.

RESIST ONLINE DISTRACTIONS

One of the many delightful things about curling up with a dog-eared copy of *Pride and Prejudice* is that Mr. Darcy *never* pops up to tell you about the seven surefire ways to burn belly fat: You'll never believe number five!

When you are reading online, such distractions are a never-ending obstacle. Maybe you can resist the belly-fat ads, but are more susceptible to the targeted ads that haunt your workday with reminders of whatever you browsed during your evening downtime: patent-leather boots, audio gear, Hawaiian vacations.

Or maybe you resist the ads, but get distracted by the hyperlinks to related stories, the exhortations to share what you're reading via social media, or the incoming email notifications that pop up on your screen while you're trying to read. This is exactly what online publications and social networks are designed to do: to pull you in and either keep you clicking, or send you off to someone who's paying for access to your eyeballs.

All of these distractions are even more perilous for the home-based worker, for two reasons. First, it's much easier to tumble down the rabbit hole of link clicking and Web surfing when you don't have to think about whether a colleague might peek over your shoulder at any moment. Second—and far more important—are the opportunity costs: any time you waste reading pointless top-ten lists or browsing the latest online sales is time you could have spent reading the material that actually advances the goals of your Business of One.

The good news is that you don't need an iron will to resist these distractions and focus on your work-related reading. If you've followed the three-step process for purposeful reading, you should always be clear on your reading goals at any given moment, as well as on the structure of the material you are reading. You should also develop some tactics for reducing distractions (see the "Four Tech Tricks for Distracted Readers" feature below), since that will not only protect you from getting blown off course, but also increase the breadth and value of your reading by making it easy for you to find, review, and retain the right reading materials at the right time.

FOUR TECH TRICKS FOR DISTRACTED READERS

1. **TURN ON "READER MODE" IN YOUR BROWSER.** Most Web browsers offer "reader mode": a one-click option that strips away all the clutter of a Web page so that you can focus on the text. Look up the reader mode option for your browser and use it whenever you're reading online.

2. **INSTALL AN AD BLOCKER.** The easiest way to resist advertiser distractions is to not see the ads in the first place. Install an ad blocker in your Web browser and the ads will magically get stripped away.

3. **USE "DO NOT DISTURB" MODE.** If you've set aside time to read on your phone, computer, or tablet, put your device into "do not disturb" mode so that you aren't interrupted by incoming email or text notifications.

4. **SELECT A DEDICATED READING DEVICE.** Yes, you can definitely read on your computer or your phone, but there is a lot to be said for reading on a dedicated device, like a tablet: there are many solid, inexpensive options if you choose an Android tablet rather than springing for an iPad.

BUILDING AN ONLINE READING SYSTEM

Once you know how to read effectively, and you're alert to the danger of online distractions, it's time to build the online reading system that can take the place of office chitchat, lunch-and-learns, or even industry conferences. It all hinges on thinking through the contexts in which you read, and then building a system that makes it easy to get the most out of each reading opportunity.

Identify Your Reading Contexts

When and why do you do work-related reading? If you build an inventory of your reading opportunities, you will be able to match any opportunity with the right kind of material for that particular moment.

Start by jotting down a top-of-mind list of the things you read (or listened to) in the past week or two. (It may help to review your browser history, phone, or e-reading device.) Here's what a partial list might look like:

- National and business news from *Washington Post, Wall Street Journal*
- Industry news I found on LinkedIn, Twitter
- A few chapters of a book on sales strategy
- Part of an audiobook on the economics of racism
- A few chapters of a novel

Next, make a list of the times of the day (or week) when you typically read—and the kinds of things you like to read during those windows. Here, a partial list might include:

- Morning coffee: national and business news, news from social networks
- Lunchtime: Kindle book on my phone/tablet (need a break from work)
- Afternoon: lots of short work-related articles while my attention is dwindling
- Afternoon walk: podcast or audiobook, can be work-related if it's really engrossing
- After dinner/bedtime: feature articles, biographies or novels, can't be too work-related

Now group your reading contexts by the kind of thing you like to read at each time. In the example above, there are four basic groups: work-related (text), work-related (audio), relaxation (audio), and relaxation (text).

Ideally, you will set up a separate app or platform for each of these: A newsreader and "read it later" file that you use for work-related stories, a podcasting app and/or audiobook app you use *only* for work titles, and then a separate app for your relaxation reading and audio. That way you won't have your sleepy time interrupted by a sales podcast that revs you up. There are plenty of great podcasting apps (Stitcher, Spotify, and Overcast are three great options) and plenty of different RSS[5] readers and news apps that will bring you news from different sources (like Feedly, Flipboard, Google News, and Apple News). Using different applications for different types of content makes it easy to keep your political news and celebrity gossip separate from your industry updates and business news.

We're focusing here on on-screen reading, but it's absolutely fine to opt for actual ink-on-dead-trees for some of your reading contexts. Maybe you prefer reading physical books, or you want to subscribe to a few business publications so that you have a screen-free way to do some of your work. What really matters is to make deliberate choices about the optimal format for each context and type of reading. And if it's a type of reading you'll need to refer to later, formulate a plan for how to capture any notes or quotes.

Set Up a "Read It Later" File

If you save the articles you want to read in the same place as the articles you've already read but might want to refer to in the future, you'll never have a tidy place to find your next read when you have a spare minute. And if you save articles by emailing them to yourself or others, well, that's just a recipe for an overflowing inbox (and annoyed colleagues).

Instead build your "read it later" list in an app made just for this purpose. The two leading platforms for this purpose are Pocket and Instapaper, so if you choose one for saving work-related reads, and one for saving fun reads, you won't get distracted by beauty advice or car reviews when you're trying to catch up on business news. Each of them makes it easy to save an article you don't have time to read right now, so that you can find it during your next reading window. You can also use the "Reading List" feature built into Safari on iOS and macOS devices. Once you've signed up for your read-it-later service(s), make sure you have one-click save enabled in any device or app where you regularly stumble across articles you want to read.

Now use the Pocket or Instapaper app to catch up on the news you've saved whenever you have your next reading window: You'll always have the right kind of reading waiting for you—work or play—when you have a moment to catch up. When your reading wish list grows beyond your available reading time, just clear the queue of articles waiting for you to read later, and start over.

Set Up a Clipping File

For those of you who don't remember the feel of actual physical newspapers, let us explain that a "clipping file" is the name for the collection of articles people used to actually cut out of newspapers, and stick in an actual folder—back in the olden days when you couldn't count on being able to access a previously read article by just looking for it on the Internet.

Happily those dark times are now behind us. And yet things disappear from the Internet all the time, or just become harder to find—or maybe you want a clipping file that lets you highlight or annotate your reading. Maybe you even want to do the modern equivalent of sending a newspaper clipping through the mail. (Yes, people really did that.) All of these are great reasons to set up a clipping file that's separate from your "read it later" file, though you may want to set it up a little differently.

Your clipping file should give you an easy way to save links or articles for future reference: It's up to you whether you prefer to keep the full text of an article on your device (where it's searchable or readable offline) or simply build a list of titles and links. Choose a tool that makes it easy for you to save items with a click, categorize what you save, and (most important) actually find it again. See the "Four Ways to Maintain a Clipping File" feature below for some options.

TECH DEEP DIVE

Four Ways to Maintain a Clipping File

1. EVERNOTE. This digital notebook includes a Web clipper that allows you to save a bookmark (that is, just the title and link), an excerpt from an article, or the entire article. It's really handy for compiling collections of related links—for example, a file of case studies you can use in future talks.

2. ONETAB. If you're the kind of person who opens new windows and tabs all day long, intending to read or refer to them, a single click of your OneTab button converts them all into a tidy list of links you can name, save, and recover. This functionality makes OneTab an excellent tool for quickly creating a clean list of links you can share: Just open all eight or ten of the articles you want to add to a Google Doc or blog post, each in its own tab (but all in the same browser window), then click the OneTab button. Voila! You now have a list of links you can copy and paste. This is also a great way of saving a whole bunch of resources you're using on a given project so that you can come back to them in a day or a week, without leaving them open in your browser.

3. CODA. This productivity app does a nice job of styling URLs as hyperlinks or embedded teasers. If you're assembling a collection of links as part of a team project you're tracking with Coda, or you want a nice-looking collection of links to publish online, Coda is an easy way to do it.

4. TWITTER. Use Twitter as a clipping file? It might sound crazy, but people do this all the time. Just choose an unusual hashtag—something nobody else is using—and include it anytime you're sharing a link you also want to refer to in the future. You can always find the clipping again by

searching Twitter for that hashtag, or better yet, use a tool like Zapier or IFTTT to build a simple workflow that saves everything with that hashtag to a Google Doc or Evernote notebook.

Turn Reading into Listening

One great thing about working from home is that it gives you lots of little windows to catch up on household chores like dishes, laundry, or tidying. If you feel guilty about doing the dishes in the middle of the workday, make that time do double duty by catching up on your reading list. Here's what will round out your online reading system:

- AN AUDIOBOOK APP. You can buy a wide range of audiobooks through Amazon's Audible or Apple's iTunes, or get audiobooks from your public library by using the Libby app from OverDrive. You can also switch back and forth between reading and listening by keeping a book synced between Audible and your Kindle.
- SENSOR EARBUDS OR HEADPHONES. Some earbuds or headphones include a sensor that detects when you take them out or off. If someone interrupts you while you're listening to a book or article, pop out an earbud and your book will pause—then resume as soon as you pop it back in. No more rewinding to find your place.
- VOICE DREAM. This app is designed for people with visual impairments, and offers a wide range of humanlike voices, making it a great way to convert your reading to listening. It integrates with Pocket, Instapaper, and Evernote, so you can use it to listen to your read-it-later articles.
- A HOME ASSISTANT. You can use a voice-controlled home assistant like Amazon's Alexa or Google Home to listen to your favorite podcasts and newscasts—handy if you're tackling a quick chore in the kitchen while your phone is still upstairs on the desk.

FROM A REMOTE WORKER

Marshall Kirkpatrick is the VP of influencer and analyst relations
for Sprinklr, which taps in to his ability to consume, retain,
and access an extraordinary volume of information.

I've always been a pretty big reader, ever since I was on the high school debate team twenty-five years ago. I found that if I could get access to good streams of information and then absorb and utilize them well, I could find a lot of success in life. That's how I ended up being the Pacific Northwest debate champion in my junior year.

Through all the phases of my career, assimilating and synthesizing information has been one of my key practices. But one thing that has changed a lot is that I now do a lot of things—like washing the dishes—while I'm reading, because my phone can read to me out loud. My house is cleaner than it's ever been since I discovered text-to-speech on mobile. I can listen at two or three times the speed, so it's way faster for me to listen than to read with my eyes.

I save articles to Pocket so I can listen to them out loud, and I've set up If This Then That so that anytime I like a tweet with a link in it, the link gets sent to Pocket. I use text-to-speech with mobile apps from Forrester and McKinsey to listen to reports like "How the Insights Center of Excellence Powers the Adaptive Enterprise." That's my idea of a good time right there.

Every morning when I wake up, I look at Feedly, which I use to scan the sources I've collected on climate change: that's my next big project. I scan through the day's articles, throw them to Pocket, and while my coffee is brewing, that's what I listen to. I also try to read from a paper book every day, and right now there are probably fifteen books I'm reading all at once. Paper feels like a different experience.

When I'm reading I take notes in Roam Research, which lets me see the connections between my notes. If I hear something interesting while I'm washing the dishes I'll dry my hands, pull my phone out, and take a note. There is something to be said for stopping and thinking about what you want to note, and being deliberate about it.

Every weekend I set some time aside to open up everything I've tagged "reading" or "best practices" in Roam, and open a separate window for Anki, which I use to make flash cards. Then I spend five minutes every day reviewing my flash cards, so that I retain what I learned; I've been doing that for four years. The theory is that right when I am about to forget something, Anki shows me the flash card again.

While I'm now at home full-time, learning like this helps me bring more to the table when I do converse with colleagues. I can't always recall a flash card perfectly but I will remember that I have a flash card and pull it up. Or if I've got a meeting scheduled with folks, I bookmark something they've written recently, go for a jog, and listen; people are delighted when you've read the things they've written.

What matters isn't just what you can retain in your brain; it's your ability to quickly discover the right information, and apply it quickly and effectively. This is my specialty: information absorption and reapplication. It could be something a lot more people do a lot more of, but so far it's a competitive advantage for me.

TAKEAWAYS

1. Online reading offers many productivity benefits, but requires you to mitigate distractions by using reader mode, ad blockers, and other tools.

2. Before you start to read any material, think hard about your purpose in reading, and stick to it.

3. Then go through a three-step process—grasping the structure of the document, reading the introduction and conclusions, and perhaps reading the paragraph tops in the body.

4. As you go through these three steps, try to actively remember the key points relevant to your purpose. Take a few notes to reinforce your memory.

5. To make the most of your reading time, select a range of reading apps that match the specific contexts in which you do different types of reading.

6. Use a "read it later" tool like Pocket or Instapaper to save your must-reads for a time and context when you can absorb them.

7. Set up a clipping file that allows you to collect readings you want to refer to in an easy-to-reference form.

8. Extend your reading capacity with audiobooks and text-to-speech tools.

CHAPTER 12

WRITING SOLO AND WITH OTHERS

When you're a Business of One, you are your words. Your boss, colleagues, and clients will all have a higher opinion of your knowledge and expertise if you express them effectively. That's why it's essential to become a good writer, as well as an effective user of online collaboration tools like Google Docs.

In a business or professional context, all that means is that you are able to produce a written document or communication that . . .

- Clearly and efficiently communicates the information and ideas you need to share
- Moves other people to required next actions
- Generally reflects the commonly agreed-upon rules of grammar and spelling

If you're able to go beyond these basics with prose that conveys a sense of personal voice or style, builds an emotional connection with your reader or colleague, or sticks in your reader's memory thanks to your powers of narration or persuasion—well, terrific! That's a valuable professional skill. But you don't need to aim that high.

The good news is that this is a matter of practice and process as much as innate ability. Just follow a writing structure that mirrors the three-part reading process we outlined in the previous chapter (which uses the document structure, introduction, and conclusion to highlight key points) and any skilled reader will be able to quickly absorb the essential content in your documents.

You will become a better writer if you write regularly, using a consistent writing process that takes you from idea to finished document. And you can use the particular challenges and opportunities of remote work as a whetstone for sharpening the blade of your professional writing.

In this chapter we'll show you how to do just that. First, we map out the four-stage process that is essential to producing any written document, from planning and outlining through to writing and revising; we also introduce you to some tools that can make this process a little easier when you're working online. Next, we talk about the challenges of collaborative writing, which makes up so much of the written work we do as professionals, but which looks quite different when you are part of a distributed team rather than based in a conventional office. Finally, we'll show you how to harness online tools that will make collaborative writing flow more smoothly, so that you can use your writing process in service of your larger team.

THE FOUR STAGES OF WRITING

If you are writing as part of your job, you need a process that will help you develop drafts and documents that serve your clients—especially if your "client" is your boss.

The process we map out here proceeds through four stages, reflecting the very different types of work and thinking that are required to create a document that reflects your goals and priorities. You will be much more effective in your writing and revising if you first do the work of planning and outlining.

Make a Plan

Before you start outlining your document, you need a plan that covers:

- KEY AUDIENCES. Who are your readers, and why are they reading this? Is this for internal consumption only, or is it a public document?
- GOALS. What are the actions, behaviors, or ideas you want the reader to take from reading this document?

- CONTEXT. How will this document actually get read: On a screen? On paper? Quickly or with some time to digest it?

Take the time to write this down, and it will both clarify your thinking and give you a useful reference if you get stuck while outlining or writing.

Here's an example of what a writing plan might look like if you're writing a business case for installing a green roof at your company's headquarters:

KEY AUDIENCES
- Facilities manager: assessing and advising on feasibility
- CFO: determining/approving budget
- Corporate social responsibility manager: assessing impact and public perception relative to other initiatives
- HR team: assessing impact on employee morale/engagement

GOALS
- Approve project plan and budget
- Mobilize facilities team (and potentially, other employees) to implement in timely manner

CONTEXT
- In theory, read ahead of meeting on-screen/on paper, but probably will read handout in first ten minutes of meeting

You can see how making this kind of plan saves you time and lets you write more efficiently. Once you've recognized that your key stakeholders will mostly be skimming your report in the first few minutes of a meeting, you realize that most of your effort should go into the first page or two of the document—conveying information in point form, or visually, so that it makes a compelling case for the feasibility, impact, and financial returns from the project. Everything else that goes into your document is just there as evidence that you've done your homework.

Create Your Outline

A good outline lays out the structure of the document you're going to write so that you have a road map for your writing. It should encompass the major sections of your document and (in short bullets) the key points to make in each section. Then all you need to do, when you're actually writing, is flesh out those points and build the connective tissue that smoothly takes the reader from one point or section to the next.

Your outline not only provides a scaffold for your draft, but also frees up your brain to focus on writing.[1] Once you are clear on the line of argument for your piece, you can use your brain to focus on the difficult work of translating your thinking into words. If you try to do that before you actually know your argument, you're going to be confused in your writing, and you're going to confuse your reader.

Some lucky people can just sit down and write an outline in the order they plan to follow when writing. But for many of us the outline process is a lot messier: a process of capturing our ideas, then thinning and categorizing them, then finally mapping out the structure. If that sounds more like you, here's how to go about the job of outlining in a more efficient way.

Capture Your Ideas, Either on Paper or Electronically

"Capturing" your ideas means jotting down everything you think you might want to include, in short form. You're not trying to write coherent paragraphs or even sentences: you're just trying to capture the ideas or information you want to share, in the fewest words you need to remember what you have in mind.

If you're capturing your ideas on paper, use Post-its or index cards so you'll find your ideas easier to rearrange. If you're doing your idea capture electronically, it's best not to use a word processor (like Word or Docs) because it's too cumbersome to rearrange your ideas. (Though you might find it feasible if you're writing something extremely short.)

A better option is a mind-mapping, outlining, or dedicated writing tool, any of which will make it easier for you to rearrange your ideas.[2] A mind map is a way of organizing ideas into a treelike or flowchart structure: tools like MindNode, MindMeister, or MindMaster all make it easy to capture and rearrange your ideas.

There are also many software programs that are designed to help people outline their ideas, like OmniOutliner or Workflowy. Scrivener, a popular writing application (see "The Writer's Toolkit" feature below) has a terrific outlining tool built into it that you can use in either linear or "cork board" mode.

And don't overlook the potential of spreadsheets as a way to organize your ideas. Start by capturing each idea in its own row—the next section will show you how to reorganize what you've captured.

With all of these approaches, the idea is to work quickly, capturing all your top-of-mind ideas: don't worry about getting every last ingredient, because you'll inevitably have more ideas as you're organizing your outline or sitting down to write.

Categorize Your Ideas

Once you have all your ideas jotted down, organize them into related themes. You're not worried about order yet: you're just trying to group related pieces of information or concepts.

For example, if you're writing a departmental review, you might label or cluster a whole bunch of points about coordination and communication as "team"; points about specific leaders would be labeled "management"; concerns about resource allocation or costs would go under "budget."

If you're using an outlining or mind-mapping tool, you'll do this clustering by dragging related ideas onto the same part of your screen, or drawing connectors between them. In a spreadsheet, you might have columns for "category" and "subcategory" that you fill in as you go through your ideas.

This categorization process is a moment when you might set some ideas or information aside as irrelevant or less than compelling; you may also have some new ideas that pop up as you work.

TECH DEEP DIVE

The Writer's Toolkit

Don't try to use the same all-purpose software for every aspect of your writing process. Depending on your needs, choose . . .

- SCRIVENER. This dedicated writing application is a must-have for anyone who regularly writes documents longer than ten or twenty pages (though it's useful for short documents, too). By making it easy for you to outline, slice up, and rearrange your work, Scrivener dramatically accelerates and improves the process of writing long documents—and brings the same benefits to writing short articles or documents, too.
- EVERNOTE OR ONENOTE. These digital notebooks are suitable for day-to-day notetaking, meeting notes, and reference.
- GOOGLE DOCS. This is the right choice for collaborating on documents where you need feedback or edits. That doesn't mean you necessarily want to use it for first drafts: write in Word, Scrivener, or OneNote, then copy and paste into Docs when it's time to get input.
- WORD. A local Word document is a good choice for writing short articles or reports, though not for getting feedback. Don't fall into the trap of having your colleagues edit their own copies of the document by sending your document out as a file attachment: That just creates a ton of work when it comes time to reconcile their various bits of feedback. Instead have them all work on the same cloud-based file using Word's built-in online collaboration features, or by uploading it to Google Docs.
- CODA. Think of Coda as an upgraded version of Google Docs. It's a great way to create an easy-to-navigate, multipage document, like a handbook or a collection of reference materials.

And unlike Google Drive, which separates text documents from spreadsheets, you can combine both in a single Coda document.

- ZOTERO. If your work involves citing research or referring back to things you've read months or years before, you need a citation manager: an application that can house your article collection, centralize your reading notes, and create bibliographies. Zotero is a widely used option that makes it easy for you to save citations or full-text sources, extract passages you highlight (using the Zotfile plugin), and insert properly formatted citations into a Word or Google Doc.

Organize Your Ideas

Once you have your ideas clustered, it's time to think about the actual flow of your document, and the order in which you want to make your points. This is where you'll want to refer back to the goals, audiences, and context you identified during your planning stage, because the order in which your document unfolds is a matter of strategy as much as logic.

For example, imagine you're writing that green roof business case. Yes, the logical place to start is with an explanation of the problems that green roofs are intended to solve: improving air quality, absorbing rainwater, increasing insulation, etc. But you know that the decision-makers reading this document may not make it past the first page or two, so you need to outline your document in a way that puts the most essential points—like the concrete costs and benefits—on page one.

It may take a few tries before you get your ideas into an order that will work for your goals and audience, and still have some kind of internal logic or flow. Use section headers, subheaders, and numbering to make this outline easy for you and others to scan, and to communicate the overall hierarchy of ideas. Your outline is now ready to share with others so that you can get feedback and buy-in before proceeding to your full draft.

WRITE FASTER BY TOUCH TYPING

If you still need to look at your computer keyboard in order to type, then learning to touch type is one of the best investments you can make in your productivity. You should be able to type at least sixty words per minute; with practice, you can and should be able to type as quickly as you think. Choose a game or app that will teach you how to place your fingers on the keyboard, and practice for a few minutes a day, testing your speed once a week.

Write a First Draft

Look at this: We're halfway into a chapter about writing, and only now are we actually getting to the business of how you sit down and actually write. This is a very accurate reflection of what makes for effective writing: an awful lot of it is about planning and outlining, and the actual writing is a lot easier if you take the time to do that initial work.

Now that you know what you're going to say and the order in which you're going to say it, you need to find the style and structure that will make your words most effective. There are only a few rules that apply to just about every document:

- Offer your readers a road map early on—certainly on your first page—so that they know what this document is for, how it's structured, and why they should read it.
- Use subheadings and boldface to draw attention to key points.
- Conclude with the next action the reader can take, even if it's just "how to learn more."
- If your document is longer than two pages, include an executive summary on the first page. In a short (three-to-twenty-page) document, this might be a single paragraph or a few bullet points; for a longer report, your executive summary might be a page.

Beyond these universal rules, your style and structure choices largely depend on the audiences and goals in your writing plan:

- AUDIENCE. Are you writing something for internal or external consumption? An expert audience or newcomers? A business or a consumer audience?
- GOALS. Are you driving the reader to a specific decision (like approving your budget or buying your product) or are you simply sharing information (illuminating last quarter's performance; building awareness of your brand and what it offers)?

Your answers to these questions will shape the tone and structure of what you write. (See table 12.1 for a cheat sheet on how to structure your documents.)

TABLE 12.1

HOW TO STRUCTURE A DOCUMENT FOR YOUR GOALS AND AUDIENCE

Goal Is . . .

AUDIENCE	ACTION	INFORMATION
INTERNAL	• Lead with desired outcomes and decision factors (pages 1 and 2) • Follow with context: back up the decision(s) you're recommending with more detailed information and arguments that people can read if they aren't convinced by what's on pages 1-2 • Write in bullet form so it's easy to scan and digest	• Start your document with the single idea or piece of information you most want the reader to understand • As much as possible, order so that the least important information is last • Make it fun and engaging to read if possible, because an information-only document is optional reading—so people will read it only if it's compelling

AUDIENCE	ACTION	INFORMATION
EXTERNAL	• Start with the reader's problem—and tell them how you'll solve it • Make a list of the key sentences you want the reader to see—these should be subheadings or callouts that are hard to miss • Build the document around those key sentences • Use short sentences and lots of dynamic language to create a sense of urgency • Every point should bring the reader back to the key action(s) you want them to take	• Start with a relatable story—an anecdote that catches attention and builds empathy • Make key information visual (e.g., with charts) or turn it into callouts/headings • Look for the opportunity to be surprising—not contrarian for its own sake, but a perspective that is different from what's already out there

Revising

As a Business of One, you want to show your clients or boss your best work. And almost nobody is at their best on the first try, which is why revising is such an essential part of the writing process.

Ernest Hemingway is credited with saying that "all writing is rewriting," and that's as true for a business writer as it is for a novelist. The more comfortable you get rewriting, the faster you'll get at knocking out those first drafts—because you'll be able to suspend your inner critic in the knowledge that yes, you'll have a chance to improve things later.

Here are a few practices that can help with the revision process:

- Whenever possible, set your document aside for at least a day before you start revising. You're more likely to spot errors and potential improvements if you are looking at your document with fresh eyes.
- Create a duplicate of your first draft before you start revising. That way if you lose something you want to restore, you can always go

back to your original document. (Google Docs's revision history can help with that, too.)

- Use a digital notebook or a separate document file to stash anything you cut from your draft. That way you can always pull pieces off the cutting-room floor if you realize the paragraph you cut three pages ago would be useful to add to your conclusion.

- "Kill your darlings" is a piece of writerly advice that's been attributed to many sources.[3] It just means that when you're revising a piece of writing, be especially suspicious of any paragraph, section, or turn of phrase you particularly love—because the more you love it, the harder it is to be objective about whether it needs to stay in your document.

- Think in terms of three rounds of revision—it may sound daunting but it will let you work faster. First round is big-picture: cutting or re-arranging big sections, or adding in any context or connective tissue that you can see is missing and necessary. Second round is tightening: reducing your word count by eliminating any section, sentence, or in-dividual word that isn't absolutely necessary to your document. Even if you're not working with a strict word or page limit, tighter prose is always more effective. Finally, do a copy edit, leaning on your software's built-in spell checker and grammar checker (or consider a third-party tool like Grammarly) to catch any errors and make sure you're consis-tent in what gets capitalized, italicized, or put in quotation marks. A fresh pair of eyes can be particularly useful at this stage in the process.

- Learn to do at least the first two rounds of editing on-screen; oth-erwise you're creating additional work for yourself by reading and annotating on paper, and then implementing your changes. You may find that printing out can be helpful in the very final revision, however, because it can be hard to spot errors in a document you've reviewed multiple times.

THE CHALLENGE OF COLLABORATIVE WRITING

When you are writing in a professional context, your writing will often involve some degree of collaboration. If you're writing a blog post for the company website, that "collaboration" might be as simple as asking someone to read your draft and catch your typos, or asking a junior colleague to fill in a few factual details you've left blank. If you're developing a major white paper or a detailed report for a client, it's likely that the collaboration will be much more involved, with different people researching or authoring different sections, and several different managers revising or editing with an eye on different goals.

Although these projects should still follow the four-stage process we've described here, you will need to consider how to enable the collaborative side of the process. When you're working with others, you are responsible for more than words written or pages produced. Your work must fulfill the goals and requirements of your client (who might be an actual client, your boss, or another internal team), and your colleagues will assess your work based on the process as well as the result. If you make it easy and enjoyable for them to provide input, if they can see that their ideas and contributions have shaped the document, and if you live up to your commitments on feedback cycles and turnaround times, your boss and colleagues are much more likely to respond positively to the final document.

It might feel like remote work puts you at a disadvantage in collaborative writing, especially at the planning and outlining stage. If you're the kind of person who relies on a brainstorming session to get the ball rolling on a new writing project, it can be hard to get past that blank screen to a plan or outline you can share with a team. You may have a harder time identifying your audiences and goals when you can't just sit down and talk them through with your boss or internal client.

These challenges can slow you down at the writing and revising stages, too. You can't pop your head over the cubicle wall when you're looking for the perfect example to illustrate your blog post, or searching for the right word to use in your sustainability report. When you feel proud of something you've written, it can be demoralizing to open a Google Doc and see dozens of critical comments from your colleagues, which may drain your enthusiasm for the all-important process of revising.

As all of these examples suggest, the challenges of collaborative writing mostly come from our mistaken vision of writing as a solitary process: when you're writing in a professional context, it's anything but. That's why you need to approach your writing projects in a way that not only addresses the obstacles to getting input and feedback while working remotely, but also uses distance to make those input and feedback cycles more efficient and effective.

MAKING THE MOST OF REMOTE COLLABORATION

Collaborative writing and document creation is one place that remote work can have an edge over the traditional office, because the challenge of writing together when you're working apart will force you to get your ideas down on (virtual) paper relatively early. Yes, a phone call might be a useful starting point for determining your goals and audiences. However, once you've got that sorted out, it's best to start outlining, writing, and revising so that everyone can see what's been accomplished and where they need to contribute.

Google Docs makes this kind of collaboration very easy. You can also use Word's "Track Changes" feature, but we don't recommend it, unless your team is using the online version of Word so that everyone is sharing their comments on the same document, in real time: otherwise you end up with multiple sets of feedback you then have to reconcile.

Here's how to get the most out of a collaborative writing and editing process when you are working remotely:

- CLARIFY YOUR ROLES AND CONTRIBUTIONS. If you regularly collaborate with other colleagues on document creation, have a frank talk (in a call or online meeting) about what each of you brings to the process. Maybe a couple of people on the team are great researchers and thinkers; somebody else has a fabulous writing style; perhaps you also have someone who's great at copyediting, or someone who's a whiz with charts and layouts. Talk about what you're good at and what you enjoy, because you'll work better together if you are each focused on the areas where you excel.
- START WITH A PLAN—OR, BETTER YET, AN OUTLINE. Even if you are writing a document that will be divided up among several people, someone

needs to get the ball rolling by putting the document plan on Google Docs (that is, the goals, audience, and context you're writing for), so everyone can refer to it. Ideally that lead writer or project manager will also share an initial outline, even if it's very preliminary: many people find it easier to contribute or to see what's needed once they have a starting point, and can see what's missing or wrong. If you're the person who gets the ball rolling, be clear if what you've shared is just a starting point, and don't take it personally if people rip it apart or change it into something quite different.

- PUT YOUR DOCUMENT IN ORDER BEFORE YOU SHARE. A good approach is to write your outline or draft in Word, and then upload to Docs. Regardless of how you get to your starter document, be sure to review it before sharing, because copying and pasting often produces strange results. Sharing an outline or document with a clear structure and hierarchy (that is, with numbered headings and subheadings) makes it easier for other people to contribute.

- BE EXPLICIT ABOUT THE KIND OF FEEDBACK YOU'RE REQUESTING. When you share a document via Google Docs, let your colleagues know the level of feedback you're looking for. For example, you might say "This is a rough draft so I'm looking for general feedback on tone, and on any crucial topics/points that are missing from the document; don't worry about copy edits." Conversely, you might say "This document goes live on our site tomorrow and has already been through multiple revisions, so please flag only actual errors or typos that are essential to fix."

- IN RESPONDING, FLAG WHAT'S GOOD, AS WELL AS WHAT NEEDS FIXING. Providing feedback isn't just a matter of telling people what needs improvement: it's also a matter of pointing out what works well. In part this is a matter of collegiality, because encouragement and appreciation feel good. But it also makes for better documents, both now and in the future: when you add a comment like "This is a great analogy!" or "Perfect example!", you are shining a light that helps your collaborators see the path forward.

- USE "SUGGESTING" MODE IN GOOGLE DOCS. When you're revising someone else's document, or asking them to revise yours, use "suggesting" mode: that way you can see what changes have been made, and rewind if you don't think they're improvements.

- ANNOTATE A GOOGLE DOC USING COMMENTS. Not every suggested change needs to take the form of a specific edit. Sometimes it's better to leave a comment like "Can you please try a different way of clarifying why this investment is worthwhile?" Comments can be useful when you're inviting feedback, too: you might leave a comment on your own document like "Can you suggest a better example for me to use here?"

- SUM UP YOUR INPUT. If you're providing a detailed review of someone else's document, step back once you've finished your edits and annotations. Are there any overall patterns in what works, and what needs improvement? Sum these up in an email or a comment at the top of the document, even if it takes a few bullets or paragraphs. For example, you might say something like "All the points are here, but the structure isn't quite right—here are a couple of ideas for how we might move things around."

- WELCOME ALL FEEDBACK. If you've put a lot of thought or time into something you've written, or you're strongly invested in your own writing, it can be really hard to hear all the ways someone thinks your work can be improved. Try to think of editorial feedback as free coaching on how to be a clearer thinker or a better writer. And remember, if it's your document, you don't necessarily need to accept every suggestion.

- EXPLOIT TIME ZONE DIFFERENCES. Collaborative writing is one place that a geographically dispersed team offers a huge advantage—one that we exploited while writing this book. If Alex finished a draft at 9 p.m. in Vancouver, she could email it to Bob before going to bed; by the time she was back at her desk the next morning, it was noon for Bob in Boston, so he'd have sent Alex his revisions. If Bob sent Alex a draft at the end of his day in Boston, she had the rest of her workday to review it, so he'd have feedback waiting by the time he woke up the next day. Working time zones to your advantage is a great way to reduce turnaround times when you're writing and editing as a team.

- SAVE ONE COLLABORATOR FOR A FINAL READ. When you're working as a team, try to save one nitpicky person for the final read-through. This is the person who will catch all the little errors the rest of you have stopped noticing because you've read the document so many times.
- REMEMBER: DON'T SWEAT THE SMALL STUFF. If you and a colleague are quibbling over word choice in an internal document, consider conceding the point and just letting them "win." If you're working on an external document, there should always be a project owner who is the ultimate decision-maker: rather than asking this person to make a ruling on each individual word battle, make sure a single person is empowered to be the final editor who determines the voice and style of the document.

If you combine these specific tactics for remote-friendly, collaborative writing with the four-stage process we mapped out in the first section of this chapter, you will create documents that are not only a credit to you as a Business of One, but also strengthen your collegial relationships and build a sense of collective pride in your work.

FROM A REMOTE WORKER

Jim Wang is a personal finance blogger and the founder of Bargaineering and, later, Wallet Hacks. Over many years as a remote worker, he has identified the habits, tools, and strategies that help him write effectively—so that he then has time available for his family.

After I graduated from Carnegie Mellon University with a degree in computer science, I went to work in the defense industry. While I was working at Northrop Grumman, I started a personal finance blog because I wanted to start a blog, but I didn't have many hobbies that are the kind of thing you write about—so I started writing about personal finance.

In the beginning, I was writing my Bargaineering blog for my friends. If we were all trying to figure out which benefit plan to buy into, I'd write about that. One of the weird things I did was share my net worth every month. A lot of other bloggers were doing it, so I joined in. I wouldn't do that now, but when you're twenty something and your net worth is a thousand dollars (even less if you factor in student loans), who cares? But the New York Times wrote about it, because they thought it was crazy—which made my parents really happy!

After a few years, the blog started making money and I opted to quit my day job and work on it full-time. Hey, I was in the New York Times: that means my blog is a real thing!

I spent most of my day writing, and even though I had the occasional phone call, it was a little lonely initially. But I got so used to being on instant messenger with other bloggers and friends that it was enough interaction, and I didn't feel lonely.

I would eventually sell my blog but that just meant I had to go into the office every six months; I still worked from home. Even before the pandemic I never worked in coffee shops, because I like my home office setup, as I have two monitors. When I work on my laptop, it feels like working in a closet after working in an arena.

I started Wallet Hacks because I wanted to get back into personal finance. It's different this time around: with my four kids at home, my ability to be creative is diminished, as is my patience. With Bargaineering, I was young with no kids, so I could write all the time: I was going to work, coming home, and then writing.

But I've changed my pace, and I don't work as much as I used to. I wake up at 6 or 6:30 and do a little work in the hour before the kids wake up. But by four o'clock my workday is over and we're doing stuff as a family. Six hours of work is plenty, because your eighth hour of creative work is never going to be as good as your first or second or third.

I don't think I'm built for office life anymore. Once you work on your own and set your own schedule, it is hard to go back to having someone dictate your time.

I did all of that, but now I'm at the point where I've done it enough. I will no longer go back to those systems and follow those rules. I think that's why

I'm no longer cut out for big corporations. Unless I'm doing something really interesting, but even that seems unlikely.

TAKEAWAYS

1. When you are working remotely, you are your words. That's why it's essential to be a good writer—which means writing in a way that communicates clearly and efficiently, and moves people to action.

2. Good writing begins with a plan that specifies the goals and audience for what you're writing, as well as the context in which your work or document will be read.

3. Work from an outline that captures your key ideas and information, categorizes them by theme or topic, and then organizes them into an order that reflects how it will be read.

4. Every document should begin with some kind of road map, but your specific structure will depend on your goals and audience.

5. All writing is rewriting. Plan for at least three rounds of revisions: one for content and structure, one to tighten your text, and one to catch any typos or errors.

6. Get better results from document collaboration by asking for the specific kind of feedback you need, and using both comments and suggestions to ask for help and track changes.

7. Choose the right tools for your particular writing job by investigating specialized writing tools like Scrivener and Zotero.

PART V

EFFECTIVE ONLINE COMMUNICATION

When you are working remotely, a great deal of your communication will take place online. That's why it's essential not only to be proficient in the essential skills we just covered, but also to master the specific practices and tools for effective online communication. This part drills down on the essential skills in part 4 by helping you learn the key ways to ingest and disseminate information online—through messaging, social media, and presentations.

Anyone who is old enough to remember working life before the advent of Slack and Teams (or perhaps even before email) can tell you that each successive change in the technologies of communication will produce a new set of challenges, and new forms of etiquette. Unlike the handwritten letter, which evolved over literally thousands of years, each new form of online communication springs quickly into our lives without any commonly agreed upon standard for how to use it courteously, let alone effectively.

That's why it's important to adopt an approach that can accommodate the wide range of expectations and practices around online communication, which can vary from person to person, as well as from organization to organization.

Chapter 13 covers email and messaging, so that you know how to handle incoming email, write effective messages, and use team messaging platforms. Chapter 14 covers social media, helping you avoid information overload and mapping out an efficient strategy for sustaining a social media presence. Chapter 15 looks at the particular demands of making online presentations, so you will know how to plan, prepare, and deliver an effective talk on the small screen.

CHAPTER 13

EMAIL AND MESSAGING
Beating Overload

When you are managing your work as a Business of One, your number one resource is your own time. Incoming email and messages can be the greatest obstacle to managing that resource: if you reply to every incoming email or message, you're letting other people dictate how you spend your time.

Instead you need to make some well-thought-out choices about which parts of your business most deserve your time and attention, and then fit your email and messaging interactions into the amount of time they actually warrant relative to your other priorities. Easier said than done, we know!

In this chapter, we map out the tech tools, configuration, and habits that can help you manage the flood of incoming information so that you can devote your time and attention to the work that matters most. And we'll show you how you can be most effective when you're driving the flow of outgoing information—writing emails, messages, or texts yourself.

EMAIL

If email is a challenge in the conventional workplace, it can be an even bigger problem for remote workers, for whom email too often serves as the primary connection to their boss, their colleagues, or their customers. That's why it's critical for remote workers to develop effective practices for dealing with their email.

Email Principles

A healthy, productive email habit begins with four key principles:

1. **YOU DON'T HAVE TO ANSWER EVERY MESSAGE.** If that feels heretical, then just ask yourself a question: Would you feel like you had to answer every single email if you received five hundred emails a day? What if it were five thousand? For each and every one of us, there is some threshold at which the volume of email is just unmanageable. Rather than waiting for that breaking point, take control of your time and attention now by accepting—indeed, embracing—the fact that you're not going to respond to everything. This is particularly crucial for remote workers, since the sheer volume of email you may receive while working outside the office can crowd out all your other work.

2. **YOUR EMAIL TIME SHOULD REFLECT HOW IMPORTANT EMAIL IS RELATIVE TO YOUR OTHER TYPES OF WORK.** If you're spending four hours a day reading and replying to email, and you have four hours of meetings every day, and you also have four hours a day of high-priority focused work, you're either putting in twelve-hour days or you're skipping meetings and missing deadlines because you're so busy handling your email. Take a hard look at whether the time you dedicate to email actually reflects your top priorities as part of the goal-setting process we mapped out in chapter 4; if not, determine the maximum amount of time email deserves in your daily schedule, and scale your inbox to that window of time.

3. **AUTOMATE YOUR ATTENTION.** Deciding which emails warrant your attention on a message-by-message basis is both a waste of time and a needless source of stress. Instead, use mail rules to filter all but the most important messages out of your inbox—what we'll henceforth refer to as your "primary" inbox—so that you don't have to spend time thinking about what's worth reading or replying to. This is the best way of sticking to the OHIO rule (Only Handle It Once), explained in chapter 6, "Don't Sweat the Small Stuff," because you won't see a message until the moment when you're actually ready

to address it. Even more important, this approach ensures you don't miss crucial messages in a sea of barely relevant correspondence.

4. **WRITE FOR ACTION.** Writing an email is not like writing an article or report: email communication is almost always about providing actionable information, so your outbound emails need to be effective and efficient in enabling your recipients to take the necessary action, even if that action consists of simply making a decision.

How to Automate Your Attention

Once you have released yourself from the obligation to reply to (or even see) every message, and you've determined how much time email should get relative to your other professional priorities, you're ready to automate your attention.

1. **IDENTIFY THE DIFFERENT TYPES OF EMAIL YOU RECEIVE,** and how urgent or important (two different things!) they are. Here's what that prioritization process might look like for Sunita, the chief financial officer of a medium-size professional services firm, who's working from home with two young kids:

   - Emails from the CEO asking her about different financial issues within the firm (urgent and important)
   - Customer emails asking about payment terms or arrangements (urgent and important)
   - Emails from direct reports asking her to authorize expenditures or approve other decisions (important)
   - Emails from direct reports or colleagues cc'ing her on company issues with financial implications (medium/low)
   - Emails from the IRS advising her of the company's tax obligations or issues (urgent and important)
   - Meeting invitations (possibly urgent, sometimes important)
   - Advisories of outstanding client payments (important)
   - Industry newsletters (low)
   - Personal purchase receipts (medium)

- Sales promotions and marketing emails (low)
- Emails from her kids' teachers advising her of their class schedule or homework (important)
- Personal emails from friends and family (medium)

2. **CREATE "ALTERNATE INBOXES"** for each type of email you receive. Your goal is to see as little as possible of your email in your primary inbox: unless a given type of email is both urgent and important, it does not belong in your primary inbox. In Sunita's case, she can have a few alternate inboxes:

   - Internal emails (anything where she's in the "to:" field, and where the "from:" field includes an email address within her company)
   - Internal cc's (as above but where she's in the cc or bcc field)
   - Meeting invitations
   - Late payments
   - Newsletters and promotions
   - Personal receipts
   - School email
   - Personal email

3. **SET UP MAIL RULES OR FILTERS** that direct your incoming email to the appropriate alternate inbox so that it *skips the primary inbox*. The specific steps for setting up rules or filters depends on the email service you use (Gmail, Exchange, etc.) and also on the specific email client you use (Web mail, Apple's Mail.app, Outlook, etc.). But here's what a few mail rules might look like for Sunita:

   - Message from internal email address that contains the words ("late" or "outstanding" or "overdue") and ("payment" or "invoice" or "bill") >> Skip the inbox, send to "Late payments" folder
   - Other messages from internal email address *unless* it's from Sunita's boss or contains the words "urgent," "time sensitive," "emergency," or "today" >> Skip the inbox, send to "Internal email" folder
   - Message contains .ics (a calendar invitation file) >> Skip the inbox, send to "Calendar invitations" folder

- Message from the kids' school or teacher >> Skip the inbox, send to "School email" folder
- Message contains "your purchase" or "shipped" >> Skip the inbox, send to "Personal receipts" folder
- Message contains "unsubscribe" >> Skip the inbox, send to "Newsletters and promotions" folder

Set Your Email Routine

Now that you have your email channeled to different places, you can make a plan for how to process your email at different windows in your day or week. This is a really good way to ensure you keep on top of crucial messages without falling into the remote work trap of handling email 24-7. Here's what Sunita's email plan might look like:

» *8:30–9:15 a.m.* Review primary inbox and address any emails from CEO, clients, the IRS, or urgent internal messages.

» *2:30–2:50 p.m. every Monday, Wednesday, and Friday.* Review "Late payments" folder and send a single email with instructions to the payment manager on how to handle each issue.

» *2:50–3:00 p.m.* Review calendar in calendar application, look for any new calendar invitations (they'll automatically appear in the calendar), and accept or decline each one.

» *4:00–4:45 p.m.* Review internal emails (first priority) and address as needed; quickly scan internal cc's.

» *4:45–5:15 p.m.* Review primary inbox and deal with any end-of-day priority emails.

» *7:30–8:30 p.m.* Review school emails, read and reply to any personal emails.

What's not on the schedule? Looking at shipment or purchase notifications (those can go straight to the "Personal receipts" file for retrieval come tax time) or browsing industry newsletters (something Sunita can do when she feels like taking a break and catching up on the news). There might also be other quick moments throughout the day—like a ten-minute gap between meetings—when Sunita takes a glance at her primary inbox to see if there are any other time-sensitive emails she can quickly read and address.

But the whole point of automating your attention is to get out of the habit of constantly checking email just in case something interesting or urgent is waiting for you. Instead aim to check your primary inbox no more than once every hour (once every two hours is better) throughout the rest of the day, and turn off the notification "ping" or pop-up message that heralds new incoming messages so that you aren't tempted to peek more often.

If your boss or your company culture is such that it's unacceptable to wait an hour or two to respond to the CEO, you can set up an email rule that sends you a text notification whenever you receive an email from your supervisor: Just find out the email address structure for your mobile phone provider (it's usually something like "2045551212@phonecompany.com") and set up a mail rule that forwards every incoming email from your boss to that number, then leaves it in your inbox. This is a good practice for anyone who's trying to provide their number one "client" with excellent service: responding swiftly to your boss is a smart way to keep them delighted with your Business of One.

MAKING THE CASE FOR *REMOTE, INC.*

Filtering Internal Email

Terrified by what you might miss, or address too slowly, if you filter internal emails or cc's out of your primary inbox? Then show your boss what you hope to accomplish by focusing on the most important emails first.

Frame this as an experiment: "I've noticed that our average email response time for client inquiries is seven hours, and a third of client messages don't even get a same-day response. I want to see if I can beat those numbers by organizing my email a little differently . . . but it will mean that I might not see internal emails or cc's until the end of the workday. Can I try that for a month, and come back to you with a report on the results?"

You'll note that *outgoing* email is also missing from the schedule. That's because the from-scratch emails you generate are typically a by-product of other tasks, so you will write these throughout the day, as the need arises. For example, if you're writing a report and realize you need some crucial background documents from a colleague, you will send her a request right then *and immediately return to your current task without stopping to look through your inbox.* Yes, it takes discipline—but it will quickly become a habit! Be careful that you send these outgoing emails only when absolutely necessary, however: every email you send just increases the volume of email you receive.

Automating your attention takes an up-front investment in setting up your alternate inboxes and email rules, and it requires a little ongoing maintenance, too: Once you've gone through any initial email backlog in order to identify the types of messages you receive and the mail rules that will help you triage, you'll still receive new newsletters or new types of email that require you to set up additional folders or rules. A handy practice is to create a "Rules needed" folder: that way, when an email lands in your primary inbox that really doesn't warrant your urgent attention, you can drag it to your "Rules needed" folder for later reference. Once every week or so, look at your "Rules needed" folder and either adjust an existing rule or add a new one, so that only the most urgent and important messages land in your primary inbox.

TECH DEEP DIVE

Clear Your Email Backlog

You can build your mail rules *and* conquer your backlog at the same time. Set aside a block of time (or possibly several blocks) when you'll go through your backlog. When you spot an email that doesn't belong in your primary inbox, think about the broadest rule that could possibly get it out of your inbox: Instead of sending emails from "newsletter@honda.com" to your newsletters folder, send *any* email that contains "from: newsletter" to your newsletters folder. Once you write or adjust your mail rule, check an option such as "Also apply filter to matching messages" (in Gmail) or use the "Run rules now" command (in Outlook). You'll get to see a big portion of your backlog vanish before your eyes!

LITTLE LIFESAVERS FOR BEATING EMAIL OVERLOAD

- Use email signatures for replies you send over and over again—like "No, thank you, we already have our vendors lined up for this quarter."
- Copy people on messages sparingly, and only when you have a specific reason for keeping them informed; get out of the "just in case they want to know" mentality.
- Use a separate email address for online purchases or Web sign-ups so that you minimize the volume of website updates and promotions that land in your work inbox.
- Reply-all only when necessary: This button is a huge generator of excess emails. Even if the whole office got that fundraising request, they don't all need to hear back about your generous donation.
- Unsubscribe from at least one email list every day. It will keep your email volume in check, and it's incredibly satisfying.
- Use "send it later" or inbox-pause tools in services like Boomerang so that you can draft emails after-hours without contributing to a culture of always-on communication. Just draft your email and set a delivery time for the next day.

Writing for Action

The success of your Business of One depends on excellent communication with your boss or clients. You want to minimize the demands on their attention; a rambling two-page email just makes it hard for your boss to give you the clear, timely feedback you need. Well-written emails make it easy for your boss and clients to reply—so your productivity doesn't get bottlenecked while you wait for a crucial answer.

Writing great emails (yes, an email *can* be great!) is all about focusing on the action you're asking the recipient to take. You are not trying to write something beautiful and evocative: you are trying to write the shortest possible message that will do the job. (Just think how much happier *you* are when you receive an email that's one paragraph, rather than one page.)

Business emails work best when they . . .

- Use a clear subject line that conveys topic and timeline
- Start with the action items needed, including deadlines
- Use bullet points or numbering, where possible, rather than paragraphs
- Provide any additional context lower down, and make it clear that this is optional reading
- Use Google Docs rather than the email to get feedback on anything longer than two paragraphs
- Convey key information quickly so that subject and urgency are clear even if someone is just glancing at your message on the phone
- Use boldface to make it easy for your recipient to see essential points they might otherwise miss

EMAIL, MESSAGE, OR TEXT?

It's not always easy to know when you should send an email, when you should send a message via Slack or Teams, or when you should just send an SMS (text) message to someone's phone. Here's a quick cheat sheet:

IT'S AN EMAIL IF . . .

- It's spelling out immediate action items: if you're asking someone to take action on more than one item, or you need to provide context or attachments, send an email.
- It's a communication that includes people outside your Slack/Teams workspace.
- It's a lot of information—but not a draft document that you'll be evolving with the people you're emailing. (That's better handled by inviting them into a Google Doc.)
- Your request or action item needs to be tracked by others in a way that ensures your recipient is accountable for responding or taking action.
- It may need to be referenced months or years down the road. Yes, you can search Slack/Teams, but it's not ideal for long-term reference. But you can and should keep your emails forever, because as long as you have a good, searchable email system, there's no better way of finding something you need five or ten years later.

IT'S A GROUP MESSAGE IF . . .

- It's very short (under one hundred words).
- It's time sensitive: you need a reply within an hour or so.
- It's a topic that's easier to sort out synchronously: that is, some amount of rapid back-and-forth will allow quick clarification or resolution.
- You're primarily speaking to one or two people (whom you should tag in your message) but your conversation may be useful for other people to see or find in later searches (even if they don't need it cluttering up their inboxes as a cc'ed email). For example, if you ask someone for the HR policy on dogs at work, anyone else who searches the HR channel for "dog" will be able to find the answer—but you don't need to cc the whole company.

IT'S AN SMS (TEXT) MESSAGE TO MOBILE IF . . .

- It's extremely time sensitive: you need a response immediately, or within the next thirty minutes.
- The person you are messaging has major issues with inbox or messaging overload, and has asked you to alert them to important issues via text (possibly as a way of letting them know you've emailed something crucial).
- It's a sensitive subject you don't want on the office servers (but not so sensitive that you don't want it in writing at all).
- It's a quick question for someone outside your messaging group, and even if it's not urgent, their reply will allow your work to move forward.

THE UNIVERSAL EMAIL

These principles are universal enough that we can use them as the basis for an email recipe: a single email structure you can use over and over again. It won't work for every single situation, but it should be your default unless you have a good reason for another structure. (See the "Example of the Universal Email" feature below for an example.) Here it is:

OPEN WITH ACTION ITEMS

- The first sentence and bullets map out what you need the recipient to do and by what date (if they read no further, this will be enough).
- Use one bullet per action item: If you need your recipient to approve your outline *and* you need them to email the India team, each of those is one bullet. If the deadlines are different, specify the deadline for each item.
- Use "unless . . . then" framings for overloaded recipients: if your recipient gets so much email that they have a hard time replying

promptly, or has mandated you to proceed with actions unless you hear otherwise, your bullet(s) can take the form of "Unless I hear from you by X date to the contrary, I will do Y."

PROVIDE SUPPLEMENTARY CONTEXT AND INFORMATION (OR LINKS TO SUCH INFORMATION)

- Provide any context your recipient might find necessary, useful, or informative in taking the actions/making the decisions you have mapped out.
- This part of your email can be more detailed and include full paragraphs (preferably still organized into bullets).
- Clarify why you are recommending this approach or asking for this action.
- Boldface the most important information in case the recipient is skimming.

CLOSE WITH THANKS

- Your conclusion can and should be minimal; if you find yourself mapping out next steps or further actions, move those to the top.

FINISH WITH A SIGNATURE

- Set up your email account with a signature line that puts your key contact details (email, phone number, Twitter handle) in every single email.
- Include this signature even if you're replying to a thread, so your correspondent never has to go hunting for your number (or the best way to message you).
- Keep your email signature concise, because people will get *really* tired of your inspirational quotes if they're appended to every message.[1]

AN EXAMPLE OF THE UNIVERSAL EMAIL

SUBJECT: Please advise by EOD on extending Acme budget by $13k
MESSAGE:

Hi Jen—

Key next steps on the ACME project:

BY EOD:

1. As per our convo please approve additional 13k on budget to cover:
   - Next week's urgent site visit ($3k airfares, $4k hotel/per diems)
   - Retaining Ken Harris (privacy consultant) to review terms of use for Web campaign ($6k)

2. Tomorrow/Monday: Lara and I are coordinating with ACME to set up call for you & CMO

CONTEXT:

- Additional media coverage for our site launch raised internal flags at ACME re: possible privacy exposure
- Their CMO is concerned to be on firm ground in addressing questions from her compliance team
- They'll cover the additional cost of the privacy consultant (i.e., $6k in scope increase) to deliver detailed review to their compliance team, but need us to retain

- We need to get on-site to meet with their legal and Web teams next week—this is partly client relations but will also expedite the next phase of work
- Their CMO was apparently very reassured to hear you have a legal background, which is why we think a call between you & CMO will help ease her concerns

Thanks,
Vanessa

Vanessa Marquez
Project Manager, CompanyName
vmarquez@companyname.com
tel 777-888-9999 mobile 777-555-4444
Twitter @vmarquezexample

MESSAGING

You will get the most from team messaging platforms like Slack and Teams if you stop thinking of them as an alternative to email or even to SMS (phone text) messaging. Team messaging platforms are their own thing, and if used properly, they can help liberate you from the tyranny of back-to-back video calls. In the context of a physical office, team messaging is often less efficient than a quick face-to-face conversation. However, when you and your colleagues are working remotely, group message is the form of communication that most often meets your functional requirements without imposing a massive footprint.

The *Remote Inc.* mindset embraces team messaging as a way of balancing the twin goals of responsiveness and excellence. Your "clients"—that is, your boss and the senior colleagues who are depending on you—want you to answer their questions or respond to their demands as quickly as possible. But they also want you to deliver excellent work, which is hard to do if you're constantly interrupted by incoming messages. With the right team messaging habits, you will find a balance between these two considerations so that you are generally responsive while also carving out windows for focused work.

TEAM MESSAGING PRINCIPLES

- TEAM MESSAGING SHOULD BE YOUR DEFAULT FORM OF COMMUNICATION AS A REMOTE WORKER WHO IS PART OF A TEAM. Properly used, it provides a broadly accessible way of efficiently obtaining information and input, in a form that is accessible for future reference, and at a pace that provides a middle ground between the inflexibility of a scheduled video call and the unpredictability of an email response. One other major virtue of working via team messaging, as editor Amy Shearn notes, is that it's self-transcribing: "When the conversation is in Slack, the conversation *is* the notes."

- PAY FREQUENT BUT NOT CONSTANT ATTENTION TO YOUR GROUP MESSAGES. You need to look at messages more often than you look at emails, but you don't need to look at them *constantly*. Turn off notifications and use the "do not disturb" setting for one or two extended (two- to four-hour) periods every day. During the hours when you are notionally available, check your dock or taskbar periodically—when you have a natural break in your focus—to see if you have any waiting messages, and address them when they're not disruptive to your own workflow. Calibrate your expectations of your colleagues' responsiveness, too: in most organizations it's reasonable to expect responses to direct or tagged messages within a few hours, but you can't expect those within minutes.

- MAKE THOUGHTFUL USE OF CHANNELS, THREADS, TAGS, GROUPS, AND MESSAGES. Team messaging platforms offer these features to keep conversations organized and searchable, and to keep people from getting overwhelmed by message volume. Make sure you understand how each of these features works, what it's for, and what the specific protocols are within your organization or team for how to use each one.

Team Messaging Basics

Any organization that relies on a team messaging platform to connect its remote workforce really needs its own protocols and guidelines: a document specifying things like how often you're expected to check messages, how to name specific channels, and when it's appropriate to flag a message for a particular coworker. If you haven't yet reviewed your company's guidelines, you should not only take the time to read and absorb them, but you should also keep them someplace handy for ongoing reference. If your organization doesn't have documented guidelines, reach out to your manager, your HR team, or your IT team to advocate for a guide: you will have no trouble finding dozens of online articles explaining why this is a crucial organizational practice, and offering every kind of guidance on how to develop your organization's protocols.

While the nuances of using different team messaging features will vary across companies, there are a few basics that it's your responsibility to grasp, even if there's no company guide:

- CHANNELS. Think of these as themes or meeting rooms for different teams, projects, or topics. They can be public or invitation-only. Most organizations put a high value on keeping each channel on topic, and may encourage keeping conversations in channels (as opposed to messages) so that they're available for future reference by your colleagues.
- THREADS. A thread is a conversation about one topic within a channel. When you're replying to a message or comment in a channel, reply to the thread (not the channel) to keep the conversation coherent and avoid cluttering the channel.
- MENTIONS. When you include an @ sign when mentioning a particular colleague by name or username, you're drawing their attention to a specific question or message.
- HASHTAGS. Depending on the messaging platform, you may be able to use hashtags by preceding a word or phrase with #. This is a useful way of categorizing related messages so you can see them in one place.

- MESSAGES. Direct messages let you have one-on-one or small-group conversations that are visible and searchable only for the people in the message/group. It's useful if you need to keep something private or if you're sorting out work details that nobody else is ever going to need to see or refer to. (Just remember that even direct messages could be shared via screenshot or accessible to managers, and calibrate your level of discretion accordingly.)

Being a Good Team Messager

There are also some basic practices that will help you preserve your sanity and ensure you get the most from messaging:

- SIGNAL YOUR STATUS AND AVAILABILITY. Make sure your status line shows whether you're available or offline (you can even indicate whether you're actually away from your desk, or simply in "do not disturb" mode). You can connect your messaging app to your calendar to do this automatically, or you can just make a point of updating your status regularly.
- MINIMIZE @ MENTIONS. If you have a message that's directed to a specific colleague, but where the answer/conversation may be relevant to others (like asking for information on a client file, or a how-to on using some part of your internal sales system), your best bet is usually to post that in a public or group channel, with a mention of the specific colleague who needs to reply. But @ mentioning someone just because you want them to see something is the group messaging equivalent of a cc, something you should do very sparingly.
- RESPECT THE THREAD. Use message threading to reply to a specific message and to keep subsequent replies or comments linked to the original message.
- SEARCH BEFORE YOU ASK. The whole genius of a team messaging platform is that it makes information and answers available for posterity. So before you ask a question of your colleagues, search your

organization's messaging platform to see if it's been previously asked and answered.

- **REMEMBER THAT TEXT ISN'T YOUR ONLY OPTION.** Team messaging platforms typically include options for audio and video calls, file sharing, and screen sharing. The beauty of having all these options in one place is that you can switch to a quick call or screen share if your text conversation is getting cumbersome or confusing.
- **PICK YOUR CHANNELS.** Not every channel requires your ongoing attention. Muting some channels is a way of ensuring you don't get overwhelmed by messages and miss notifications in the conversations that really need your attention.
- **PAUSE BEFORE SENDING.** If you're communicating something that needs a few sentences, don't hit send until you've got the whole thing written—it's annoying to get a paragraph one sentence at time.
- **RESPECT BUSINESS HOURS.** Some organizations attempt to protect their employees' personal time by setting hours when group messaging turns off or is officially discouraged, but that's not always practical if people are working across multiple time zones. To protect your own personal time and show respect for colleagues, save your after-hours messages until the next workday.
- **KEEP IT PROFESSIONAL.** It's fine to be casual, but keep your grammar and spelling tidy.

TECH DEEP DIVE

Mixed Messages

It's easy to get mixed up by all the different kinds of messaging out there. Here's a cheat sheet:

- **TEAM MESSAGING** (e.g., Slack, Teams) is the focus of this section. These platforms are designed to help teams or companies manage their day-to-day internal communication.

- SMS MESSAGING, sometimes also referred to as text messaging, is what's baked into your phone. Unless a colleague or client specifically tells you that they prefer you to message their mobile number, think of SMS as a last resort for emergencies only.
- SOCIAL MEDIA MESSAGING is available through all the big social media platforms (Facebook, Twitter, Instagram, LinkedIn). These can sometimes be a useful way of establishing or reestablishing a collegial connection.
- SECURE MESSAGING. Many users have security and privacy concerns about mainstream messaging apps, particularly those affiliated with social networks. A 2014 survey found that 80 percent of social media users are concerned about third parties accessing data they share via a social networking site.[2] There are a few messaging platforms, notably Signal and Telegram, that aim to address this concern with end-to-end encryption of voice calls and text messages. It's good to keep an encrypted messaging app on your phone for sensitive conversations that need to be safeguarded from potential government or competitor intrusion. As of this writing, Signal is the most trusted application of this kind because it's open source, which means lots of security experts have had a chance to look for holes or gaps in its security.
- OTHER TEXTING APPS. WhatsApp, GroupMe, Apple's Messages, and a few other services exist as their own platforms for one-on-one or group messaging. WhatsApp (which is owned by Facebook) has a massive user base and in many countries is the prevailing platform for both text and group calls.

When you make effective use of email and messaging, you reduce the amount of time waiting for replies or in meetings that cut into your focused work. You can beat email overload by automating your attention with mail rules that prioritize incoming messages, and you can communicate more efficiently by making smart choices about when and how to use email, texting, or messaging. This allows your Business of One to operate more efficiently—and makes you a considerate, valued colleague.

FROM A REMOTE WORKER

Soren Hamby is a user experience designer who has turned remote work, email, and messaging into tools for navigating their vision impairments and autism, as well as for educating colleagues who are unfamiliar with nonbinary people who use they/them pronouns.

As someone who is neurodivergent, I like expectations to be communicated clearly. It's not just "Can you provide me with the design I need for my work?" but also "Can you read between the lines and understand what clients mean by 'jazzy' or 'snazzy'?"

I have learned to use adaptive tech to meet myself where I am. Remote work helps because I have my workstation set up exactly as I need. Having everything be adjustable and customizable is important for vision and for people with ADHD or autism, so we can control the amount of stimuli we're receiving. If it's a day where things are overwhelming, I can turn down the volume of a conference call; I can't do that in a live meeting.

Email and Slack make communication easier because I can make the screen bigger and use dark mode—white text on a black background. But messaging apps tend not to be well designed for people with accessibility concerns. In Slack, there is a red line that shows you which messages are new, but I didn't even know that line was there until someone took a screenshot for me and zoomed in.

Because so many tools don't take accessibility into account, it's even more important to have our own coping techniques and workflow. I have different email addresses for personal and work stuff but they go to the same inbox. That helps me categorize my incoming email because I can filter based on which address it was sent to.

I place things from different senders in different categories, instead of using the prebuilt categories in Gmail, which didn't work for me. Whenever I start working with a client, I create an email folder for them and move it to the top of the folders list.

Automatic sorting makes sure I don't miss things. If I get an email about a job I've applied to, it goes to the address I use for jobs, interviews, and guest speaking. I know to check that folder a couple of times a day so I won't have a situation where someone wants to interview me but I don't see that email for a week.

Remote work means the teams I work with don't have as many opportunities to misgender me. I've started jobs where, out of the gate, I've said "Here are my pronouns and here is the name I would like you to use." But gender is hard for them because they should be able to look at you and know how to address you and approach you.

If someone misgenders me in a group setting, sometimes it's better to address it through a private chat. If we're on a conference call, I'll send them a message. Sometimes I've had to do it over email, which always feels like a big thing; keeping things on a messaging platform, it feels smaller. I leave it very light and short, and try to just make it like an FYI, not a "You did a bad thing and now I'm correcting you." More like "I fact-checked this for you, and that's not the pronoun I use."

It's a designer's job to think about how tech affects marginalized groups—groups that have their own cultures, which aren't necessarily defined by ethnicity or geography. I think of inclusion as user experience: we need to change the conversation from "we are making accommodations" to "we are being inclusive of different cultures."

TAKEAWAYS

1. You don't need to reply to every email message. Decide how much time your inbox deserves relative to your other objectives and tasks, and then scale your email usage to fit inside that window.

2. Automate your attention so that you see the email that matters most, and don't miss crucial messages due to inbox overload. Use

"alternate inboxes" and mail rules to ensure that only the most important, urgent messages land in your primary inbox.

3. Make an email routine so that you can spot and reply to urgent, important emails quickly, but process other messages at a later time, as your other priorities allow.

4. Write your emails so that action items come first (and note deadlines), followed by any contextual or supplementary information.

5. Send your emails only to those with a real need to know, and try not to hit the reply-all button.

6. Use text messages when you need an immediate response, or you are having trouble getting a person's attention by other means.

7. Treat team messaging as your default form of communication for the team, and rely on public channels as much as possible so that your communications are visible and searchable for your colleagues.

8. Master the basics of your organization's team messaging platform so that you can be an efficient, respectful colleague, and follow the guidelines set out by your employer. If your organization doesn't yet have its own documented guidelines for team messaging, advocate for them to be developed.

CHAPTER 14

SOCIAL MEDIA
Projecting Your Presence

Your Business of One needs a public face—and when you're working remotely, that face will primarily be online. In order to strengthen your collaborative relationships, maximize your opportunities in your current role, and position yourself for future career growth, you need an online presence that demonstrates your skills and expertise, helps you build and sustain collegial relationships, and reminds other people that you are an actual three-dimensional human being.

When you're working as a Business of One, social media serves several crucial purposes:

- STAYING INFORMED. The curse of overload is the flip side of social media's great blessing: an abundance of timely information on every conceivable subject.
- BUILDING RELATIONSHIPS. When you're outside of a traditional office, social media is your best bet for building ongoing relationships. We'll show you how to focus on quality, not quantity.
- SHARING EXPERTISE. Social media gives you a way to share your knowledge and insights with your colleagues and the world, which helps you build a reputation for your expertise.
- BEATING ISOLATION. A home office can be one lonely workplace! Social media can help—if you're thoughtful about how you use it.

While these are distinct benefits, they're also deeply intertwined. The industry leader you follow to stay informed may evolve into a valued professional relationship; the tips you share in the form of short social media posts can generate the conversation that keeps you from feeling quite so alone.

That's why it's useful for a remote worker to approach social media as an integrated system. This chapter will show you how to build that system by organizing your attention, establishing your voice, and implementing an approach that lets you maintain a useful social media presence in three hours a week.

DEFINING SOCIAL MEDIA AND SOCIAL NETWORKING

People spend a lot of time arguing about the definition of "social media" and "social networking." For the purposes of this book, we mean "social media" to include any online platform where the content comes from the site's users, whether we're talking about a blogging site (like Medium), a photo- or video-sharing site (like TikTok, Instagram, or YouTube), or a social network where people follow and connect with one another (like Twitter, LinkedIn, or Facebook). As these examples illustrate, there's a fuzzy line between social networks and other kinds of social media, so we're going to talk generally about "social media."

ORGANIZING YOUR ATTENTION ON SOCIAL MEDIA

Social platforms like LinkedIn, Twitter, YouTube, Instagram, and Facebook are major contributors to information overload. Figuring out what to pay attention to and what to ignore is absolutely essential to staying focused on your top priorities as a Business of One, while also looking to the long-run future of your personal *Remote, Inc.*

• • •

Principles for Managing Your Social Media Attention

An effective system for organizing your online attention rests on three key principles, as elaborated below:

- DON'T KEEP UP. Social media platforms and social media "influencers" (people with big online followings) work hard to convince us that it's our job to "keep up" with social media, whether that means joining the latest platform or knowing about the latest meme. By definition, however, keeping up is all about *other people's* priorities. If you're going to focus your time and attention on the activities that matter to your own goals and objectives, you'll need to resist the pressure to keep up.
- ORGANIZE YOUR ATTENTION AROUND YOUR ROLES AND GOALS. Organize your social media usage around your own top priorities and objectives by looking at your specific objectives for this year or quarter, and then thinking about the people, relationships, and information that will help you achieve them. (See the section below, Organizing Your Attention with Lists.)
- PRUNE RUTHLESSLY. Pay attention to the people who inform and inspire you, and the time you spend online will fuel your growth, expand your mind, and regenerate your spirit. Your social media intake is the "crew" you hang out with in your virtual work life, and you're under no obligation to stay engaged with people who are ill-informed, self-aggrandizing, or simply make you feel lousy.

Organize Your Attention with Lists

Social networks are literally designed to pull your attention away from *your* priorities, and instead allocate that attention to the information or ads that are prioritized by the platform you're using.[1] To resist that distraction and manipulation, ask yourself two questions: Which relationships will help my Business of One achieve its objectives? What emergent information is absolutely essential to the performance and growth of *Remote, Inc.*?

Answering these questions will let you organize the way you view your favorite social networks so that you pay attention to the people *you* want to see instead of what the social network decides to put in front of your eyeballs.

The easiest way to do that on Twitter or Facebook is with lists. On Twitter, you can make public or private lists of the different kinds of accounts you follow; consider naming these lists so they remind you of why you want to interact with each person or organization (for example, "Inspire," "Support," or "Pitch"). You can use a similar approach with Facebook friend lists; on Facebook, the lists that let you pay attention to different people also let you post your own updates so that only certain people can see them.

Here's an example of how this might work. Imagine you're a management consultant who wants to dazzle her current boss and business clients while setting herself up for a longer-term pivot into a public service role in human services. You might have a "Support" list made up of your company's key executives so you can strengthen these valuable relationships; a "Learn" list of academic experts on human services who share resources that will help you learn about your new field; and an "Inspire" list of public sector leaders who pivoted from the business world, and can help you think about your possible career path.

Once you have each of these lists set up, you can set aside some time every day or week to look at each one. Instead of just scrolling through the Twitter home feed, you might set aside thirty minutes to look at that "Support" list to see what is on the minds of your executives and clients; or when your energy dips for the afternoon, a few minutes with that "Learn" list is more useful than thumbing through Instagram.

MISINFORMATION HAZARD

Nothing will damage the credibility of your Business of One like resharing or even referencing inaccurate information. But misinformation is rampant online, and we're all vulnerable to "confirmation bias"—that is, believing information that confirms what we already believe. Fact-check anything you read online before resharing or even internalizing it by making sure it's information that's been published in a reliable source. If you follow anyone who regularly shares information without citing a source, or whose posts you have fact-checked and found wanting, unfollow them.

Beat Distractions

Here are some simple habits to keep your social media usage intentional instead of compulsive:

- SET A TIMER. A little social media surfing can make a great break in the workday, help you reset between tasks, or mitigate the solitude of remote work. If you tend to fall into an abyss once you let yourself log on, set a timer so you remember to return to your work after five or ten minutes.
- MOVE YOUR SOCIAL MEDIA APPS OFF YOUR PHONE'S HOME SCREEN. If they aren't right there, beckoning to you, it may be easier to exercise restraint.
- USE PARENTAL CONTROLS. You can use parental controls on your own phone or computer to limit the total number of minutes you spend on social media every day, or to block your access to social media sites during certain times of day.
- DON'T LET SOCIAL MEDIA BE YOUR FIRST OR LAST STOP OF THE DAY. Try to hold off on checking social media for the first thirty to sixty minutes after you wake up, and don't look at your social networks in the hour or two before bed.[2]
- SET GUIDELINES FOR WHOM YOU WILL FRIEND, FOLLOW, OR CONNECT WITH. Belonging to any social network is a recipe for getting endless friend or connection requests. Decide on whom you want to connect with on each network, and make that your explicit rule. For example, you might decide you'll accept Facebook friend requests only from

people you actually know, or who have at least five friends in common with you; you might decide that you'll accept LinkedIn requests only from people you've worked with as colleagues or clients or who are in recruitment positions. If you get a request from someone who doesn't meet those criteria, you can drop them a quick note saying you only connect with people you've worked with directly. Just take care to set criteria that broaden your view of the world, rather than reinforcing it: following people from different backgrounds, generations, or experiences is a lot more useful than following hundreds of people who look (or think) like you.

FINDING YOUR VOICE

Your Business of One needs to have a clear and visible value proposition: a domain of excellence that ensures your employer, colleagues, and clients see your particular strengths and contributions. Your social media presence should be an expression of that value proposition, so that even if you spend all or most of your workdays at home, nobody forgets what you bring to the table. To establish that presence, you need to define your turf (the subject area you'll speak to) as well as your medium (text, podcast, photos, etc.) and your tone (erudite, engaging, playful, etc.).

It's very hard to become the go-to expert on a big subject like human resources, real estate, or marketing technology. A better bet for building a useful, credible position of expertise is to situate yourself at the intersection of two or three fields, or one to two fields plus a location. For example, instead of positioning yourself as the expert on small business sales strategy, aim to be the expert on the latest business books on sales strategy for a small business reader; sales strategy for small businesses that are trying to get past $5 million in revenue; or perhaps you want to be the expert on sales strategy for direct-to-consumer startups.

Before you commit, see if anyone else has already carved out the turf you have in mind, and assess whether general-purpose sites (like the leading sales strategy blogs) are already meeting the need you hoped to fill. Be sure to pick a niche you're going to enjoy: you're much more likely to maintain a consistent and valuable presence if it's actually fun and interesting.

When you're choosing the medium you'll use to express yourself online— and it can be more than one—think both about what works in your field *and* what you personally enjoy. You might be in a field that's driven by video, but if you *hate* going on camera or editing video, you'll need to find another way to share your voice. Conversely, it doesn't matter how much you love writing: if all the top experts in your field are on Instagram, you'll need to find a way to express yourself through images, too.

You can (and probably should) choose more than one platform: a good rule of thumb is to think in terms of choosing one platform that will let you express yourself in some depth (like a blog, YouTube channel, or podcast) and at least one social network that you use to promote your in-depth posts, share real-time insights or discoveries, and converse with other people in your field or the community at large.

Just about everybody needs to maintain at least a bare-bones LinkedIn presence—essentially an up-to-date résumé—because it's often the first place new colleagues or prospective clients will go to get a sense of your background. Depending on your particular field, goals, or interests, you may find it useful (or even essential) to maintain a Twitter, Instagram, or Facebook presence as well.

When you're trying to figure out the tone to take in your social media presence and posts, approach it like you'd think about choosing your clothes for your first day at a new job: you want to present your Business of One in a way that looks and sounds professional, but you also want to convey your personality and taste. While there's no obligation to share every detail of your personal life (and there are very real professional and security risks to over-disclosure), it's often easier to form strong, meaningful professional connections online if you show up as a whole person. However, even if you're letting your hair down a little bit, and including some humor or personal details in your social media posts, be careful not to push it too far. Humor should *never* veer into territory that refers to sex or ethnicity; even on a not-for-business social networking profile, personal disclosure should always pass the front-page test. As in, How would you feel if your boss read this on the front page of tomorrow's paper?

Last but not least, try not to be *too* strategic when you're mapping out your online presence. When you're working remotely, social media is not just a way to keep yourself on your boss's or colleagues' radar: it's also a way to combat isolation and get the intellectual, creative, and emotional benefits of interaction.

You're unlikely to experience those benefits if you're always gaming everything out in professional terms. Instead of thinking of social media as a stage, or a place to promote your "personal brand," think of it as a really awesome business lunch. Yes, your colleagues are there, and yes, you're probably going to exchange some industry gossip, lessons learned, or business insights. But you might also catch up on personal news, argue over your favorite TV shows, and talk about the latest political headlines. All of that is appropriate on social media, too.

GET FEEDBACK ON YOUR SOCIAL MEDIA PRESENCE

If you already have a social media presence—whether that's a blog, a Twitter account, or an Instagram feed—you may find it useful to take a careful look at your existing profile so you can assess whether it's actually serving your goals. Here are three quick exercises that can give you a fresh perspective. Try one, or all three:

1. Ask a respected friend or colleague to look at your current social media presence, scrolling back a few weeks to get a feel for the way you post and engage. How would they describe the person they are seeing online? Do they think that your social media self reflects what they know of you personally and professionally? Use their answers to determine whether your online presence is projecting your ideas, expertise, and personality the way you'd hoped.

2. Use a social media analytics tool to assess your blog posts, tweets, or other online content. What are the posts that get shared the most? What generates the most discussion? Con-

sider categorizing your posts by topic, type (how-to, personal story, opinion, etc.) and tone *before* you let yourself look at the numbers. You may find that the topics or post types other people respond to most are different from what you enjoy posting or see as valuable.

3. Pick a role model—someone whose online presence reflects your goals in terms of the way people respond to or share their content, and their following or reach. Stay "in character" as your role model for the next few weeks, posting and participating online as if you've got equivalent reach. After a couple of weeks or a month, look at the new you: What changed in your tone or content? Did you enjoy social media more or less while you were in character? Let your answers inform the way you handle your social media life going forward.

MANAGING SOCIAL MEDIA IN THREE HOURS A WEEK

As a remote worker, you can maintain a very thoughtful, engaging social media presence in two or three hours a week. That might sound like a lot, but just remember, it's an investment in your professional profile that can save time in other ways: if you're scanning and participating in regular social media conversations, you may not need to spend as much time on webinars or industry journals.

It's much easier to engage and post consistently on social media if you have at least a couple of tools in place: A newsreader (like Feedly or Flipboard) that centralizes all your news sources in one place, and a social media dashboard (like Buffer) that can manage multiple social media presences. Look for a dashboard that lets you build a schedule of posts so that you can queue up ten or twenty social media updates at a time.

• • •

TECH DEEP DIVE

Customize Your News

In addition to the existing sources you add to your newsreader, consider creating your own "source" in the form of a custom Google News search, so that you see articles in your field even if they appear in publications or sites you would not otherwise see. Once you have figured out the search terms that will bring you relevant stories, use Google Alerts to subscribe to that search by email or in your newsreader.

For example, our would-be DTC sales expert might create a search on something like (*direct-to-consumer* or *DTC*) and (*sales*) and (*start-ups* or *startup* or *start-up*).

If you don't want these search results cluttering your email inbox, look online for detailed instructions on subscribing to a Google News search by RSS. RSS (Really Simple Syndication) is a data format that makes it possible to subscribe to multiple blogs or news searches so that you can see them all in one place using your newsreader.

Once you have both your newsreader and dashboard in place, here is what you can accomplish in two or three hours each week.

One Hour per Week:
Review News and Build a Queue of Posts for the Week

In this hour, scan your newsreader and social networks for the latest news and opinion pieces in the fields you are aiming to bridge; in the case of a sales strategist who's carving out a niche around direct-to-consumer brands, that would be stories related to DTC brands, startups, or sales strategy. As you find noteworthy quotes or interesting stories you want to share, turn each one into a short original social network update that includes a link to the item you're discussing. The sales strategist might queue up the following tweets or updates:

- Sharing a news story about a DTC that ran into trouble: *This article is a must-read if you want to understand why DTCs so often run into a revenue trough as they scale.*
- Sounds like someone needs to realize that not ALL sales strategies are about $$$$ companies—this "genius" strategy would be a total bust if you haven't made it to $100m. (Sharing a sales column he found aggravating because it talked only about massive global brands.)
- This >>> is a DTC #CMO to watch. She is a #leadgen machine, and this interview tells you why. (Sharing an interview with a DTC CMO he's hoping to pitch on his services.)

Thirty to Sixty Minutes per Week: Create One Piece of Thoughtful Content

Once every week or two, set aside some time for what's often described as "thought leadership": sharing an original idea, story, or how-to that will be illuminating for other people in your field. This could be a short blog post, a thoughtful collection of slides for Instagram, a "tweet storm" (a short article or argument written as a series of linked tweets), a Facebook live session, a podcast interview . . . it all depends on what you choose as your medium.

If it's hard to imagine creating any one of these in under an hour or two, remember that it gets easier with practice, especially if you find a go-to format (see the "Four Starting Points for Your Thought Leadership Posts" feature below). While your spontaneous or queued-up social media posts may span a range of networks and formats, it's best to choose a consistent platform and rhythm for your weekly deep dive—for example, a Wednesday morning LinkedIn post or a Sunday evening image collection.

FOUR STARTING POINTS FOR YOUR
THOUGHT LEADERSHIP POSTS

1. **A USEFUL ARTICLE WITH ONE GREAT QUOTATION YOU CAN RIFF ON.** Quote the relevant sentences and then write two or three short paragraphs (or bullets) explaining why it's relevant to your particular niche or audience.

2. **AN OPINION PIECE YOU FOUND INFURIATING.** Make a list of the three to five points you want to refute, and then use that as the basis for a social media post, blog post, or tweet storm.

3. **A PERSON YOU FIND FASCINATING.** Invite them to join you for a podcast or Facebook Live interview.

4. **A WEEKLY THEME OF IMAGES YOU'RE GOING TO CAPTURE AND COMMENT ON.** For example, a collection of shop signs that reveal a common mistake in customer service.

Ten to Fifteen Minutes a Day:
Scan and Engage with Your Social Networks

Once or twice a day, check in on the social networks you've prioritized and posted on. Respond to anyone who has commented on something you've shared (unless it makes you angry, in which case, *don't* reply until you've calmed down and run your draft reply past a trusted friend or colleague). Next, scan the latest updates from the people or topics you follow; comment on or reshare one or two items you find especially interesting or thoughtful. These real-time posts complement your weekly queue by ensuring some of your updates are relevant to whatever's happening online that day.

You don't have to check on every single platform every single day, but you don't want to go more than twenty-four hours without looking at a network where you've queued up updates. The most efficient practice is to do two or three very quick "tours" through those social media presences every day, but look *only* at your notifications: All you need to see is if someone has commented on something you've posted, and if so, whether you need to reply to them. You'll know you've found the right approach to your social media presence when it feels not like a chore, but an eagerly anticipated part of your workday.

FROM A REMOTE WORKER

Dawn Myers left her career in the law to launch her own
hair-tech startup, and social media has been a key part of how
she builds connection with her all-remote team, as well her brand.

I started The Most because everyone kept telling me: "You've got to do something in hair." I kept thinking, I'm not a beauty CEO. Then one night I saw a TV spot that inspired me to come up with the Most Mint, an appliance that applies curl-care products.

In ten months, we've grown to a team of ten. The whole team is remote: we have folks all over, from here in DC to Denver to Miami, and even in the UK.

We aren't a bunch of twenty-two-year-old boys who don't have responsibilities. These are grown women with responsibilities and kids. And when you trust your people to get their work done, it gives them the flexibility to take care of those responsibilities. I always felt that people would be more productive if they could build their work into their lives in a more seamless way, and that's what it's like for our team: we are working even when we're playing. We want to avoid extremes where you are working sixteen hours a day, but when you can figure out how to make work a part of your life, that is the ideal scenario—it all feels like play.

It's worked better for me, too, because I'm an extroverted introvert. I can do people-ing well, but only to a certain extent, so the Covid lockdown has given me a chance to shine. Going out to coffee or a networking event takes a huge chunk out of me, but I can do Zoom all day. We've been able to make a lot of big moves as a company because I can network all day now.

I talk to my CMO for four hours a day, every day, but I've never actually met her in person. Even if we just have an hour or two of work calls, we are texting throughout the day. In the social media, text-messaging age, relationships are made up of messages like "Something crazy happened," or "I saw this meme that I know you'll be interested in." That's really how you form those relationships.

We use Instagram to build an audience for our brand. We've built this world where curls and Afro-textured hair and brown skin are valued and beautiful and seen. A lot of our niche is fiending for that reality. So we built that reality on Instagram, and it brings people who are fiending for that into our world.

LinkedIn has been pretty pivotal for me, too. I'm the same person that I was a year ago but because I have been using LinkedIn a lot more often and letting people know what I'm doing, all of a sudden people are perking up and giving me kudos or reaching out or asking me to be on panels. People just recognize you as an authority in the space a little bit more. It's one of those uncomfortable but unavoidable things where you've got to toot your own horn a little bit.

Social media is such a big part of my life that it's hard to avoid overload. Your fingers almost build up a muscle memory where they go to Twitter to see if anyone has replied to that advertisement. I definitely have moments where it feels overwhelming and I don't want to be there. I try to be conscious of when it just feels like too much, and then hit that "X" button.

TAKEAWAYS

1: Don't keep up with social media. Instead determine which relationships will advance your objectives, and focus your social media usage on developing those relationships.

2. Use lists to organize your social media attention around the different types of relationships you want to cultivate, and minimize the degree to which network algorithms determine what gets your attention.

3. Choose a niche for your social media presence that positions you at the intersection of two or three fields, or one to two fields plus a location.

4. Choose a medium and platform you're really going to enjoy posting and participating on, because you won't sustain your social media presence unless it also sustains you.

5. Every week or two, post a thought piece with an idea or comment in one of the fields where you are building your social media presence.

6. Make sure anything you post on social media passes the front page test: you'd be comfortable having your boss read it on the front page of tomorrow's paper.

7. Set up a toolkit and routine that allow you to sustain your social media presence in three hours a week by queuing up posts once a week, then checking in very briefly every day.

8. Get feedback on your social media presence from friends or colleagues, who can give you an objective perspective.

CHAPTER 15

PRESENTATIONS
Making an Impact

Even the most talented and charismatic business speakers need to rethink their tactics and style when they shift to presenting over video or webinar. For remote workers, video presentations may account for a significant portion of their professional visibility. When you deliver a presentation, you're representing your Business of One just as much as you're representing the organization that signs your paycheck.

If you're already comfortable speaking to small groups or large audiences, that ability will serve you well online, though you will need to rethink your style and approach. And if you're entirely new to public speaking, we'll help you get comfortable and give you a basic approach that can support you in both on- and offline presentations. Indeed, getting started as an online speaker while working remotely will help you develop your approach without having to deal with the additional anxiety of seeing your audience members lose focus or fall asleep.

Your presentation process will follow three discrete stages: planning, preparation, and delivery. This chapter walks you through each of them, focusing on the particular challenges of online presentations.

PLANNING A PRESENTATION

When you're planning a presentation, you need to answer three questions: Who is your audience? What are the goals of your presentation? And what type of presentation are you actually going to deliver?

QUESTIONS TO ASK ABOUT YOUR AUDIENCE

- SIZE. How many people will you be speaking to? This matters even in a virtual presentation because it affects the options for discussion.
- COMPOSITION. The more you understand the makeup of your audience, the better you can tailor your content and tone: What industry or roles are they in? What are their interests or pain points relative to your topic? How senior are they in their organizations?
- SENSITIVITIES. Find out if there are any "third rail" topics or sensitivities you need to navigate carefully, like competitors you shouldn't mention.

Questions to Ask about Your Goals

In most cases your goals for a presentation boil down to wanting your audience to *learn* something new, *think* differently about your topic, or *feel* something new or different; you need to select these goals in consultation with your host or manager. Discuss:

- WHAT SPECIFIC INFORMATION OR SKILLS DO WE WANT THIS AUDIENCE TO **LEARN** THAT WILL BE CONCRETELY USEFUL TO THEM? This could be a big-picture strategic concept, a crucial historical lesson, or a nuts-and-bolts tactic. However, if you are planning to get pretty tactical, try to tie that to a larger goal around *thinking* or *feeling* so that your tactics really stick with your audience.
- HOW DO WE WANT TO SHIFT OR EXPAND OUR AUDIENCE'S PERSPECTIVE ON THIS TOPIC, SO THAT THEY **THINK** ABOUT IT DIFFERENTLY? Sometimes you are trying to equip them with the knowledge to deliver on what they already believe, or help them feel great about what they already think.
- HOW DO WE WANT OUR AUDIENCE TO **FEEL**, BOTH WHILE THEY ARE LISTENING/ WATCHING AND AFTER THEY LEAVE THE (VIRTUAL) ROOM? You might want your audience to feel joyful, inspired, energized, challenged, motivated, or some combination of these.

You may well have more than one type of goal: when Alex speaks about data-driven storytelling, for example, she wants people to *learn* that original data can help them attract attention to their posts and articles, *think* that they can relax their research standards when they're creating data-driven content for marketing purposes, and *feel* that it's within their power to do that effectively.

Remember that there is only so much people can remember from listening to a talk, as opposed to reading an article. So you need to limit your goals to a maximum of three key points you *really* want people to take away from your talk. These goals should reflect what your host or audience has asked you to address, and will ideally provide you with an opportunity to showcase the unique expertise of your Business of One.

QUESTIONS TO ASK ABOUT YOUR FORMAT

- DO YOU NEED A DECK? Not every presentation needs slides.
- HOW WILL THE AUDIENCE PARTICIPATE? While a few minutes of end-of-talk Q&A should be your *minimum* level of audience participation, find out if you can also do mid-presentation discussion or breakout rooms.
- HOW LONG DO YOU HAVE? Find out the total number of minutes allocated to your presentation, and how many of those are reserved for Q&A.
- WHAT IS THE SUPPORT PLAN? Ideally you have at least one person available to run your slides, troubleshoot connectivity issues, and track any incoming questions.

PREPARING YOUR PRESENTATION

Drafting Your Presentation

What works for a twenty-minute internal presentation may not be right for a fifty-minute public keynote, but it's almost always useful to think in terms of a three-part structure:

1. **YOUR OPENING**, which should connect with your audience emotionally (using humor or a personal story), establish the tone and structure for your presentation ("I will share three key practices for any
   security-conscious organization"), and let your audience know
   what this presentation is going to do for them. For example: "In the
   next twenty minutes I will show how our team's latest development
   project has improved system performance, and share the lessons
   this project offers for future performance challenges."

2. **THE BODY**, which should deliver on what you want your audience
   to learn, think, or feel; offer at least three actionable insights or
   nuggets of information, tied to anecdotes or visuals that give them
   emotional impact and lock them into memory; and drop bread
   crumbs that remind your audience of where you are in the overall
   arc of your presentation.

3. **THE CONCLUSION**, which should reflect on what you've covered but
   leave your audience with a final nugget of inspiration.

A RECIPE FOR EVERY CONCLUSION

When Alex is preparing a presentation, she uses the four-step conclusion recipe developed by her husband, speechwriter Rob Cottingham:[1]

1. **THE CHALLENGE** sums up the problem your speech has been trying to solve.
2. **THE CALL** is the action you're inviting your audience to take.
3. **THE RECIPE** is the brief set of concrete steps that your audience
   needs to take to fulfill the action.
4. **THE REWARD** describes the positive change your audience will
   see as a result.

Outlining your presentation in this three-part structure will help you
think through the content you need to develop in order to deliver on your
vision and goals. Ask yourself: What are the one to three ideas or insights I

want the audience to take away from this presentation? What are the personal anecdotes, business stories, or historical examples I can use to illustrate my points? Where would visuals help clarify, anchor, or amplify my argument?

Once you've answered these questions, you are ready to draft your talk. Even if you start by writing out a notional script, reduce this text to point form, and get used to delivering your presentation from these point-form notes—the fewer and shorter, the better. Your goal is to sound lively and spontaneous, which is why you want to ensure you're talking from notes rather than reading from a script.

CONQUERING SPEAKER'S BLOCK

If the idea of preparing your presentation has you frozen like a deer in the headlights, try this trick: imagine that you have to deliver this presentation today . . . in five minutes.

Take those five minutes to jot down a few quick notes, then deliver the presentation to yourself (or a trusted friend) by speaking more or less off-the-cuff, and recording yourself (either on camera or just as audio). You don't have to give a full-length presentation, but try to speak for at least five or ten minutes on the subject at hand, and keep going until you run out of things to say or simply exhaust yourself.

Then sit down and capture anything you heard yourself saying that belongs in your presentation, any questions you now realize you need to answer about your goals or format, or anything you need to research in order to fill in the blanks you left while speaking. You're likely to realize that you're further along than you thought: you have something to say, you just need to figure out the right structure and delivery.

Creating Great Slide Decks

Do *not* create your deck until you know what you want to say. Properly used, a slide deck can anchor your audience's attention, make it easier to follow your presentation, and engage your audience emotionally with humorous or powerful images. To achieve these benefits, you need a vision for how you want slides to function in your presentation, and what that implies for your design approach.

If your talk isn't *intrinsically* visual—that is, if you don't have specific charts, photographs, or technical diagrams you need to show in order to communicate your key points—you have some freedom in how you develop and theme your slides. You can use our universal deck recipe (see the feature below) or you might think of a compelling metaphor that can bring some depth or humor to your entire deck.

THREE SLIDE MISTAKES—AND HOW TO AVOID THEM

1. **STEREOTYPES.** If you're using photos in your slide deck, they should reflect the diversity of the audience, topic, or industry you're addressing. Make sure you're showing people of different backgrounds, and make sure your choices don't reflect ethnic or gender stereotypes.

2. **UGLY SLIDES.** You don't have to rely on PowerPoint's preloaded templates. Instead look for an upgraded template that you can buy and use for your presentation. There are many websites and online marketplaces, like Creative Market, where you can find excellent templates and purchase illustrations for your deck.

3. **MISSING SIGNPOSTS.** If too much text is the most common mistake in offline presentations, too *little* text can be a mistake when you're speaking online. In a virtual presentation, audiences need a little extra help to stay anchored to your structure and narrative. Use slides with an agenda, section headings, and useful titles to help your audience stay with you.

As you're preparing your deck, remember that every slide change or build is a chance for you to fall out of sync with your images, so don't use more slides or builds than absolutely necessary. And remember, not every talk requires a deck, period.

THE UNIVERSAL DECK

This recipe will work for most slide presentations. You can use it as your default, unless you have reason to do something more detailed or creative—or you're comfortable doing without a deck altogether.

1. TITLE SLIDE. Name of talk, name of event, your name, your Twitter handle, hashtag for event (so people know how to tweet about your talk. You should keep your Twitter handle and hashtag in the footer of every subsequent slide, too).

   [Turn off the deck or insert a blank slide after your title slide so people can see your face and connect to you while you share an opening story or joke.]

2. FRAMING SLIDE. A compelling image that reflects your overall theme, which you leave up while you introduce your theme.

3. OUTLINE SLIDE. A text-only slide that maps out the three to five key points of your deck in *succinct* form (one to five words per bullet, the fewer the better). This is the most text-heavy slide in your deck.

   [Revert to camera briefly to reconnect with the audience.]

4. For each key point in your outline slide, you will have the following:

   a. SECTION TITLE SLIDE. The section title on this slide should match the way you referred to this section on your outline slide.

   b. THEMATIC SLIDE. An image that evokes the key point you are discussing.

   c. KEY LESSON(S) SLIDE. 1 to 3 bullets *briefly* summarizing what you just said.

   [Revert to camera to invite clarifying questions, then repeat for next section.]

4. **CONCLUSION TITLE.** A text slide with a key question or idea that sets up your conclusion.

5. **MEMORABLE IMAGE.** A thematically appropriate image that reflects your concluding lesson or insight.

6. **THANK YOU.** A text slide with your name and contact information.

Planning for Participation

It's easy for people to lose interest or focus in an online presentation. An effective plan for audience engagement keeps people attentive and on track.

Plan to take questions at various points in your presentation: A good way to do this is by pausing between every major section to invite clarifying questions. During those pauses, you can ask those with questions to signal you (in many apps there is a "raise hand" option). Try to think through the most likely questions in advance, and plot out your answers, but recognize that you really might get asked something you haven't thought through. If so, it's perfectly acceptable to admit that you need some time to think over (or look up) the answer, or simply don't know. You can always follow up later by posting your answer on Twitter (with the event hashtag) or asking your host to share your comments with attendees.

Here are three approaches to participation that work well in online presentations:

- LIVE BRAINSTORMING. Use a virtual whiteboard like Miro or a collaborative mind-mapping tool like MindMeister to elicit ideas from your audience, capture them visually, and then cluster or connect related ideas.
- INSTANT WORKSHOP. Ask one person in the virtual room to share a challenge related to your topic and invite the audience to help generate solutions. (Ask your host to line up some potential challenges in case nobody volunteers.)

- POLL. If your presentation platform includes a polling feature, quick polls are a nice way to add simple feedback to your talk. Ask people to respond to a poll question, briefly address the consensus of the room, and then ask if anyone can elaborate on their answer.

Delivering a Compelling Presentation

Once you have your talk outline, your deck prepared, and your participation opportunities mapped out, you're almost ready to hit the virtual stage. But first: practice!

Rehearsing Your Presentation

No matter how much you hate rehearsing, at least one run-through is necessary to check your running time, catch any breaks in the flow of your talk, and get comfortable with slide changes.

Particularly if you're new to speaking, you may find it helpful to recruit a speaking buddy: think of this as Toastmasters for Two. Your speaking buddy is someone you can talk with as you're thinking through your presentation, and even more important, they're your practice audience and sounding board once you're ready to rehearse.

Start by printing out your deck and notes—yes, on actual paper! Working backward from the time you need to wrap up, mark what you think are the one-quarter, halfway, and three-quarters marks, and indicate the run time and actual time it should be when you get to that point. When you're rehearsing, you'll use these marks to figure out if your talk is running long or short, so you can make a game plan for where you can cut a few minutes from your presentation if you're running long, or add an interesting story or two if you're running short.

When you're rehearsing *and* when you're delivering your presentation, try to stand up: this shifts your energy and helps you project your voice so that you're at your most compelling.

Finally, take some time to test out the logistical setup for your virtual presentation. Set up your presentation space exactly as you plan to use it on the day of your presentation, including lighting, power for your computer, and a tidy background; see how it looks on-screen and take some webcam snapshots. Do a platform and audio check with the *exact* software you're going to use in your presentation, so you're sure there are no connectivity issues, and arrange for an emergency backup plan—even if it's just an exchange of phone numbers. Most important, make a plan to have a *silent* environment while you're presenting: find a quiet space where you'll be able to speak without interruption.

You may want to think through a few other personal details in advance. Pick out your clothes and make sure they look good on camera. If your face is shiny in the light you've set up, figure out the makeup you'll use to fix the problem. Yes, gentlemen, you can use face powder, too: you may find that a little stage makeup is a good investment if you are making regular presentations on camera.

Once you've got all these pieces in place, do one last run-through in game-day conditions. The more familiar your setup, the more smoothly you'll be able to deliver your presentation.

CHEAT WITH YOUR PHONE

If you are delivering a live, in-person presentation, here's a tech trick that creates the illusion that you're speaking entirely off-the-cuff. Distill your speaking notes down to five to ten essential prompts of no more than four words each; then write these points down in a large-size font, and capture them as a screenshot. Save that screenshot to your phone and set it as your phone's lock screen. If you lose track of where you are in your talk, and need a prompt, you can hit your home key to wake up your phone and take a quick glance at your notes. From your audience's perspective, you're just checking the time.

Connecting with Your Audience

The most challenging part of a virtual presentation, particularly for those of us who are used to speaking live, is the lack of audience feedback. When you're speaking to a roomful of physically present humans, their body language lets you know whether you've got their attention (which can be a blessing or a curse, depending on how the talk is going!).

In a virtual presentation, you need to come up with strategies that bring your audience to life for you as a speaker, and keep them engaged throughout your presentation. For a smaller audience, consider starting with a round of introductions; for a larger group, consider some form of audience participation early in your talk. Even if you're just hearing from two or three different audience members, it will break your sense of speaking into a void, and give your audience members a sense that this is a collective experience.

When you stop for questions at the points you've planned, give people time to chime in; it often takes a minute or two of uncomfortable silence before anyone will pipe up online. If you're getting absolutely *nothing* in the way of questions, ask a question of your own. For example, if you've just finished talking through the legal considerations around employee social media access, and nobody has any questions about your material, you might ask a really open-ended, hot-button question like "Do you ever feel concerned about the way you observe your colleagues using social media during the workday?" *That* should get you a few raised hands.

COPING WITH GLITCHES

Even the best-laid plans can go awry when you're giving an online presentation. In these situations, the best thing to do is to acknowledge the issue directly: Interrupt your flow to ask the person running the slides to skip ahead, or leave folks with a question to ponder while you call in and reconnect by phone. Particularly if you handle the situation with grace and humor, these human and technological failings will only make you seem more relatable, strengthening your audience's sense of connection to you and to one another as you collectively navigate a few awkward moments. And a sense of connection is the very thing a good presentation creates.

Wrapping Your Presentation

A graceful exit is an important part of your job as a presenter. Beyond the way you actually conclude your talk, you need to be sure you're gracious about the opportunity to connect with this particular audience. Thank your hosts for the invitation while the whole audience is still tuned in, and if your audience has been at all participatory, thank them for their thought-provoking questions and comments. If you're planning to share relevant links or answers to any remaining questions, tell people how and when they can find that—for example, by giving them your Twitter handle or blog URL.

Then share the news on social media: You gave a great presentation! Celebrate with a Twitter thread, LinkedIn post, or blog post sharing some of the key insights from your talk. Make sure to graciously acknowledge your hosts and audience, and keep your content the focus of your post. You had something useful to say, so you want it to be useful to as many people as possible. Telling the story of your presentation, just as much as delivering the presentation itself, helps build the profile of your Business of One.

FROM A REMOTE WORKER

Hiro Boga is an entrepreneur and business strategist who has worked remotely for over a decade, and applied her innovative thinking to moving in-person training online.

For most of my adult life, I haven't had a job where I had to be at a certain place by a certain time without a choice in the matter: I set my world up that way.

My dad was a lifelong entrepreneur, and it never occurred to me that I had to have a job or that I'd ever even want one.

I was born two years after India gained its freedom from British colonial rule. When I came to North America in 1972, it was just after the Vietnam War, and things seemed creatively chaotic. I'm a self-structured person. My experience is that when the entrepreneurs I mentor struggle, it's often because they're trying to impose an external structure on their natural way of working instead of structuring their business to support their own values and their unique way of working.

Before I took my business online in 2007, I had renovated an old mine rescue station that had been derelict for many years and made it my business's headquarters. The biggest challenge in moving my business online was re-crafting my group entrepreneurship programs.

My programs are highly experiential, and many of the practices and pro-cesses I'd created over the years depended on people being in a room together. I struggled with it until I let go of trying to replicate the depth of in-person work, and recognized that working online is a completely different culture. I had to put a lot more faith in people's ability to follow their noses and pace and manage their own learning.

There is a different assumption online: The assumption is that the par-ticipants' focus is on me instead of each other. That's a very solar-system way of thinking, which is common in the old culture of business, where there is a central sun or leader around whom the rest of the workplace revolved, like planets in orbit. Once I caught on to that, I changed the class structure, us-ing small breakout groups to keep people connected and engaged with each other. This way of working is more like galaxies: Each person is a star with a unique field of gravity yet part of a larger system that orchestrates harmony and keeps these stars from colliding.

I continued to offer private, in-person planning retreats, a couple of times a year, but stopped that a few years ago. I was just done. I felt a push-pull between the energy I needed for my own creative work and my capacity to be really present for my clients. I've worked to fine-tune the balance between the two because I won't take on more than I can show up fully for.

As I'm aging, I'm slowing down, and experimenting with structures in my business that give me more space and time—a pace that feels good to me. During the last quarter of this year, I reconfigured my schedule so that I worked with clients on alternate weeks and had every other week free for my own creative work. My weeks with clients, I am really happy. And my weeks to myself, I'm really happy.

This phase of my life is calling me to other things. The horizon is much closer than it's ever been, and there are books I want to write and art I want to make.

TAKEAWAYS

1. An effective presentation needs to be planned around the specific audience you're speaking to and the format of the talk.

2. You need to get clear on the goals for your presentation: What do you want the audience to learn, think, or feel by the time you conclude?

3. Draft your presentation around a structure that includes an emotional connection to your audience in your opening minutes, and a conclusion that includes a clear call to action.

4. Focus on a maximum of three ideas or insights that you want your audience to retain, which are related to your goals, and build your talk around these one to three key points.

5. Deliver your talk from point-form notes, printed on paper, with time notes that will help you adjust your running time as needed.

6. Use slides to anchor your audience's attention and support different learning styles, but avoid using too many slides or too much text.

7. Include some participatory elements in your talk, including a pause for questions, so that your audience stays engaged.

8. Rehearse your talk and tech setup so that you are confident in your run time and in how you will connect on the day of your talk.

9. Use social media to share key links with the audience, get feedback, and share insights from your talk.

PART VI

THRIVING IN A WORLD OF REMOTE WORK

B y now you have seen how thinking like a Business of One can help you thrive as a remote worker. You have learned the key strategies that drive productivity, discovered the secrets to getting organized when you're working remotely, and honed the essential skills and communication practices that help you work effectively as *Remote, Inc.* No matter how long you choose to sustain your current Business of One, we are confident that these strategies and skills will serve you well for years to come.

But what if things change—as they certainly will? After all, we're writing this in the midst of a pandemic that changed the rules of remote work overnight, and we are confident that those rules will be revised again as we recover and reinvent the workplace. Sadly, the people who equipped our home offices forgot to include a crystal ball. It doesn't take psychic power to anticipate that the world of work is going to change, however, in ways we can barely see from here.

In this final part of the book, we'll look around the corner to the day when people can choose how to combine remote and on-site locations. Indeed, some organizations are already coming up with clever new ways to rotate employees in and out of the workplace so they get the benefits of collaboration at the office and concentration at home. We call this hybrid model the Goldilocks plan, with not too much or too little time at home.

In the conclusion, we map out the benefits that the Business of One model offers you and your employer or clients—creating a win-win situation. And we invite you to become part of the pioneering generation of remote workers who will establish the new norms of the Goldilocks plan and the new culture of *Remote, Inc.*

CHAPTER 16

THE GOLDILOCKS PLAN

This chapter shows how to design a Goldilocks plan that is uniquely suited to your work and life: a plan that combines time at home and at the office. We will begin by explaining why the Goldilocks plan will become the dominant mode of working in the years to come. Then we will present ten reasons to work at home and ten reasons to work in the office, so you can develop the blend that is best for you. Finally, we will discuss different ways you might want to grow *Remote, Inc.* over time in light of your personality as well as your personal and professional values.

Thanks to your efforts so far, you have the knowledge and skill to pursue those choices as a Business of One. Now let's turn the page and see what the future workplace has in store.

THE CHANGING LANDSCAPE OF WORK

Remote work doesn't have to be all or nothing—for you, for your organization, or for your clients. Relatively few organizations will embrace a fully remote workforce outside of a pandemic.

Instead many remote workers will spend at least some time in the office, and many organizations will include at least some remote workers. As soon as an organization has more than one location, it starts adapting to the challenges of distributed work: setting up group messaging platforms that connect employees in different cities; implementing videoconferencing systems that cover several boardrooms; organizing calls that accommodate different time zones. Once you have a team that spans multiple corporate offices, it's only a short hop to accommodating home offices.

We refer to this mix of home and remote work as the Goldilocks plan, in which each employee spends not too much or too little time at home. It's a model that provides the best of both worlds for employers, too: They can get the cost savings from allowing some work from home, while retaining the coordination and creativity associated with office work. An organization that offers a mix of the two—where on any given day, some workers are at home and others are at the office—will be the dominant mode of work in the years to come.

The Goldilocks plan has significant implications for the success and productivity of your own Business of One, because it requires you to reckon with the larger dynamics of your employer or clients: When you are working within organizations that adopt a hybrid approach, there may be certain types of work that you are expected to do on-site, which in turn affects how you make optimal use of the days when you work remotely. If you can shape the balance of your on-site and remote work around the particular demands of your job as well as your own personal situation, you will make much more productive use of your time both in and outside the office.

WHY GO GOLDILOCKS?

If you dream of the day when you can work part-time from home, and part-time from the office, you're not alone.

Few professionals want to spend *all* their time at the office. In a survey conducted for us by polling firm Maru/Blue, two-thirds of respondents said they would prefer to work from home at least part of the time. Among respondents with a college or graduate education, the preference for remote work was even more pronounced, with only 22 percent saying they would like to go back to the office full-time. On the other hand, only 34 percent of our respondents want to work from home full-time. And that result was consistent across every demographic.

Our survey confirms what has been found in other studies: An IBM survey of 25,000 employees at multiple companies found that 75 percent said they would like to work from home at least part of the time.[1] A study from

Global Workplace Analytics found that a third of employees would change jobs for the opportunity to work remotely some of the time, and more than a third would take a pay cut of up to 5 percent in return for that option.[2] And when Slack surveyed 9,000 knowledge workers in 2020, it found that across six different countries, anywhere from 65 to 77 percent of workers expressed a preference for the hybrid model.[3]

It turns out that most people want the Goldilocks plan: not too much time at home, and not too little. But how you define the "just right" of the Goldilocks plan varies from person to person, as Stanford economist Nicholas Bloom uncovered in a 2019 survey of 2,500 working Americans (see figure 16.1). Among the 80 percent of respondents who said they would like to work remotely at least some of the time, a quarter said they would like to work from home only rarely, and nearly a third said they would like to work from home full-time. The remainder—nearly half of these would-be remote workers— differed as to whether they would prefer to work from home one, two, three, or four days a week.[4]

FIGURE 16.1

Employee demand for remote work
Percentage of respondents for each answer to the question,
"In 2021+ (after COVID) how often would you like to have paid work days at home?"

Source: "How working from home works out," Stanford Institute for Economic Policy Research

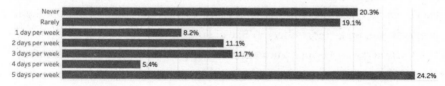

However, only 56 percent of the US workforce holds jobs that are compatible with even part-time remote work, according to Global Workplace Analytics, because many jobs involve customer contact or physical work that by definition requires you to be on-site.[5] Indeed, one of the reasons that Covid disproportionately affected people of color in the United States is because

Black and Latino people were less likely to be in jobs that could be done remotely and, conversely, more likely to be in roles that involved continued contact with the public and greater risk of exposure.[6] And when employees of color do have the option of working remotely, it can be a mixed blessing—potentially leveling the playing field, but potentially also rendering them invisible or further marginalized.[7]

Employers should be flexible and creative about combining remote work with time at the office, so that their employees can find the right mix for each person, role, and team. As economist Bloom put it, "Nobody should be forced to work from home full time, and nobody should be forced to work in the office full time. Choice is key—let employees pick their schedules and let them change as their views evolve."[8]

But what is the *right* choice: the particular combination of remote and onsite work that will work best for you and for your employer? To answer that question, you need to think thoroughly about what you do best at home, and what you do best at the office.

DESIGNING YOUR OWN GOLDILOCKS PLAN

If you're in an organization that allows a mix of office and remote work, you may be able to have the best of both worlds. Indeed, most of the strategies we've mapped out for working effectively as a remote Business of One will also help you make more effective use of your time in the office.

But that won't happen automatically: It pays to do some hard thinking about how you're going to make the combination work. That means thinking about which parts of your Business of One benefit from the context of the office, and which parts work better at home or off-site. In general, you'll find that office time is helpful for the more collaborative and interpersonal aspects of your job, while remote time is helpful to the pieces that require concentration. However, there are lots of exceptions to that general rule, so you'll need to look at your goals, projects, and tasks to figure out the right balance.

Plan on making that a recurring process, because you will need to rethink your particular combination of remote and office work, as well as the way you schedule it, every year or two. Your own personal Goldilocks plan will work best if it's tailored to the types of tasks required as part of your highest-priority work, as well as to your professional relationships and your own home or personal life. Whenever one piece of that picture changes, it's time for a fresh review.

That means thinking about the specific advantages you get from spending a day at the office, as well as the specific advantages of spending a day working remotely—whether that's at home, at your favorite coffee shop, or at a coworking space. These advantages and disadvantages will depend partly on your preferences and partly on those of your employer or client. To help you assess your situation, we have made a list of the most common advantages to working in the office or at home.

TEN REASONS TO GO TO THE OFFICE

1. **COLLABORATION.** As much as you can, tackle your collaborative work at the office. If that's a big portion of what's on your plate, then you need to spend more time at the office than at home because it's much easier to collaborate when you can throw around ideas and talk informally in person. If you can get into that kind of interaction with your colleagues and collaborators, you'll maximize the creative benefits from office time for you and your employer.

2. **INFRASTRUCTURE.** If your work makes even occasional use of specialized infrastructure like a 3D scanner or printer, a powerful computer workstation, or laboratory equipment, you will need to spend time at the workplace whenever you need to access that gear.

3. **EXPERTISE.** Access to the right people is at least as important as access to the right equipment, whether you're getting tech support, advice on how to work with customer data, or training in your new financial management system. It's often easier or more useful to meet with the experts in person.

4. **KICKOFFS.** In our experience, it is really helpful to meet your clients or colleagues in person when you start working together—either for the first time, or on a new project. Your initial meeting helps you put a face to the voice and establish a friendly relationship. Once you've made that personal connection, you can use the phone or email for subsequent communications such as agreeing on a set of deliverables and evaluating the final results.

5. **TOUCH POINTS.** Even if you've kicked off a working relationship with an in-person meeting, plan on additional face-to-face touch points throughout the project. This is particularly important when you're working directly with the boss, or with a client: by and large, the more you see each other in person, the stronger your working relationship will be.

6. **ONE-ON-ONES.** With both your boss and your direct reports, aim for regular in-person one-on-ones. Even if you're only in the office rarely, and need to do most of your check-ins by phone or video call, two or three in-person meetings each year can make a big difference to the caliber of your working relationship and the chances of your getting promoted.

7. **CULTURE.** Coming into the office regularly is crucial for absorbing your organization's culture: It's only from spending time on-site that you'll pick up on the little jokes and traditions, the allegiances and enmities, the achievements that get applauded, and the strict no-go zones. If you're a new hire, you can certainly front-load this learning by spending extra time at the office early on, and then scaling back once you've learned the ropes.

8. **FOMO.** Fear of Missing Out isn't just a neurosis: Sometimes a work-from-home lifestyle really does cut you out of the loop. There are all kinds of updates you may miss unless you show up for regular on-site meetings. At the very least, plan catch-up calls with team

members so your work can support the current priorities of your organization.

9. **SOCIAL CONNECTION.** Spending time at the office reduces the amount of time when you're alone in the house. When you see colleagues regularly, you will also feel a greater sense of connection when you talk to them via phone, video call, or even text message.

10. **JUMP-STARTS.** If you find yourself stalled in work you are undertaking at home, consider jump-starting your project and boosting your energy levels by spending a few days at the office.

GOLDILOCKS GOES FREELANCE

The Goldilocks model applies to freelancers as much as it applies to employees. If you are self-employed, you need to be just as thoughtful about the circumstances in which your Business of One needs to go on-site to catch up with clients, customers, or suppliers. Even if you're in a business that requires zero face time, consider booking days at a coworking space or making coworking dates with a friend, so you can get benefits like collaboration and infrastructure.

TEN REASONS TO WORK REMOTELY

1. **CONCENTRATION.** The number one reason to book a day away from the office is the number one advantage of remote work, period: freedom from interruption. Workers at the office are, on average, interrupted every eleven minutes, and they take twenty-five minutes to get back to work, according to a study at the University of California at Irvine.[9] This risk of disruption is particularly high if you don't have your own room at the office. So balance your work

versus home time based on your relative need for collaboration or concentration.

2. **INSPIRATION.** Depending on your temperament and home work environment, you may find it easier to do creative thinking when you're in a home workspace—especially one you've designed for inspiration.

3. **TEDIOUS TASKS.** Save up your backlog of brainless tasks for days at home, like organizing your files or submitting your travel expenses. You may be able to complete a whole bunch of annoying to-dos from the comfort of your sofa.

4. **INCLUSIVENESS.** When two or three people are in a boardroom to-gether, while three or four are dialing in from parts unknown, it creates an imbalance that makes the in-person team the core of the meeting, and leaves the rest of the virtual room struggling to stay engaged. In this circumstance it can be more inclusive and more productive to ask everyone to dial in from their own phone or computer—which means you might as well be at home.

5. **TIME SHIFTING.** If you have colleagues whose nine-to-five hours have only a little overlap with your own, working remotely makes it easier for you to align your schedules and book calls. Perhaps you want to work from home on the days that you meet with your team in India, so that if you start your day at 6 a.m., you can wrap up by two or three and walk your kids home from school.

6. **CANCEL THE COMMUTE.** If you have a long commute, work from home on days when you can't afford to waste time or energy on the pro-cess of getting to the office.

7. **FAMILY.** If you have children or other caregiving responsibilities (like elderly parents who need your help), that should absolutely factor

into your work-from-home schedule. Work from home on the days that you want to pick your kids up from school or take on daytime caregiving. Conversely, plan your office days for the days when your kids stay late for after-school activities.

8. **SENSORY LOAD.** Everything about the office imposes some level of sensory burden, whether it's the noise of an open floor plan, the glare of the fluorescent lights, or the discomfort of your own business suit. When you spend a day at home in your coziest sweatpants, you reduce that sensory load and free up more energy for your actual work.

9. **LOGISTICS.** Book personal appointments for the days you are working from home. In many cases that will remove the disruption (you can keep preparing that presentation while the plumber gets down to work); in other cases it will reduce the transit time (for example, if your dentist is closer to home than to the office).

10. **REGENERATION.** Spending your workday at home makes it easier to fit in a mid-morning walk, a little advance prep for a healthy dinner, or a mid-afternoon meditation break.

MAKING THE CASE FOR *REMOTE, INC.*

Getting More Time at Home

If you would like your Goldilocks plan to include two or three days a week at home, you may need to make that case to your manager. Use our "Ten Reasons to Work Remotely" as a starting point, and frame it as a time-limited experiment in what you can accomplish with more time at home: you want to convert your commuting time into work time, do better in-depth work on the projects that require concentration (be specific about which ones those are), or coordinate more effectively with clients and colleagues in other time zones.

Point out the cost savings from this approach: You and another employee can now use the same cubicle on alternate days. To demonstrate your continued commitment to collegial relationships, suggest a schedule that will allow you to show up in person for team meetings and one-on-ones.

Planning Your Schedule

In addition to the question of how much time you want to spend at the office, you should give some thought to the specific schedule you set for your personal Goldilocks plan. Making smart choices about which days you work on-site can ensure you get more value from your time at the office and buy you more latitude for your remote work. Here's what you need to consider.

- SYNCHRONIZATION. If you are part of a team, build your office schedule so that it maximizes the opportunity to connect with your closest colleagues and collaborators, as well as with your boss and clients. In an organization that rotates different employees in and out of the office on a fixed schedule, your team should aim to come into the office on the same days. If your office doesn't have a fixed schedule for different teams, try to arrange this for yourself by talking with your colleagues about the days when you can all reserve time for in-person collaboration and brainstorming.
- NEW PROJECTS AND TEAM BONDING. When you are starting a new project, try arranging a few days or even a couple of weeks for the whole team to get underway in person, by spending time at the office together. Keep your lunch breaks open for collegial dates on these office days, and try to stay for at least occasional after-work bonding.

- OPTICS. If you have remote workdays on a weekly basis, don't make those days Mondays and Fridays. One or the other might be OK, but if you spend only the middle of the week in the office, it starts to look like your life is a series of long weekends.
- OFFSET HOURS. If commuting time is a major factor in your desire for remote work, consider negotiating an offset schedule where your office days are ten to six, seven to three, or some other nonstandard timing that gets you out of the commuter rush.
- CYCLICAL ADJUSTMENTS. Just because you normally work from the office on Mondays, Wednesdays, and Fridays doesn't mean you need to stick to that schedule fifty-two weeks a year. Move things around to enjoy seasonal outdoor workdays or reduce the number of slow, snowy commutes.
- THE GUEST APPEARANCE. Not every day at the office needs to be a full day. It's perfectly fine to put in a guest appearance by attending a crucial meeting, and then head off to your house or your favorite coworking space. In fact, this can be a very smart way of handling a meeting that requires you to come into the office on a day when you're usually at home, because it signals to your boss and colleagues that they can't simply lure you into the office by putting one crucial meeting on the calendar. (If this is a recurring problem, you'll need to renegotiate your Goldilocks plan so that your must-attend meetings are clustered on the days you're actually in the office.)
- LESS CAN BE MORE. You may not need a schedule that's based on spending a set number of days at the office every single week. Depending on your distance from the office and the nature of your work, you may find it a lot more efficient to spend the vast majority of time working remotely, with only occasional visits to HQ.

As you review the relative benefits of office versus remote work, you will find that some of your objectives, projects, and tasks really call for more office time, while others benefit from additional time working remotely. To help find the right balance between these two sets of considerations, go back to the

FIGURE 16.2

Go to the office for...
Collaboration
Infrastructure
Expertise
Kick-offs
Touch points
One-on-ones
Culture
FOMO
Social Connection
Jumpstarts

Work remotely for...
Concentration
Inspiration
Tedious tasks
Inclusiveness
Time shifting
Cancel the commute
Family
Sensory load
Logistics
Regeneration

Finding the right balance between office
and remote time

list of goals and priorities you developed for your Business of One (see chapter 4), taking into account the objectives of your boss or client.

Are your higher-priority goals mostly tied to tasks you need to do at the office, or projects that are better pursued in the relative sanctuary of home? Let that answer shape the relative balance of home versus office time, just as much as you consider your gut-level preferences or family logistics. At the end of the day, your Business of One will succeed only if you are consistently advancing your top-priority goals and projects, so you need to take your business to the place where you can do that work most effectively.

YOUR REMOTE WORK VISION

The ultimate purpose of a successful Business of One is to help you create the career and life you really want. So in addition to thinking about how you can balance home and office time in order to maximize your success, you should

think about how to use your success to achieve the balance of home and remote work that makes you truly happy and fulfilled.

That begins with making some basic decisions about whether and how
much you want to work remotely. Since you've made it all the way through a
book on remote work, we'll assume you want to work remotely at least *some*
of the time.

But even if you know you want to work remotely at least some of the time,
you may still want to rethink how much time you spend at home, or how it's
structured. There are two key factors to consider in thinking this through so
that you can develop your remote work vision—that is, the game plan for how
you want to work remotely during the next decade or so.

First, your personality shapes your likelihood of finding remote work
sustainable and rewarding. Not everyone is equally suited to remote work,
as a number of organizational psychologists have found. Certain personality
types appear better suited to the solitude and independence of remote work,
such as people with a high level of emotional stability, combined with a high
degree of autonomy,[10] because they have lower needs for relatedness and can
handle the strain of solo work. But people with a high degree of extrover-
sion can succeed too, if they also have a high level of agreeableness, because
they're likely to form social connections that replace what they're missing outside the workplace.[11]

Second, your personal values shape the trade-offs you're willing to make
in order to get your dream balance between home and office. Are you trying
to maximize your earnings, your accomplishments, your free time, or some
combination of the above? Remote work can either raise or lower the costs
of working, depending on how much you save on costs like dry cleaning or
spend on expenses like office gear. The key is to stop thinking in terms of
total salary or total revenue, and instead think of your net income, once you
factor in *all* of the costs, savings, and tax benefits of remote work. Your sense
of impact may depend on how much interaction and feedback you get in a
remote role. And your day-to-day enjoyment of remote work will depend
on how much you value workplace interaction relative to the chance to dive
deeply into your own solitary work.

All of these considerations may shift over time. If you've got young kids,
maybe you want to spend time working from home (or maybe you want to get

the heck out of the house for eight hours a day, and leave the rug rats to your partner, your nanny, or your day care). If you're longing for the freedom to travel, maybe you want to "go nomad" for a few years by shifting to remote work you can do from anywhere. If you're approaching retirement age without a pension plan, transitioning to self-employment in time to build a thriving consultancy may provide you with the possibility of extending your earning years.

The point is, there's no single answer to remote work—not even for one person. What works for you may change a lot over the course of your life and career.

The Goldilocks plan isn't just about the balance between on-site and re-mote workers in a given organization, or the amount of time you spend at home or at the office in any one phase of your career. The Goldilocks plan is a lifelong vision for balancing and rebalancing office and remote work, over and over again, so that you continually refine and improve your own Business of One.

FROM A REMOTE WORKER

Vice-President, CFO Solutions at LPL Financial, Nakeita
Norman provides financial and strategic business support to
a nationwide network of financial advisers, which gives her a
unique perspective on combining in-person and remote work.

I always had the opportunity to work remotely, and I took advantage of that to work from home once a month, if I had a lot I needed to get done. When my grandfather passed away, I was able to go to his funeral and work from Atlanta without missing a beat, because the company is set up for people to work remotely.

That is very different from doing it every day, however. Because of the pandemic, about 93 percent of LPL is now fully remote.

Sometimes people idealize the work-from-home environment. They see it as the panacea where you can focus on your work.

But it takes more discipline to work from home. You have to be diligent about setting a schedule, creating boundaries, and taking time for yourself. It's easy to lose track of time without the cues of people leaving the office.

I was only a month into managing my team when we went remote. Our schedule accelerated because the advisers we work with needed more help to shift to a virtual world. The amount of work escalated dramatically, so my productivity went through the roof. So many meetings got put on my calendar.

If you don't prioritize your own time, someone else will do it for you. Last year, there wasn't a month I wasn't traveling. Now that I don't have all that travel time blocked on my calendar, if I have a little bit of time between meetings, someone might book that window on my calendar. I went from three to four meetings a day to six to nine meetings.

That told me I need to block out time in my calendar. Now I have some "zero meeting" days so I can get my work done.

I would absolutely do a hybrid model. In Covid, I don't want to be in an office where I'd be fearful of germs, plus it's easier to get into a flow state when you work at home and don't have people interrupting. But nothing can replace the ability to see people and be able to connect with them. If I could choose, I would work from home, either half and half or maybe 70 percent at home, 30 percent at the office. I'd like to be able to connect with coworkers and colleagues and not do it all from home.

Everyone on my team would prefer a hybrid model. Traditionally we go to each adviser's office on an annual basis. That's how we get down and dirty with the nuances of their business, to see what's working well and what can be improved. It's like a lawyer doing a discovery: I can talk to you all day long but if I come to your home there are things I learn because I'm in your environment. It's not like I can't do my work from here, but it's about building a trusting relationship. We miss that, and the advisers miss it too.

But we are getting to know one another in new ways through video. One of my advisers saw my bike in the background; she is an avid cyclist, and we connected that way. The question is, always, What are the things in the background that give me an entrée into their personal life? Maybe they introduce you to their pet, or take you around their home. Once their guard is down, they are more apt to accept your recommendations and build a deeper rapport.

TAKEAWAYS

1. By enabling flexible combinations of office and remote work, the Goldilocks plan allows workers to spend not too much or too little time at home.

2. While most workers now say they want to work at least part-time from home, not every job is compatible with remote work.

3. To create your personal Goldilocks plan, look at whether your highest-priority objectives mostly involve tasks that are better suited to the advantages of the office, or better suited to the advantages of remote work.

4. Time in the office offers benefits like enhancing collaboration, building trust with your boss, staying in the loop, and jump-starting yourself when you get stalled at home.

5. Remote time offers benefits like supporting concentration, inspiration, and self-care, and providing some flexibility to work across time zones or locations.

6. The frequency and timing of your office hours should be shaped by factors like the schedule of your boss and colleagues, the optics of your days at home, and the goal of setting consistent expectations.

7. Freelance employees can get the benefits of the Goldilocks plan by finding a coworking space or coworking buddies.

8. Consider your own personality and values in determining your ideal balance of office and remote work, and expect that ideal to change over the course of your career and lifetime.

CONCLUSION

The transition to remote work is a big challenge—for individuals and for organizations. Even people with long years in the home office may struggle to adapt to the new expectations that emerge as remote work goes mainstream. As we adjust our workplace habits and organizational cultures to distributed collaboration, we are still figuring out what translates well and what needs to get adapted or reinvented.

Reading *Remote, Inc.* has equipped you to be a leader in this transition. Whether you've worked through the book chapter by chapter, implementing one recommendation at a time, or devoured it all in one sitting, you now have a road map for increasing your productivity and satisfaction with remote work, and delivering better results for your employer or clients. You now know . . .

- THE BUSINESS OF ONE MINDSET. Thinking like *Remote, Inc.* helps you focus on delivering great results instead of getting hung up on the eight-hour workday.
- KEY PRODUCTIVITY STRATEGIES. Learning to prioritize your goals, focus on the final product, and stop sweating the small stuff will help you concentrate your time and attention on the work that matters most to you, your employer, and your clients. Translating those strategies into specific systems for organizing your time, tech, and workspace will help you follow through on these strategies each and every day.
- REMOTE WORK SKILLS. Strengthening fundamental skills like reading and writing, and becoming a better online communicator and meeting participant, means that you will be more efficient and effective in all of your projects and tasks.

The mindset, strategies, and skills you have acquired can deliver immediate, tangible benefits for both you and your employer or clients—creating a win-win situation. In these final pages, we will suggest not only what these benefits mean to you and your employer, but also what they mean for the nascent culture of remote work.

THE BUSINESS OF ONE BENEFITS YOU

Now that you know how to think and work as a Business of One, you can expect to be more productive and more satisfied with remote work. But you don't have to take our word for it: You now have a set of practices and tools that will let you see the impact for yourself. The success metrics you set with your boss or clients, the time-tracking software you use to automatically track where your hours went, and the weekly review you conduct to see what you accomplished: all of these give you a structure for assessing how your new strategies and habits translate into better results in less time.

We encourage you to pick an assortment of professional and personal metrics right now, so that you can see the payoff as you implement and build on what you've learned. Consider some easily quantifiable indicators like the number of sales you close or the number of software bugs you fix or the number of customer issues you solve. Include more subjective indicators like how you feel at the end of each day (you can log that with a mood-tracking app) or a self-assessed quality rating for each of your deliverables or the satisfaction of your customers. (See the "Seven Quick Wins for Remote Workers" feature below for some starting points that can give you quick, measurable boosts in productivity.)

As you track these metrics, you can expect to see two specific benefits from your newfound savvy: Your productivity will increase, and you will like working from home a lot more. These are the key payoffs from working like a Business of One.

SEVEN QUICK WINS FOR REMOTE WORKERS

Wondering where to start your journey to *Remote, Inc.*? Here are seven recommendations from throughout the book that are easy to

adopt and quick to pay off. Try one or several so you can see immediate benefits from this new way of working.

1. ONLY HANDLE IT ONCE. If you can embrace the OHIO rule for even
   part of your incoming email, you'll see huge time savings.

2. THE TWO-SIDED SCHEDULE. Start making a daily practice of noting your goals for each meeting on your calendar.

3. ASK FOR AN AGENDA. Every time you receive a meeting invitation, ask for an agenda to help you prepare; this will help you
   identify meetings you don't need to attend.

4. CREATE A COUPLE OF DAILY ROUTINES. Find a couple of recurring
   decisions you can eliminate or simplify by turning them into
   routines.

5. START USING A DIGITAL NOTEBOOK. Centralizing all your notes in a
   single note-taking application will save you hours of hunting
   for that key file.

6. SET UP SOME EMAIL FILTERS. Creating a couple of initial email
   filters to keep bulk email and cc's out of your primary inbox
   will reduce email overload.

7. SEND ACTION ITEMS FIRST. Adopting our email template will help
   you write actionable emails more quickly, and get better
   results.

THE BUSINESS OF ONE BENEFITS YOUR ORGANIZATION AND CLIENTS

Adopting the model of a Business of One will benefit not only you, but also
the organization you work for. When your boss or clients see that you can
produce better results when you have some latitude in how you organize your
time and tasks, that will help them embrace the *Remote, Inc.* model. Your
boss or clients will continue to set objectives for your work, and you will need

to collaborate on identifying the right success metrics for those objectives. Nevertheless, you will gain considerable autonomy in how and when you work to meet those metrics and objectives.

Some companies have already recognized the performance benefits of embracing a results-oriented model that gives remote employees this kind of autonomy. At Automattic, the company behind WordPress and many other major Web success stories, founder Matt Mullenweg observed, "For most roles at Automattic, what you're accountable for is a result. You could work . . . 20 hours [a week] and do a ton."[1] In announcing a new mobile work policy at Siemens, Europe's largest industrial manufacturing conglomerate, deputy CEO and labor director Roland Busch described the policy as a "further development of our corporate culture" that would be "associated with a different leadership style, one that focuses on outcomes rather than on time spent at the office."[2]

When employers know that they can get great results from remote employees without constant management oversight, they will become more enthusiastic about how the Goldilocks plan can help a distributed team do its best work. It helps that this plan provides tangible cost advantages: since companies now spend an average of $10,000 to make space for each on-site worker, they can reap huge savings if they reduce their space requirements by encouraging their employees to work remotely at least part of the week.[3] Moreover, if remote employees learn to work effectively in this more autonomous model, managers will not feel obliged to provide hourly or daily oversight. That frees up a lot of senior capacity that can be applied to generating new opportunities or resolving major problems.

Finally, employers that embrace the Business of One model can expect to see significant benefits in terms of employee engagement and retention. A Gallup survey conducted before the pandemic concluded that "flexible scheduling and work-from-home opportunities play a major role in an employee's decision to take or leave a job."[4] And an article in the MIT Sloan Management Review noted that when employees get remote work benefits like "having more flexibility and autonomy in their jobs and being more available to deal with family responsibilities . . . [t]his often translates into greater job satisfaction, lower absenteeism and higher employee retention."[5]

If you are a manager or executive reading this book, you are in a good position to help your organization make the most of the benefits of the *Remote, Inc.* model. In organizations where this model represents a big shift, treat your own immediate team (or a specific department) as a pilot: start by defining a set of success metrics that you will use to track progress on your key objectives, and then use the results to make the case for *Remote, Inc.* (See the "Seven Big Wins for Organizations" feature below to get more ideas for specific changes you can pilot.) Meanwhile, engage other organizational leaders (and clients) in a conversation about why and how to evolve your workplace-centered management model so that you can be more effective with a distributed workforce. (You can use this book to jump-start that discussion.)

SEVEN BIG WINS FOR ORGANIZATIONS

The *Remote, Inc.* model can deliver significant productivity wins at scale. When an entire team or organization adopts this mindset, along with core strategies and practices, you can get more done separately and together. Here are seven changes that can have a big impact when they're led or supported by a manager or executive.

1. **ESTABLISH GROUND RULES.** Draft and share an online document that specifies guidelines for working hours, meetings, email, and messaging to simplify your work as a team.

2. **EMBRACE PUNCTUATED COLLABORATION.** Use online meetings to catalyze, parcel out, and check in on collaborative projects, while taking advantage of remote work to accelerate solo tasks.

3. **SCHEDULE WEEKLY ONE-ON-ONES.** Institute weekly one-on-ones for managers with each team member to help everyone continually improve their performance.

4. **TIE PERFORMANCE TO OBJECTIVES.** Work with each team member to set prioritized objectives with success metrics, and make this the foundation of your frequent performance reviews.

5. **STOP HOURLY MONITORING.** Once managers can readily see success metrics, they can stop using videoconferencing as a way to hold employees accountable, and may also be able to reduce reliance on timesheets or computer tracking.

6. **ENABLE ALTERNATE SCHEDULES.** Invite employees to negotiate alternatives to the strict nine-to-five schedule if it gives them the flexibility to work effectively with overseas colleagues and clients, or support family obligations.

7. **THINK LIKE GOLDILOCKS.** Move to a hybrid model where the organization allows employees to choose where to work and for how many days per week, subject to team needs.

THE BUSINESS OF ONE ENABLES A NEW CULTURE OF REMOTE WORK

If you were trying to welcome a new group of employees to your workplace, you probably wouldn't choose to onboard fifty million of them at once.[6] And yet that's exactly what happened in the spring of 2020, when millions of American workers switched to working remotely. Employers across the United States had to onboard their teams to the home office—and all over the world, other businesses and organizations were grappling with the same challenge.

A year into that experiment, we can see the seeds of a new world in the way these freshly minted remote workers have adapted to the home office. It's a world in which employees achieve better results while enjoying greater work-life balance, because they've tapped into the productivity gains that come from punctuated collaboration. It's a world in which organizations get better results (and higher profit margins) because their workforce is more effective, with less oversight and overhead. And it's a world in which freelancers and small business owners can work hand in hand with full-time employees, because the line between them is steadily eroding.

But it's also a world that is just beginning to emerge. Those of us who are new to remote work, as well as those of us who were working at home before Covid, get to shape this new world. As you have doubtless discovered from adjusting to remote work with the help of colleagues, friends, and fellow readers, remote workers are a generous bunch: They love to pass on their best tricks and tips, so that others can be a little more effective in their home offices. It's through passing on this wisdom that we establish norms and expectations for remote productivity and satisfaction. The people who are figuring out these norms and expectations are laying the foundations for a new culture of remote work.

Now that you understand what it means to think like *Remote, Inc.*, you're ready to join them. The productivity strategies you can now implement will help you become a model and mentor for those who are still trying to figure out how to work remotely. The results you generate for your organization and clients will build understanding and support for the Business of One model, because you will demonstrate what's possible to achieve through remote work. And the generosity with which you share your new skills, strategy, and mindset will help to build a thriving culture of remote work. These are the biggest payoffs from learning to work like *Remote, Inc.*

ACKNOWLEDGMENTS

This book is proof that remote work succeeds on the strength of collaboration—and not just our own. We wrote this book without ever meeting each other, and have yet to meet many of the people who made this book possible.

Our research assistants, Peter Hoffman and Kevin Downey, undertook wide-ranging research in record time so that our recommendations could include insights from management and psychology, among other fields. Their ability to identify and synthesize the most important sources related to remote work—as well as their willingness to work at all hours, across time zones—was absolutely essential to our successful completion of this book. We are also grateful to Jesse Wickstrom, who provided additional research support.

Our agent, James A. Levine, was a generous adviser in the process of developing a book that could speak to this peculiar moment. Thanks to his guidance and support, we somehow went from a book idea to a book deal in less than four weeks—a miracle that set the pace for the rest of this endeavor. From our initial conversation to our finished draft, Jim's comments have helped us find the appropriate scope and focus for our advice to remote workers.

Hollis Heimbouch, our editor at Harper Business, has truly been our partner in bringing this book to publication. From our very first conversation, she has articulated a clear vision for how *Remote, Inc.* could build on the success of Bob's previous book, *Extreme Productivity*, by serving the millions of people who are now adjusting to remote work. Her detailed input was incredibly valuable in editing the final manuscript. We are also grateful to Josh Karpf, the copy editor whose meticulous work is visible on every page of this book.

The team at polling firm Maru/Blue generously provided access to their omnibus panel so that we could survey remote workers and gather our own insights on the impact of autonomy on remote work. Andrew Grenville provided crucial guidance in developing our survey and analyzing the results. John Wright helped us connect that survey to Maru's ongoing research on the shift to remote work, so that we could build on the time series data tracking remote worker sentiment over the course of the pandemic. Daniel Faziluddin fielded the survey questions and delivered results in record time, so that we could go to press with fresh data.

We would like to thank four early readers of our manuscript for thoughtful input that had a dramatic impact on our tone and guidance. Jerome Kagan helped us tune our attention to the particular challenges the Business of One model poses for developing employees. Courtney Paganelli encouraged us to streamline the chapters on social media and presentations in order to focus more specifically on the challenges of remote workers. Renee Fry helped us consider the Business of One from a remote employer's perspective so that we have a book that managers will want to share with their teams. Morgan Brayton's feedback was the inspiration for our features on making the case for *Remote, Inc.* and, even more important, ensured that we two dog owners acknowledge that some home offices include cats.

Many other people made specific suggestions that found their way into these pages—or onto the cover! The sofa and laptop you see on the jacket were the suggestion of Haig Armen, associate professor of design at Emily Carr University. Nicole Summitt at Sprinklr is the source of our guidance on writing an email around recommended actions, in just one example of how Alex's ongoing work with the Sprinklr team has shaped her thinking about digital collaboration. Several chapters include recommendations Alex has written about previously, so she would like to thank the editors who helped her develop these ideas: Larry Rout, Elizabeth Seay, and Rob Toth at the *Wall Street Journal*; Amy Shearn and Cari Romm Nazeer of Medium's *Forge*; Joanna Weiss at *Experience* magazine; and Ania Wieckowski at the *Harvard Business Review*.

Most important, we would like to thank our families for enabling the writing process so that we could get this book into our readers' hands as quickly as possible. Alex's husband, Rob Cottingham (who was also an early, insightful reader); her children, Micah and Jonah; and her mother, Deborah Hobson, all pitched in with meal preparation, dog walking, emotional support, and as human thesauruses. Bob's wife, Liz, was an incredibly supportive partner who endured several hectic months of drafting and editing. Her patience and wisdom have always been a source of inspiration to him, and her emotional sensitivity has guided him through almost forty-five years of marriage.

Finally, we want to thank the many remote workers who shared their experiences so that we could offer you the benefit of their knowledge and insights. We are particularly grateful to the sixteen people who spoke with us at length for the profiles you found throughout this book: Huw Evans, Maggie Crowley Sheehan, Adin Miller, Simone Alexander, Amy Lightholder, Katrina Marshall, Corey Branstrom, Michael Morgenstern, Hollis Robbins, Beth Kanter, Marshall Kirkpatrick, Jim Wang, Soren Hamby, Dawn Myers, Hiro Boga, and Nakeita Norman. But there are many other remote workers whose input influenced these pages: our friends and colleagues, our social media buddies, the respondents to our surveys, the remote workers whose interviews did not wind up in the pages of this book, and the people who shared their struggles with remote work during chats at the dog park. At times it felt like 2020 was just one long conversation about how to adjust to working at home, and we were very lucky to eavesdrop on that conversation in so many different contexts.

Now it is up to you to continue that conversation with your own colleagues, friends, and family. We hope that this book, and all the many people who made it possible, will make a great starting point.

APPENDIX: ABOUT THE DATA

To understand how people were adapting to remote work, we asked Maru/Blue to conduct an online survey of more than 3,000 Americans, of whom 1,826 were currently working; of these, 1,047 were working at least part-time from home. These are the remote workers we focused on in our study, conducted from October 1–7, 2020.

We measured autonomy by asking respondents how much they agreed or disagreed with certain statements. For each of these three statements, autonomy was indicated by strength of agreement:

- While I have deadlines and meetings, I can make a lot of my own decisions about how to schedule my work.
- I have the flexibility to decide on my own how to go about doing my work.
- As long as I get my work done, I have a lot of control over how and when I do it.

For each of these two statements, autonomy was indicated by strength of disagreement:

- I don't feel like I have any real say on when I work and what I do.
- I don't really have much control over my work schedule.

To measure productivity, we asked:

When you are working, would you say you are . . .
- More productive working at home?
- Equally productive inside and outside the home?
- More productive working outside the home?

Respondents who indicated that they were more productive at home or at the office were asked to say whether they were "somewhat more" or "much more" productive in their more productive location.

To measure satisfaction with remote work, we asked:

If you had to choose, would you prefer to . . .
- Work from home all the time?
- Work outside the home all the time?
- Work partly from home, partly outside the home?

Source: Maru/Blue Omnibus survey field, October 1–7, 2020.

NOTES

CHAPTER 1: YOUR BUSINESS OF ONE

1. Peter Cochrane, "Company Time: Management, Ideology and the Labour Process, 1940–60." *Labour History* 48 (May 1985), 54, https://doi.org/10.2307/27508720.

2. Jared Lindzon, "It's Time to Stop Measuring Productivity in Hours," *Fast Company*, April 24, 2020, https://www.fastcompany.com/90492964/its-time-to-stop-measuring-productivity-in-hours.

3. Jon Messenger, *Working Time and the Future of Work*, ILO Future of Work Research Paper Series (Geneva: International Labour Organization, 2018), 13, http://englishbulletin.adapt.it/wp-content/uploads/2019/03/wcms_649907.pdf.

4. Bobby Allyn, "Your Boss Is Watching You: Work-from-Home Boom Leads to More Surveillance," NPR, May 13, 2020, https://www.npr.org/2020/05/13/854014403/your-boss-is-watching-you-work-from-home-boom-leads-to-more-surveillance.

5. "Nearly Half of U.S. Employees Feel Burnt Out, with One in Four Attributing Stress to the COVID-19 Pandemic," Eagle Hill Consulting, April 14, 2020, https://www.eaglehillconsulting.com/about-us/news/announcements/nearly-half-of-u-s-employees-feel-burnt-out-with-one-in-four-attributing-stress-to-the-covid-19-pandemic/.

6. Maru/Blue, "Eight Months and Counting: How Americans Are Feeling about Covid-19 Headed into Autumn," October 26, 2020, https://marureports.com/wp-content/uploads/2020/10/MaruReports-COVID19-Tracker-Eight-Months-and-Counting-US.pdf.

7. Ibid.

CHAPTER 2: MAKING THE NEW MODEL WORK

1. Eli Rosenberg, "Gig Economy Bills Move Forward in Other Blue States, after California Clears the Way," *Washington Post*, January 17, 2020, https://www

.washingtonpost.com/business/2020/01/17/gig-economy-bills-move-forward
-other-blue-states-after-california-clears-way.

2. Bernstein, Ethan, Jesse Shore, and David Lazer. "Improving the Rhythm of Your Collaboration." *MIT Sloan Management Review* 61, no. 1 (Fall 2019): 29–36, https://www-proquest-com.libproxy.mit.edu/scholarly-journals/improving -rhythm-your-collaboration/docview/2335160250/se-2?accountid=12492.

CHAPTER 3: MANAGING A REMOTE TEAM

1. Rebecca Knight, "How to Manage Remote Direct Reports," *Harvard Business Review*, February 27, 2020, https://hbr.org/2015/02/how-to-manage-remote-direct-reports.

2. Nick Routley, "6 Charts that Show What Employers and Employees Really Think about Remote Working." World Economic Forum, June 3, 2020, https://www .weforum.org/agenda/2020/06/coronavirus-covid19-remote-working-office -employees-employers/.

3. Theresa Minton-Eversole, "Virtual Teams Used Most by Global Organizations, Survey Says," Society for Human Resource Management, July 19, 2012, https://www .shrm.org/resourcesandtools/hr-topics/organizational-and-employee-development /pages/virtualteamsusedmostbyglobalorganizations,surveysays.aspx.

4. Boris Groysberg, Jeremiah Lee, Jesse Price, and J. Yo-Jud Cheng, "The Leader's Guide to Corporate Culture," *Harvard Business Review*, January-February 2018, https://hbr.org/2018/01/the-leaders-guide-to-corporate-culture.

5. Annamarie Mann, "3 Ways You Are Failing Your Remote Workers," Gallup, August 1, 2017, https://www.gallup.com/workplace/236192/ways-failing-remote -workers.aspx.

CHAPTER 4: PRIORITIZE YOUR GOALS

1. Frankki Bevins and Aaron De Smet, "Making Time Management the Organization's Priority," *McKinsey Quarterly*, January 2013, https://www.mckinsey.com /~/media/McKinsey/Not%20Mapped/Making%20time%20management%20 the%20organizations%20priority/Making%20time%20management%20the%20 organizations%20priority.pdf.

CHAPTER 6: DON'T SWEAT THE SMALL STUFF

1. Lakshmi Mani, "Hyperbolic Discounting: Why You Make Terrible Life Choices," *Medium* (blog), August 1, 2017, https://medium.com/behavior-design/hyperbolic -discounting-aefb7acec46e.

2. Dan Ariely and Klaus Wertenbroch, "Procrastination, Deadlines, and Performance: Self-Control by Precommitment" (Cambridge, MA: Massachusetts Institute of Technology, 2011), https://erationality.media.mit.edu/papers/dan/eRational/Dynamic%20preferences/deadlines.pdf.

3. Laura Solomon and Esther Rothblum, "Academic Procrastination: Frequency and Cognitive-Behavioral Correlates," *Journal of Counseling Psychology* 31, no. 4 (1984), 503–9, https://psycnet.apa.org/record/1985-07993-001.

4. Elaine Mead, "Letting Go of Perfectionism in Pursuit of Productivity," *Medium* (blog), September 17, 2019, https://medium.com/swlh/letting-go-of-perfectionism-in-pursuit-of-productivity-2e8ce9a08471.

5. "Perfectionism," GoodTherapy, November 5, 2019, https://www.goodtherapy.org/learn-about-therapy/issues/perfectionism.

6. "Multitasking: Switching Costs," American Psychological Association, March 20, 2006, https://www.apa.org/research/action/multitask.

7. Peter Bregman, "When Multitasking Is a Good Thing." Forbes.com, https://www.forbes.com/sites/peterbregman/2015/01/28/when-multitasking-is-a-good-thing/.

8. Eric H. Schumacher, "Virtually Perfect Time Sharing in Dual-Task Performance: Uncorking the Central Cognitive Bottleneck," *Psychological Science* 12, no. 2 (2001), 101–8, https://journals.sagepub.com/doi/pdf/10.1111/1467-9280.00318.

CHAPTER 7: ORGANIZING YOUR TIME

1. Drake Baer, "Always Wear the Same Suit: Obama's Presidential Productivity Secrets," *Fast Company*, February 12, 2014, https://www.fastcompany.com/3026265/always-wear-the-same-suit-obamas-presidential-productivity-secrets.

2. Laura Scroggs, "The Pomodoro Technique," Todoist, 2020, https://todoist.com/productivity-methods/pomodoro-technique.

3. Conor J. Wild, Emily S. Nichols, Michael E. Battista, Bobby Stojanoski, and Adrian M. Owen, "Dissociable Effects of Self-Reported Daily Sleep Duration on High-Level Cognitive Abilities," *Sleep* 41, no. 12 (2018), zsy182, https://doi.org/10.1093/sleep/zsy182.

4. Sara C. Mednick, Denise J. Cai, Jennifer Kanady, and Sean P. A. Drummond, "Comparing the Benefits of Caffeine, Naps and Placebo on Verbal, Motor and Perceptual Memory," *Behavioural Brain Research* 193, no. 1 (2008), 79–86, https://doi.org/10.1016/j.bbr.2008.04.028.

5. "Sleep Inertia," The Sleep Council, January 28, 2020, https://sleepcouncil.org .uk/advice-support/sleep-hub/sleep-matters/sleep-inertia/.

6. Jacob Daniel Drannan, "The Relationship Between Physical Exercise and Job Performance: The Mediating Effects of Subjective Health and Good Mood" (master's thesis, Bangkok University, 2016), http://dspace.bu.ac.th/bitstream /123456789/2249/1/drannan.jacob.pdf.

CHAPTER 9: ORGANIZING YOUR SPACE

1. Trina N. Dao and Joseph R. Ferrari, "The Negative Side of Office Clutter: Impact on Work-Related Well-Being and Job Satisfaction," *North American Journal of Psychology* 22, no. 3 (May 2020), 397–419, https://www.researchgate.net /profile/Joseph_Ferrari3/publication/341322270_The_Negative_Side_of _Office_Clutter_Impact_on_Work-Related_Well-Being_and_Job_Satisfaction /links/5ebaab36458515626ca18df0/.

2. Henna Mistry, "Music While You Work: The Effects of Background Music on Test Performance amongst Extroverts and Introverts," *Journal of Applied Psychology and Social Sciences* 1, no. 1 (2015), 1–14, https://ojs.cumbria.ac.uk /index.php/apass/article/view/209/320.

3. Canadian Centre for Occupational Health and Safety, "OSH Answers Fact Sheets: Ergonomic Chair," October 28, 2020, https://www.ccohs.ca/oshanswers /ergonomics/office/chair.html.

CHAPTER 10: MAKING THE MOST OF MEETINGS

1. Leslie A. Perlow, Constance Noonan Hadley, and Eunice Eun, "Stop the Meeting Madness," *Harvard Business Review*, July–August 2017, https://hbr.org /2017/07/stop-the-meeting-madness.

2. A. H. Johnstone and F. Percival, "Attention Breaks in Lectures," *Education in Chemistry* 13, no. 2 (March 1976): 49–50.

3. Marcia Blenko, Michael C. Mankins, and Paul Rogers, *Decide & Deliver: Five Steps to Breakthrough Performance in Your Organization* (Boston: Bain & Company, 2010); J. Richard Hackman and Neil Vidmar, "Effects of Size and Task Type on Group Performance and Member Reactions," *Sociometry* 33, no. 1 (March 1970), 37–54, https://doi.org/10.2307/2786271.

4. Suzanne Hawkes, "Facilitating Virtual Meetings for Humans." LinkedIn, April 30, 2020, https://www.linkedin.com/pulse/facilitating-virtual-meetings -humans-suzanne-hawkes.

5.   Elizabeth J. McClean, Sean R. Martin, Kyle J. Emich, and Col. Todd Wood-
     ruff, "The Social Consequences of Voice: An Examination of Voice Type and
     Gender on Status and Subsequent Leader Emergence," *Academy of Management
     Journal* 61, no. 5 (October 2018), 1869–91, https://doi.org/10.5465/amj.2016
     .0148.

6.   Don H. Zimmerman and Candace West, "Sex Roles, Interruptions and Silences
     in Conversation," in *Language and Sex: Difference and Dominance*, ed. Bar-
     rie Thorne and Nancy Henley (Rowley, MA: Newbury House, 1975), 105–29,
     https://web.stanford.edu/~eckert/PDF/zimmermanwest1975.pdf.

7.   Libby Sander and Oliver Bauman, "Zoom Fatigue Is Real—Here's Why Video
     Calls Are so Draining," May 19, 2020, TED Ideas, https://ideas.ted.com/zoom
     -fatigue-is-real-heres-why-video-calls-are-so-draining/.

8.   Clive Thompson, "What If Working From Home Goes on . . . Forever?," *New
     York Times*, June 10, 2020, https://www.nytimes.com/interactive/2020/06/09
     /magazine/remote-work-covid.html.

9.   Betsy Morris, "Why Does Zoom Exhaust You? Science Has an Answer," *Wall
     Street Journal*, May 27, 2020, https://www.wsj.com/articles/why-does-zoom
     -exhaust-you-science-has-an-answer-11590600269.

10. Liz Fosslien and Mollie West Duffy, "How to Combat Zoom Fatigue," *Harvard
     Business Review*, August 29, 2020, https://hbr.org/2020/04/how-to-combat
     -zoom-fatigue.

CHAPTER 11: READING ONLINE AND OFFLINE

1.   Sara J. Margolin, Casey Driscoll, Michael J. Toland, and Jennifer Little Keg-
     ler, "E-Readers, Computer Screens, or Paper: Does Reading Comprehension
     Change across Media Platforms?," *Applied Cognitive Psychology* 27, no. 4
     (2013): 512–19, https://doi.org/10.1002/acp.2930.

2.   Nicholas Carr, "Author Nicholas Carr: The Web Shatters Focus, Rewires
     Brains," *Wired*, May 24, 2010, https://www.wired.com/2010/05/ff-nicholas
     -carr/.

3.   Yiren Kong, Young Sik Seo, and Ling Zhai, "Comparison of Reading Perfor-
     mance on Screen and on Paper: A Meta-analysis," *Computers & Education* 123
     (2018):138–49, https://doi.org/10.1016/j.compedu.2018.05.005.

4.   Lucia Moses, "'The Money Is Real; That's the Problem': Publishers Turn a
     Blind Eye to Content-Recommendation Ads," *Digiday*, November 15, 2016,
     https://digiday.com/media/links-web-ad-units-terrible/.

5. RSS stands for Really Simple Syndication, a publishing format that allows you to pull blog posts, news articles, or other online content into a single location like a newsreader application.

CHAPTER 12: WRITING SOLO AND WITH OTHERS

1. Ronald T. Kellogg, "Competition for Working Memory among Writing Processes," *American Journal of Psychology* 114, no. 2 (2001), 175–91, https://doi .org/10.2307/1423513.

2. If you are new to mind mapping, we recommend looking at the work of Tony Buzan, who has many useful resources that can get you started, including several books.

3. Forrest Wickman, "Who Really Said You Should 'Kill Your Darlings'?," *Slate*, October 18, 2013, https://slate.com/culture/2013/10/kill-your-darlings-writing -advice-what-writer-really-said-to-murder-your-babies.html.

CHAPTER 13: EMAIL AND MESSAGING

1. Jen Doll, "The Right Way to Close Out an Email. (Skip That Inspirational Quote.)," *New York Times*, December 15, 2019, https://www.nytimes.com /2019/12/15/smarter-living/the-right-way-to-close-out-an-email-skip-that -inspirational-quote.html.

2. Mary Madden, "Public Perceptions of Privacy and Security in the Post-Snowden Era," Pew Research Center, November 12, 2014, https://www.pewresearch.org /internet/2014/11/12/public-privacy-perceptions/.

CHAPTER 14: SOCIAL MEDIA

1. Nir Eyal, *Hooked: How to Build Habit-Forming Products* (New York: Penguin Business, 2014).

2. Lawrence Robinson and Melinda Smith, "Social Media and Mental Health," September 2020, https://www.helpguide.org/articles/mental-health/social-media -and-mental-health.htm.

CHAPTER 15: PRESENTATIONS

1. Rob Cottingham, "Challenge, Call, Recipe, Reward: How to Write the Conclusion of your Speech," *Rob Cottingham* (blog), October 30, 2017, https://www .robcottingham.ca/2017/10/write-speech-conclusion/.

CHAPTER 16: THE GOLDILOCKS PLAN

1. Jessica Snouwaert, "54% of Adults Want to Work Remotely Most of the Time after the Pandemic, According to a New Study from IBM," *Business Insider*, May 5, 2020, https://www.businessinsider.com/54-percent-adults-want-mainly -work-remote-after-pandemic-study-2020-5.

2. "Latest Work-at-Home/Telecommuting/Mobile Work/Remote Work Statistics," Global Workplace Analytics, October 10, 2020, https://globalworkplaceanalytics .com/telecommuting-statistics.

3. "Moving beyond Remote: Workplace Transformation in the Wake of Covid-19," Slack, October 7, 2020, https://slack.com/intl/en-ca/blog/collaboration/work place-transformation-in-the-wake-of-covid-19.

4. Nicholas Bloom, "How Working from Home Works Out," Stanford Institute for Economic Policy Research, Stanford University, June 2020, https://siepr .stanford.edu/sites/default/files/publications/PolicyBrief-June2020.pdf.

5. "How Many People Could Work-from-Home," Global Workplace Analytics, June 8, 2020, https://globalworkplaceanalytics.com/how-many-people-could -work-from-home.

6. "Ability to Work from Home: Evidence from Two Surveys and Implications for the Labor Market in the COVID-19 Pandemic," Monthly Labor Review, US Bureau of Labor Statistics, June 1, 2020, https://www.bls.gov/opub/mlr/2020 /article/ability-to-work-from-home.htm; ReNika Moore, "If COVID-19 Doesn't Discriminate, Then Why Are Black People Dying at Higher Rates?," American Civil Liberties Union, April 8, 2020, https://www.aclu.org/news/racial-justice /if-covid-19-doesnt-discriminate-then-why-are-black-people-dying-at-higher -rates/.

7. Nelson D. Schwartz, "Working from Home Poses Hurdles for Employees of Color," *New York Times*, September 6, 2020, https://www.nytimes.com/2020 /09/06/business/economy/working-from-home-diversity.html.

8. Nicholas Bloom, "How Working from Home Works Out," Stanford Institute for Economic Policy Research, Stanford University, June 2020, https://siepr .stanford.edu/sites/default/files/publications/PolicyBrief-June2020.pdf.

9. Jeremy Boudinet, "Working from Home vs. Working in an Office: Pros & Cons," Nextiva Blog, August 20, 2020, https://www.nextiva.com/blog/working-from -home-vs-office.html.

10. Sara Jansen Perry, Cristina Rubino, and Emily M. Hunter, "Stress in Remote Work: Two Studies Testing the Demand-Control-Person Model," *European Journal of Work and Organizational Psychology* 27, no. 5 (2018), 577–93, https://doi.org/10.1080/1359432X.2018.1487402.

11. Thomas A. O'Neill, Laura A. Hambley, and Gina S. Chatellier, "Cyberslacking, Engagement, and Personality in Distributed Work Environments," *Computers in Human Behavior* 40 (November 2014), 152–60, https://doi.org/10.1016/j.chb.2014.08.005.

CONCLUSION

1. David Gelles, "An Evangelist for Remote Work Sees the Rest of the World Catch On," *New York Times*, July 12, 2020, https://www.nytimes.com/2020/07/12/business/matt-mullenweg-automattic-corner-office.html.

2. Justin Bariso, "This Company's New 2-Sentence Remote Work Policy Is the Best I've Ever Heard," *Inc.*, July 27, 2020. https://www.inc.com/justin-bariso/this-companys-new-2-sentence-remote-work-policy-is-best-ive-ever-heard.html.

3. Amar Hussain, "4 Reasons Why a Remote Workforce Is Better for Business," Forbes.com, March 29, 2019, https://www.forbes.com/sites/amarhussaineurope/2019/03/29/4-reasons-why-a-remote-workforce-is-better-for-business/.

4. Niraj Chokshi, "Out of the Office: More People Are Working Remotely, Survey Finds," *New York Times*, February 15, 2017, https://www.nytimes.com/2017/02/15/us/remote-workers-work-from-home.html.

5. Jay Mulki, Fleura Bardhi, Felicia Lassk, and Jayne Nanavaty-Dahl, "Set Up Remote Workers to Thrive," MIT Sloan Management Review, October 1, 2009, https://sloanreview.mit.edu/article/set-up-remote-workers-to-thrive/.

6. Calculated from data in *The Employment Situation: September 2020*, October 2, 2020, Bureau of Labor Statistics; May Wong, "Stanford Research Provides a Snapshot of a New Working-from-Home Economy," Stanford News, Stanford University, June 29, 2020, https://news.stanford.edu/2020/06/29/snapshot-new-working-home-economy/; and "Latest Work-at-Home/Telecommuting/Mobile Work/Remote Work Statistics," Global Workplace Analytics, October 10, 2020, https://globalworkplaceanalytics.com/telecommuting-statistics.

ABOUT THE AUTHORS

Robert C. Pozen is a senior lecturer at MIT Sloan School of Management and a senior non-resident fellow of the Brookings Institution. He was president of Fidelity Investments and executive chair of MFS Investment Management and served as a senior official in both the federal and state government. He is also the author of seven books, including *Extreme Productivity*, one of the top-rated business books of 2012. He offers MIT courses for executives on personal productivity and has been teaching online since the spring of 2020. He lives in Boston, Massachusetts.

Alexandra Samuel is a tech speaker and data journalist who has worked remotely for most of her twenty-five-year career. Her writing on digital productivity appears frequently in the *Wall Street Journal* and the *Harvard Business Review*. The cofounder of the groundbreaking social media agency Social Signal, Alex's work as a tech and data journalist has included working with some of the tech companies mentioned in the book, including Sprinklr, Twitter, Zapier, and LinkedIn. She holds a PhD from Harvard University, and works remotely from Vancouver, Canada.